VOICES
FROM THE
HEART

the adoption experience

HTTPS://TWAGAA.COM

Mumbai (MH), India
Website: https://twagaa.com
Email: hello@twagaa.com

First published by TWAGAA INTERNATIONAL
Copyright ©Dipika Maharaj Singh
All Rights Reserved.

Title: Voices From The Heart - The Adoption Experience

ISBN: 978-93-90488-94-0

First Edition
Published in India

Ordering Information:
Quantity sales: Special discounts are available on quantity purchases by corporations, associations, and others. For details, contact the publisher at the address or email above.

All disputes are subject to Mumbai jurisdiction only.

VOICES FROM THE HEART

the adoption experience

Dipika Maharaj Singh

HTTPS://TWAGAA.COM

This book is dedicated to families around the world who
went beyond the boundaries of biology to embrace an
enriching form of kinship which is rooted in the depths of
the heart and held together by the strength of emotional ties.

It is a tribute to my Gurus and Mentors whose wisdom and
guidance have illuminated my path.

It is in gratitude to colleagues and organisations with
whom I have shared fifty years in the field of child
development and adoption.

It is a silent acknowledgment of lost birth parents who let go
of their children in traumatic circumstances, whose journeys
I have also shared.

Above all it is a tribute to countless young children with
whom I have shared all the stages of the adoption journey ,
and whose experience and perspective have added volumes
to my book of life...

> **"**
>
> *Kunti should have given her son to an adoptive family instead of leaving him adrift in the Ganges*
>
> **"**

Words of a young boy to his adoptive parents, when they shared the story of Kunti and Karna from the Indian epic Mahabharata

ACKNOWLEDGEMENTS

Lockdown has been a time for introspection. We embarked on this journal when COVID hit us and families were locked in together. We requested parents across the diverse geographical landscape of India to share the highlights of their journey of parenting through adoption.

Through their writings we gained new insights into the issues and areas of concern in domestic adoption. Their experience, recorded in the following pages , covers a span of more than three decades. It provides a valuable guide for those who are just venturing on this path and those who are concerned with adoption.

It is our hope that the Voices From The Heart which we hear in the following pages, will provide a compass to find the way forward on an uncharted path and a key to this complex but fulfilling relationship called adoption.

Our sincere thanks to all who contributed to this effort, most specially:
- *Adoptive parents*, for responding with such overwhelming warmth and trust. Our concept became a reality only because they shared their very personal and moving stories with us. All identities have been changed to protect confidentiality.
- *SPARCC team members* who poured in their ideas, experience and efforts to produce this book: *Madhuri Abhyankar, Vinita Datye, Sharika Glover, Jayashree Puranik, Kalyani Saraf, Rama Panchanadikar*
- I express my special and heartfelt thanks to SPARCC

volunteer, *Jayashree Puranik*, for her dedicated and invaluable support and contribution to our services.

- *Mr. Rupendra Mukherji* for the space and infrastructure to write the book.
- *Prof. Madhu Khanna* for review of the manuscript.
- *Britt Marie, Eva, Monica* and *the* **Board of FFIA** for their constant support.
- *Aditya Maharaj Singh* for giving us a great office to carry out our work.
- *Family members and friends* who have encouraged, sponsored and stood by us.
- *SAMARPAN FOUNDATION* for facilitating our efforts and services.
- *Patrick Sanfrancesco*, Chairperson & Mentor of Samarpan Foundation, a beacon of light and hope, for inspiring us to spread love, peace, happiness and kindness through our humble initiatives. In his words:

'Let me lose my sense of Self,
Let me gain my sense of Oneness.'

***

It is our hope that this book will open our eyes and hearts to a beautiful concept of kinship which crosses over the frontier of social divisions , surmounts the barriers of blood and overcomes isolation and separation.

A feedback from you , dear readers , will be greatly appreciated.

Dipika Maharaj Singh   *Madhuri Abhyankar*
Founder Director   *Programme Director*
SPARCC   *SPARCC*
sparccindia@gmail.com

FOREWORD

Fresh from the Pune based Film & TV Institute of India, I had just begun making documentary films in the mid-seventies, with a particular focus on social issues.

It was in that phase that I encountered Dipika(Jha) Maharaj Singh, who gave me a glimpse into the world of institutionalised children who had found a new life through adoption. It was a fateful encounter as I was to find out later.

In an effort to promote the idea of adoption in our country, especially adoption of the girl child, Dipika asked me to make a short film. During the course of my filming I interviewed lots of adoptive parents to learn about their experience of this somewhat unique path to parenthood.

It came as a great surprise to me that adoption was nearly a taboo subject which parents were so afraid to speak about, due to the social stigmas attached to the issues related to adoption of children who do not share your bloodline, indeed even questioning the validity of this bond. The prejudices were particularly surprising since adoption is such an ancient, time- tested relationship which has been so vividly portrayed in Indian mythology and folklore.

It amazed me that most of the parents I spoke to, were firm in their view that they would never reveal the fact of adoption to anyone, not even their child. It would remain a family secret. Personally I believed that it would strengthen the bond if the truth was revealed to the child with sensitivity and understanding at appropriate times in a child's life, because trust and truthfulness are essential components of a strong and loving relationship.

It was during these interactions and the overwhelming experience I had at the child care homes which I visited, that I developed the urge to nurture a child without parents. It was late in the eighties when I came across Palna, a child care center in Delhi where I had volunteered my time and services to help take care of the children. And that is where I met the little girl, Disha, who came into my heart and home and changed the course of my life.

When Disha turned seven years old, I took her to her child care home and showed her the crib through whose protective bars we had reached out to each other to begin our journey together as father and daughter. "This is where God left you for me," I told her. There was no other explanation for our wondrous relationship. Today, some decades later, she has grown up to be a film producer, developing her own scripts and making her own movies. We do not share genes but we are on the same wavelength and similar career path! Adoption is full of possibilities...

From the articles that parents have so candidly shared in this book, and from my own experience , I see what a long way adoption has come in our country and how greatly the adoption landscape has changed. However the experiences shared by such a wide spectrum of parents also reflect the undercurrents of prejudices still prevailing in our society towards such an enriching relationship.

The voices of parents heard in this book have so well conveyed the nuances of the rather complex relationship of adoption, and highlighted certain issues that still need to be understood and addressed, most particularly from the perspective of the child.

I see this book as a guiding light for all whose lives are touched by adoption.

~ Prakash Jha
FilmMaker
Mumbai, India

CONTENTS

PART 1

VOICES FROM THE HEART

VOICES FROM THE HEART

'Love is blind', so it has been said.

In the world of adoption this is not just a saying but a fact.

An anonymous birth mother relinquishes the custody of her child. An unknown stranger or a group of strangers take over the care of her child. A mediator introduces the child to strangers who are seeking to fulfill their longing for a child by taking care of a child born to an unknown other. A little finger reaches out to the wayfaring strangers and their heart reaches out to this tiny being who has manifested from an unknown origin. A bond is sealed. The bond called Adoption, perhaps one of the most complex relationships in the world, where one set of parents takes over from another in an unseen exchange of responsibility, in a blind process of trust and acceptance... truly a blind love!

The umbilical cord is transplanted to an unrelated family line and a new genetic fusion is created. The process of fusion begins with a 24 hour vigil, sleepless nights, diaper changes, feeding schedules, and meeting the needs of the child with consistency. It involves being present, emotionally and physically, with a gentle touch, a soothing voice, a comforting embrace and reassuring response to an infant's cry through continued interaction.

The parents did not give birth to the child but the child gave birth to them as parents. It is a huge responsibility.

The newborn parents have to work hard to create the fusion, to help their child cross a huge gap of loss and trauma which came as a legacy from the premature separation from birth parents. It is a formidable task.

The task does not end when their child begins to relax in the reassuring response they give to their child's needs. As the child evolves from one stage of development to another, awareness grows. Socialization exposes the child to a world outside the comfort zone of a protected home environment. The child experiences herself in relation to a world that questions her (adopted) identity and her very presence. The word Adoption which stood for fusion, becomes a cause for confusion. People question the reality of this parental bond.

The child does not resemble the distinct ethnic features of the adoptive family. Questions start playing around in the child's mind. If the parents have initiated an age appropriate and sensitive conversation on adoption based not just on fairy tales and legends but on reality, the child is on firmer ground. The child who knows nothing about his adoption has no foundation on which to build his life because the foundational pieces are missing. Complex behaviour patterns arise from this confusion as this relates to the most important fact of human life: birth.

Our physical presence on earth is the outcome of biology. Most human beings are Born. But a transplanted child is Adopted, never born. The term 'adoptee' seems to refer to a species who are not biological beings but adopted entities whose presence and identity is certified by a Court Order. It more or less sets the point of their existence to the time of their adoption, thereby closing the door to a traumatic or unsavoury past and de-recognizing their origin and birth.

Birth parents have retreated from their role in a situation of crisis. Adoptive parents are interested in starting a new chapter by sealing the pages of a painful past. While the adults have had time and space to reflect, grieve and take control of their lives, the child has not.

Adoptive parents have to give their child missing pieces of themselves, initiate adoption conversations to help their child understand the circumstances which led to separation from their birth families and provide the child space to come to terms with losses and grief. Otherwise somewhere between the dark story of birth and the Happy Adoption story, there will remain a blank page, a dividing line. It is this blank page, this dividing line, which creates a crack in the psyche of many young people.

This fractured identity crisis, when it has not been addressed with empathetic communication at different stages of development, have led to most crisis situations in domestic adoption.

Defiance replaces compliance and parenting involves grappling with unexplained oppositional behaviour. In young children it is often viewed as a disciplinary issue. In older children it is sometimes branded as the product of unknown genes. In reality it is the play of ambivalent forces inside the child's mind. Even doctors and therapists address the behaviour instead of the cause since adoption is not well understood. All children come into the fold of adoption from a background story of pain and loss. It is only natural that they will have a greater reaction to situations of stress and potential loss than a child born into the family, who has not faced disruption.

Therefore disciplinary measures as suggested by many advisors and specialists will suppress rather than address the underlying concerns. Hyperactive behaviour and poor concentration on academics are not due to lack of intelligence or effort but due to inability to apply the mind to the logic taught in a mathematics class when there is no logic in their own lives. Unfortunately children are given labels and medication rather than therapeutic measures to address early life trauma.

Why am I an Adoptee when everyone else in my class is not?
Why did my birth mother leave me?
Adoptive parents have given a life long commitment to care for me. Why didn't my birth mother fulfill her commitment?
Something wrong with me perhaps?
Am I the problem?
Will adoptive parents also abandon me if I am not good?
I need to test their commitment.
What if they die, who will take care of me ? I am not related to anyone in this world.
I need to be in control.
My parents left me. I cannot trust adults. I have to rely on myself.
Teacher wants us to draw a Family Tree... my tree is standing on top of the soil. It has no roots...
If I was with my birth parents, how would my life have been?
If she had not opted to leave me, perhaps I would not be alive...
If my birth mother returns perhaps my parents will return me...
Perhaps she would have understood me better and not scolded me...

Perhaps, perhaps, perhaps.

When there are no logical answers available, a state of dissonance arises. Children flounder wondering what is wrong with them. Parents flounder trying to understand where their love and care went wrong.

So many concerns haunt the vulnerable psyche of young adopted people. One of the greatest challenges adoptive parents face is how to address those concerns, which requires great communication skills as well. Many parents have difficulty with communication of ideas. Culturally too, there is difficulty in addressing issues concerning birth stories relating to unwed motherhood, poverty, violence and other painful circumstances in which the child may have lost birth parents.

In the background of distinct social classes which characterize our society, 'upper' class parents have to guard the social origins of their child from the superficial values of their social circuit. They also do not want to hurt their child by speaking about his less privileged social origins, or the surrounding pain, so the subject is taboo. The child internalizes the signals which this family secret may convey. Comparisons with cousins and extended family members also alienates them. A sense of unworthiness develops from within and stays locked inside. Minor stress may produce a volatile reaction ignited by the hidden issue. Some children develop a dual identity and always wonder which self is real. Adoptive parents are often beaten with the stick of adoption by their child, taking the brunt of their child's hurt, confusion and helplessness. This is manifested in anger outbursts.

The culmination of all volatile behaviour takes place at adolescence when emotions are at their peak. There is no harmony in the hormones.

Psychiatrists explain that the prefrontal cortex of the brain which enables a matured adult to self regulate behaviour patterns, has not developed in the teen even though physical development has taken place. Adolescence is most often the time for domestic war, a war behind closed doors when adoptive parents are as bewildered as their child, but they have to lock up their issues from a society which does not understand them. Teens swing between a love-hate relationship with their adoptive parents, a reflection of the war waging within themselves.

In-Utero losses are now known to impact hormonal balance in the infant. So even those adopted as infants can be impacted by greater reaction to stressful situations. But parents begin to see themselves as dysfunctional and question everything including the unknown genes of their child. Typically they go back to the child care center from where they adopted, after years of no contact. 'Did the birth mother have mental problems? Depression?' are the most often asked questions. Usually the answer is 'No'. She was just another woman caught in circumstances beyond her control. Holding on to a child against all odds is an act of maternal courage. Letting go of a child in certain circumstances sometimes takes even more courage... circumstances in which a mother knows she cannot fulfill her child's most fundamental need — the need for security.

A residual anger with the birth mother is often transmitted to the adoptive mother. The sense of rejection is carried forward to enact a rejection of the adoptive mother and parents are often at the receiving end of violence which is actually a distress call for help and understanding.

Some children retain a clear memory of their life experience prior to adoption, usually a traumatic situation which continues to haunt their young minds. While parents cannot take away the pain, bringing the pain out into the open, trying to help the child speak rather than suppress the events can release pent up stress. However difficult it can be it is important for parents to open a dialogue about a difficult past. Letting in the shadowed birth parents rather than denying their existence goes a long way in healing fractured identity where parents can share their child's story with empathy and without being judgmental.

Building trust is one of the most important tasks that adoptive parents have to work on. A truthful sharing of the adoption story is a fundamental part of a trustful relationship between the parents and child. If children learn their adoption story from a third party it shatters trust. In the words of an adopted youth, relationships are like glass, beautiful when they are transparent and handled with care, but if shattered, the pieces become weapons.

The sharing of the adoption story really begins at the beginning, prior to adoption. Some children are lost and found. Retracing footprints to the earliest point can also be a therapeutic exercise in re construction of the self for children who are trying to join the dots. Sharing the complexities of the early life story is not a one time event but an ongoing process which has to take into consideration the child's stage of development and emotional state. It is one of the most difficult tasks for adoptive parents to handle yet it is remarkable how many parents have helped their child cross over from trauma to healing by the sheer force of their parental commitment, love and understanding. It is a huge challenge. The adoption experience has shown that with support, it is possible to meet that challenge.

In today's scenario adult adoptees are able to search for birth families. Those who have found their past fulfill their curiosity and need for closure, then move forward without the ghost of an unknown past.

DNA testing is now enabling those with no information to launch a search with a view to establishing a concrete identity in case they view themselves as lost people. Recreating the self can be a lifelong process.

Children who come to their parents through adoption are often resentful that their adoption was not their parents first choice but a last option, and hold this as a grudge. In fact in life our circumstances often lead us into situations which may not have been our first choice nevertheless it was the most meaningful outcome for all concerned, including the challenges which came along the way. Certainly the adoption route took parents on a laborious path to attain parenthood. It did not come easy. It took hard work, commitment, compassion and courage to walk on an uncharted path.

It is important to understand that adoption is not the problem. Adoption is not a dysfunctional relationship. It is the circumstances in which adoption is rooted which pose problems when surrounding trauma has not been understood or adequately addressed. Adoption is a very wholesome response to a complex web of human problems. It is a transformative, life changing relationship.

Eventually adopted people who have been supported to explore their unusual lives, learn to integrate their past into their on going life journey. In that way they can view their lives not as fragmented pieces but as a continuous flow of events which are in fact linked to each other... not as uncontrollable Fate but unfolding Destiny.

In the following pages parents by adoption across India's diverse landscape have openly shared their parenting experience with its highs and lows. The life lessons that we gather about the parent-child relationship are so truly expressed in the words of Sufi poet, Khalil Gibran

"Your children are not your children..
They are the sons and daughters of Life's longing for itself
They come through you but not from you
And though they are with you yet they belong not to you.."

In the end adoption is an interactive relationship in which the interplay of a multitude of human emotions nurture and impact the psyche of all concerned.

The child who emerges is not a photocopy of the adoptive parents who nurtured him, not a fruit from the cultivated and curated orchard of their family lineage, but a fruit from a great forest of trees generated by Mother Nature to keep alive the diversity and creativity of this vibrant and symbiotic universe.

~ Dipika Maharaj Singh
Founder Director, SPARCC

THE PSYCHOLOGY AND NEUROSCIENCE OF ADOPTION

THE PSYCHOLOGY AND NEUROSCIENCE OF ADOPTION - A COGNITIVE NEUROSCIENCE PERSPECTIVE

Take a Rs. 5 coin in your hand and push it in some clay. For the impression of the coin to occur in the clay, the clay needs to undergo certain changes and change its shape.. The kind of impression that will occur will depend on the clay's density, while its flexibility will be determined by the temperature. Now think of the human brain as the clay – in response to experience or incoming information (i.e. the coin being pressed in the clay), the brain needs to reorganize itself.

This incredible capacity of the human brain to adapt, reorganize, and change with experience is known as neural plasticity. Neural refers to the nerve cells (known as neurons) that are the building blocks of the nervous system and brain, and plasticity refers to the brain's malleability or ability to change. For many decades, the brain was thought to be like an extraordinary machine – capable of amazing things but incapable of growth and change. However, growing scientific research has now presented strong evidence that from birth till the day we die, our brain can reorganize itself by forming new connections and pathways between neurons and neural circuits, rewiring to adapt to new circumstances.

You might have heard about changes occurring in the brain due to prolonged exposure to music. That is, renowned musicians not only show a change in neural circuitry, but neural connections made during music training are also thought to affect other factors outside of music such as human communication. Or you might have met a visually impaired person who has a heightened sense of hearing – the event of losing one sense rewires the others. While these are positive outcomes of neural plasticity, sometimes events that affect the brain can leave undesirable effects.

While plasticity occurs throughout our lives, the first few years of life are a time of rapid growth with the immature brain growing and organizing itself. As we age, brain plasticity decreases; a child's brain is thought to be more sensitive and responsive to experience or learning compared to adults. Thus, children can recover from injury much faster and more effectively than adults. While the basic structure of your brain will be established by your genes before birth (in our clay example, the density of the clay is its genetic makeup), its continued development depends on environmental enrichment (the temperature surrounding the clay and the kind of stimulation it receives). Because children's brains are constantly growing, adapting, and developing, each new experience structurally and functionally changes the brain.

Low-stress and responsive environments during childhood lead to healthy development whereas chronically adverse experiences such as neglect or family chaos fundamentally alter the functioning of neural circuits that are engaged in basic processes such as learning a new skill, memorizing things, or even regulating our own behaviours. When children are relinquished for adoption, they are separated from their mother and move on from the womb to an institutional setting and group care. Separation of the young from the parent is one of the most drastic adversities that produces profound changes in the brain that can even be long-lasting. In humans, as well as other animals such as primates and rodents, the young are not born with all the functions necessary to live, they need to develop these through interactions with others and their environment. However, if they are deprived of these interactions, these functions may not develop to their full extent.

Additionally, in both humans and animals, attachment cues are important. That is, at a very young age, we can recognize our primary caretaker such as a parent, with our senses (sight, voice, touch, or even smell). These cues make us feel safe. Think back to the time of your childhood when a familiar voice singing a lori or narrating a story perhaps made you feel happy and relaxed. However, when children do not feel such cues around them (for instance, when the child cannot hear the voice they have heard when in the mother's womb), children do not feel as secure, leading to changes in the systems that process stress in the brain. Early trauma and separation therefore may increase an adopted child's risk to interpret situations as more threatening and stressful when they are not, leading to aggressive or more exaggerated responses in stressful situations.

In addition to alterations to the stress systems, adverse early experiences, particularly during infancy and toddlerhood, also lead to significant changes in the development of brain systems that govern executive function. Think of executive function as a traffic police – in a crowded city like Pune or Mumbai, an efficient policeman will ensure the smooth functioning of traffic, remember to control vehicles coming in from all four lanes of the crossroads, multi-task, and adapt in new situations such as when an accident occurs, or rains flood the roads. In a similar way, executive function includes abilities such as working memory, flexible thinking, and the ability of self-control, allowing us to plan, focus, remember instructions, adapt when needed, and multi-task successfully. Executive function deficits are often seen in adoptees - typically because of adverse experiences such as separation, and neglect in institutional care that they may have faced before they were adopted. Executive functioning is also thought to be crucial for effective cognitive, social, and emotional progress, and adoptive children often show deficits across these domains of development, also leading to a heightened risk for psychosocial disorders. Compared to non-adopted individuals, adopted individuals may show higher levels of loneliness, and experience more stressful life events due to circumstances surrounding their birth and relinquishment.

However, just as the development of neural systems can be negatively impacted by early-life adversities, the notion of neural plasticity definitely applies to the potential for positive changes in the brain and associated improved behavioural outcomes. Given the malleability of children's brains, positive changes in their environment post adoption have reversed early stress effects on children's brain development. For instance, children who receive therapeutic interventions and/or are nurtured in enriched environments show better regulation of the stress systems in the brain compared to children who continue to live in stressful environments. In particular, since between birth up to 24 months of age appear to be extremely crucial to physical and cognitive development, children adopted at infancy are likely to be more well-adjusted compared to children adopted at a later age. However, even in later growing years, children show impressive catch-up in domains of development that they earlier showed deficits in, including intellectual functioning, executive function, and achievement in school.
Of course, there is substantial population variation in the

mental health and cognitive functioning of adopted children. While some show typical development and complete catch-up in cognitive development, others show more persistent delays. A number of factors are thought to influence these individual differences, including both genetic and environmental factors. Resilience (or the ability to recover from life's adversities) is often considered an important factor in characterizing children who show fewer vulnerabilities after stressful events. Resilience may depend on the genetic factors of the adopted child but is also primarily dependent on resilience-promoting environmental factors such as a supportive and cohesive community, and a responsible and responsive caregiver. Another factor is the sensitivity to different environmental contexts - highly sensitive individuals may both thrive in positive environments and struggle in poor environments, whereas less sensitive individuals may be less affected irrespective of whether the environment is poor or positive. This is of course not a *one-size-fits-all* approach where every highly sensitive or highly resilient individual will behave in the same way. Both genetics and environment are important in this regard. Environments differ to a large extent, and depending on the child and the context, the type of adoptive parenting also needs to change. We need to remember that the goal is not to *change* a child to mold them in a certain way ignoring their past experiences and neural changes, but to encourage them to achieve their full potential as *who they are* and not *who you want them to be*.

The author notes that most research in the field of neuroscience is based in Northern America and UK/Europe. Even so the basic principles of neural plasticity still stand, and although early adversity can lead to profound changes in the brain that might result in adverse behavioural outcomes, these changes have been known to reverse given the right environmental support from adoptive parents and the community as a whole.

References:

- *Finet, C., Vermeer, H. J., Juffer, F., Bijttebier, P., & Bosmans, G. (2019). Remarkable cognitive catch-up in Chinese Adoptees nine years after adoption. Journal of Applied Developmental Psychology, 65, 101071.*

- *Fisher, P. A., Mannering, A. M., Van Scoyoc, A., & Graham, A. M. (2013). A translational neuroscience perspective on the importance of reducing placement instability among foster children. Child welfare, 92(5), 9.*

- *Harlow, E. (2019). Attachment theory: developments, debates and recent applications in social work, social care and education. Journal of Social Work Practice, 1-13.*

- *White, L. O., Schulz, C. C., Schoett, M., Kungl, M. T., Keil, J., Borelli, J. L., & Vrtička, P. (2020). A Social Neuroscience Approach to Interpersonal Interaction in the Context of Disruption and Disorganization of Attachment. Frontiers in Psychiatry, 11, 1437.*

*~ **Kohinoor Monish Darda***

PART 3

THE
PARENTING EXPERIENCE

EXPERIENCE REMAINS A GREAT TEACHER

When people declare that they are going to adopt a child, the first question asked is: Why are you adopting? Is there any problem?

Questions like this need to be answered.

Our adoption story began nearly three decades ago. My husband and I lived in a rural area near Pune. We both come from responsible families who believe in fulfilling their social obligations. Our parents had seen the struggle for Independence from close quarters. My husband's parents had devoted their lives to the freedom movement. We both grew up with a strong sense of social responsibility.

We have made this introduction with a view that when we adopt and people ask us questions about our motivation for adoption, our answers should be clear and honest.

Within a month of our marriage, we decided that we would give birth to the first child and we would adopt the second child. We were aware of the changing times and changing social circumstances. We were firm about being financially independent first before starting our family. If we had a son we would adopt a girl and if we had a daughter we would adopt a boy. Our problem was not the inability to have a child, so our ideology was the reason for adoption.

We completed our family of four by adopting a girl. We

completed the adoption process at the right age. My husband and I discussed it very logically. We had decided on some criteria for adoption...

- First and foremost, we decided to have our children by the time we were thirty years old.
- The difference between the two children should not be more than 2 years.
- Of the two children one should be our "own" biological baby and the other should be adopted.
- Of the two children, one should be a son and the other a daughter.

After 2 and a half years of marriage, a son was born to us. When he was 1 and a half years old we made our first visit to the childcare and adoption agency. At that time it was certain that we would adopt a daughter. A series of social workers guided us. The adoption agency's Social Worker gave us information about the Agency and the childcare center. Another Social Worker took care of the adoption-related process.

At that time the adoption process was very different from the current process. My husband and I were asked to fill a questionnaire with about fifty questions without discussing or communicating with each other. We had to submit many important documents along with our questionnaire. A few days later the social worker who had been assigned our case, paid us a home visit early one morning. It was more comforting to be interacting in a homely atmosphere rather than in an impersonal office. From morning to evening she carried out our interviews. She asked our neighbours about their opinions about us, observed the atmosphere of our home etc. and then submitted her report to our Agency.

During all this time we developed a different kind of relationship with the Social Workers at the agency...a comfort level. They were very respectful of our emotional needs. They would welcome us warmly whenever we visited the Agency. It was very reassuring that we were not alone on this uncharted path.

Finally came the great day when we were to welcome our little baby home.

The atmosphere was very festive. A big rangoli was drawn at the entrance of the Agency. My husband and I, together with our son, were made to sit down. We were garlanded and the little baby was placed ceremoniously on our laps. Our Social Worker performed a traditional ceremony to bless us. Our son jumped with joy when he saw the little baby. He danced around in ecstasy. He was 2 and a half years old. It was a dream come true. We distributed sweets to everyone. We spent a happy and unforgettable day at the Agency.

At home, we bustled about. Baby food tins, special baby items, medicines, milk tins, clothes, all the new things filled the whole house. The everyday routine for all of us changed. I had taken leave for the first three months. A woman had been appointed to give the baby an oil massage and a bath. In the beginning, the baby was a little weak and could not digest even cow's milk. She had a wound on her head, which slowly disappeared on its own. Three months fled by just watching her grow.

The emotional involvement between the four of us grew with the lisping and innocent gurgling of the baby. Our relatives' hesitations decreased and their participation increased. As many colours blend together to make one colour, our baby along with us, became an integral part of our family and our lives.

As the years went by, an independent personality developed. Of course, our daughter started behaving/interacting in her own individual style with everyone. Since both of us were working, the siblings took good care of each other.

Today when we observe her as a person we realise that she has become someone who thinks independently and chooses and handles her path on her own. We are her trusted guides. She discusses any topic with us freely and asks us for our opinions, and also convinces us about her opinions. She's a happy and joyful person. She got married two years ago and has created a separate and respected position for herself in her new family with her in-laws.

As her parents, we have understood an important issue relating to children by adoption: their identity development... how they view themselves when they grow up. This is the biggest challenge for parents to support. It is important that a child is strong physically, but it is much more important for us to help our child to be mentally strong and to develop a healthy self-esteem as well as a satisfactory thought process. When children realize they are adopted they become unsettled, restless, emotional, sensitive, self-pitying, and sometimes aggressive. Many times, they feel lonely and isolated. This period is difficult for parents as well. Parents have to understand their child's feelings and prudently and sensitively handle those feelings. Parents too may feel bewildered. While explaining that they love their children immensely, parents may have to go through some strange situations. I too felt at a loss.

Fortunately, there are good people around us. I visited our social worker in troubled times, she listened to my grumbling and told me that 'You have to find a solution to this situation and solve the problems yourself as you are her mother and closest to her. You love her the most. You know what is going on in her mind and you know how to ease her stress'. I realised that I would be the best person to solve the ' problems ' and after that things became easier to handle.

We, as parents, are our children's first true counsellors and our counsellors are people such as our Social Worker, who are experts, knowledgeable, and practitioners in the field. We should definitely consult them whenever necessary.

There is absolutely no difference between bringing up a biological child and an adopted child. However, the issues and challenges they face in some aspects of their growing experience are different. All parents face these challenges. Sometimes they consult counsellors and then become good peer counsellors themselves. Experience is a great teacher. We too have grown substantially alongside our child.

IS THERE ANYTHING LIKE TRUE OR FALSE PARENTS?

I am a single parent, and my daughter came home to me via an adoption process. We keep talking about adoption. Adoption, parents, and children are an integral part of the fabric of life.

In general people around us come to know about adoption very easily. It becomes common knowledge and the subject of gossip or personal questions.

Of late in my housing society, my daughter was questioned multiple times.
"Yeh tumhari mamma sachi hai ya jhothi hai?". 'Is this your true mother or false?'

"Jis parents ne tumhe birth diya wo mar gaye isliye tum ye mamma ke pas ho kya?" 'The parents who gave birth to you died, is that why you have come to this mother ?'

"Tumhe papa nahi hai?" 'You don't have a father?'

She has to answer endless questions to explain her presence in my life. I am glad that my daughter discusses these incidents with me, and I get the opportunity to clear up her doubts and clarify the answer to such probing questions. As a parent can we ask a few questions to ourselves and equip our children to have an appropriate response to curious and insensitive questions.

1. How much are you aware of the adoption process?
2. Can adoption be shared with your children as just one way of completing a family?
3. Can you equip your child not to pass on comments to other children on this process?
4. Are we allowing people to label our children as "adopted"?
5. How would you feel if someone comes to your child and says, "Are you a forceps baby or cesarean baby?" and that label sticks on you throughout your life?
6. Are you aware that you and your children are creating emotional stress in someone's life? Do you care about that?
7. Are you contributing towards making a mess or creating confusion in someone else's life? What exactly is your motivation in doing so?

Believe me, just the shift in our thoughts will bring a lot of change in the lives of children coming to a family via adoption. Let us be more sensitive while talking about adoption and create peace and harmony around ourselves.

My daughter, Nandita, and I were watching one video on Facebook, where this girl is born different (without legs) and now she is a gymnast. In her story, she says that she was given up for adoption after her birth. As a child, she was inclined towards gymnastics and she was seeing herself in another gymnast who is from Romania. Then she came to know that the famous Romanian gymnast is her younger sister.

After seeing this video, my daughter, Nandita, asked me these questions:
Nandita: Do you know my birth parents?
Myself: No, in India during adoption the organisation does not disclose the identity of birth parents.

Nandita: In future, is it possible to find out if I have a younger sister?

Myself: Maybe, when you become 18 years old you can ask your organisation to help find your birth parents.

Nandita: I don't wish to meet my birth parents.

Myself: Any reason?

Nandita: No, you only are my mother, no one else can claim to be my mother.

Myself: Yes, But she gave birth to you.

Nandita: I just wish to know if I have an elder or younger sister.

I shared with her the story of her birth mother …a single deserted mother. I made it a point to make it a realistic non-fictitious story, while also reinforcing only positive feelings about both her parents.

Nandita: One should get married, and at the age of 24-25 years think of having a child.

Myself: You know beta, you are my daughter. So your birth mother's role was giving birth to you. That's why you both chose each other, while We both chose each other to live together in this life.

Nandita: Yes...even the grandmother in that house is not loving, my grandmother is very loving.

Myself: How do you know that! Are you sure about it?

Nandita: I know it...I can sense it…

Nandita is my daughter. We share a very close bond. But she has strong intuitions about her birth family. We all seem to be connected by an invisible thread which is not cut off by adoption.

PARENTHOOD IS
CHALLENGING BUT NOT DIFFICULT

I am proud and love to be known as Rudra's mother. It had been three years since I, Kanta and my husband Manoj were married, and we did not conceive a child. Instead of undergoing numerous medical examinations and tests that were not only expensive but would also have been very painful mentally and physically, especially for me, we opted for adoption. It was a positive choice.

We were blessed that our families on both sides were modern in their outlook and accepted our idea of adopting. They expressed that we were free to make our own decision. They would always support us. With the whole family's support, the process of adoption became easy. We completed all the requirements and procedures, then we had to wait.

In the case of a biological pregnancy, one knows one waits for nine months & nine days before a child arrives. In the case of adoption, we had no idea how long we would have to wait for our baby. We were excited and eager but sometimes we would panic a little. We were happy to make financial arrangements to provide for the security of our forthcoming child. We also changed our daily routine to prepare for and adjust to the arrival of our baby. At last on a very special date, after an 11-month long wait, a beautiful flower, Rudra, bloomed in our life. He was transplanted from an institution into our home and our lives changed completely. Days and nights flew by in caring for Rudra. We had to plan our daily schedule to suit Rudra's routine. Initially, I was always alert and on my toes to look after Rudra day and night. Gradually I realised that as a caregiver and a mother I had to take care of my personal health as well. Both of us were working and ours was a nuclear family. We had to plan our work and schedule. Though it was a balancing act it gave us great pleasure. Gradually we managed Rudra's routine according to our office timing. I stayed home during the day to take care of Rudra and at night Rudra's father took care of him.

When he was three years old, Rudra started going to a well-known English Medium school. I am in full agreement that no child should be compared with another. However, as a parent, it is important that one should observe the child's abilities alongside his peers. We became aware that Rudra was not able to do things that a child his age should normally be able to do. Also, Rudra was behind his classmates in his studies. One of our friends who knew about us and our adoption experience suggested that we should consult a counsellor. We took his timely advice and consulted a reputed counsellor in our city. The counsellor said Rudra had dyslexia, a learning difficulty, but this diagnosis would be confirmed only when he turns six years old, after certain tests relating to intelligence and brain development. When we did the first tests Rudra was just 4 years old.

Dyslexia was a new challenge for us all. We had just started sharing the fact of his adoption with Rudra. Our Social Worker was helping and guiding us in this challenging issue in adoption. As new questions arise in the adoption journey we continue to seek her support. We had heard of physical illnesses before, but we were unaware of learning difficulties. Could it be cured with medicine? Would the treatment be very expensive? All such doubts bothered us. At the same time, Rudra's school too informed us that Rudra was falling behind the class in his academic curriculum. The school counsellor too expressed her doubts that Rudra may be suffering from dyslexia.

In order to understand dyslexia and get as much information as possible about this condition, we referred to the internet. It was encouraging to learn that famous people like Albert Einstein, Leonardo da Vinci, Abhishek Bachhan, also had dyslexia. Dyslexia is not a disease but a certain type of disability. We also learnt that a person who has Dyslexia will often have an average or a very high I.Q. which psychiatrists call Superior I. Q. Rudra has an I.Q. Of 125, i.e. Superior I.Q. We decided that we would not become disheartened but accept this challenge happily and positively. It would be useless to blame the circumstances as the facts would not change. By facing the challenge, we will definitely find a solution.

Now we had to overcome two challenges at the same time. On the one hand to break the news gently and gradually to Rudra that he was not a biological child and on the other hand to deal with his dyslexia. At that time, I was teaching in a school while Rudra's father was working in a Government office. Our child would now require a lot more attention from us. We had to give more time to his challenge, so I decided to reduce my hours of teaching in the school. I talked to the school principal and she allotted me a timetable of 4 hours. We realised at this time that Parenting, whether biological or through adoption, needs the support of Society. We were going to need a special educator for Rudra. Special Educators or Remedial teachers teach dyslexic children by a play-way method giving them basic education and forming their own learning pattern which is Remedial teaching. Children suffering from dyslexia need counselling and Remedial teaching. This is the treatment for dyslexia. Dyslexia remains with the person for life. It never gets 'cured' but its intensity can be reduced. We started Rudra's remedial sessions on the advice of his counsellor. She said that the sooner it was started the better.

In order to understand remedial teaching and to make sure that I was going along the right direction which, I thought, was equally important, I attended 50 sessions of remedial teacher training. From now on two days in the week before school from 10.30 a. m. to 11.30 a. m. Rudra's remediation was started. He attended school between 12.00p.m.to 6.00 p.m.. For all these routines it was very important to take care of Rudra's health. A lot of attention had to be paid to his diet, stamina, and mood. We also had to plan for the time all this would take and money it required. Remedial Teaching and counselling are quite expensive. Family members were not aware of these things, so their reaction was: Why all this fuss.? Once the children grow up they automatically learn. Why this new fad? Unnecessary and wasteful spending of money. We had to hear such comments time and again. We had to control ourselves. When working on all these problems, parents have to be strong, both mentally and physically.

Parents have to find and give time to themselves and only then is it possible to be more positive. To achieve this state of mental and physical health, every morning I left home and spent an hour doing yoga. Similarly, I spent time at night and read my favourite authors' books. While doing this I had to take care that Rudra was not being overloaded. For example, if the Remedial Session was in the evening then on that day Rudra could skip homework even if it irritated his teacher. It had to be managed carefully. Our friends whom we referred to earlier stood by us in all our efforts and strongly supported us. "Do whatever you think is right even if it is not productive, at least no harm will be done". Such positive support from them gave us special positive energy.

During this time, (repetition) we continued the process of sharing with him the fact of his adoption. We told him the story of Karna. We took him to an adoption agency in our city expecting some questions after his visit. Rudra started questioning who were the children in the care home and why did they live there? Where were their parents? We replied that they did not have a mother or a father. Then he asked if they would get mother and father, to which his father replied that some other mothers and fathers would come for them and take them home. Then Rudra said let us take a baby home. His father replied that he and Rudra's mother had come there one day to meet the babies and one baby smiled at them and they took this baby home and this baby was none other than our Rudra. He was overjoyed and hugged his father. There ended the subject of adoption. The process of sharing the fact of adoption with an adopted child continues for a long time. We too were overjoyed that he accepted his adoption with ease, however the process of sharing this fact with an adopted child is not a one time activity; rather it continues for a long time. As the child grows up his understanding becomes deeper and so do his/her questions.

Rudra turned six while balancing both these things. He was tested in the hospital where we were given to understand that Rudra had two learning difficulties. He had dyslexia and dyscalculia. It was difficult to understand both these problems and to think positively. Rudra also had a difficulty of eye-hand coordination. His motor skills had not developed. Motor skills allow the gaps between fingers to get a good grip. Similarly, it strengthens the hands for writing. Occupational therapy was needed. All these indicators are seen in dyslexic children. Again, there was a need to make time and financial adjustments.

All these difficulties depressed us for a while. Why did WE have to face these problems? Will everything work out fine? At this time Rudra's counsellor helped us. She was like an aunt to Rudra. We felt encouraged again because of her. The school informed us that we should make Rudra repeat Sr. K. G. We agreed. Now the question was how to convey it to Rudra as all his friends would be going to the first standard. However, Rudra accepted this when we said he had yet to complete six years and children below six years are not allowed in the first grade. This satisfied him. Such small testing moments kept presenting themselves. They still do.

Continuing the process of sharing the fact of adoption was also important as it was absolutely necessary to let him know that he was not a biological child. Who is better able to convey this difficult reality to him than us, his parents, as children have more trust in their parents than anyone else. Rather than avoiding the questions asked by children they should be answered in a way suitable to their understanding. Our experience is that children accept it more easily if we tell them ourselves. One night, Rudra asked where his birth mother was. We said she must be very far away as she had not come for so long and would probably not come at all. On hearing this Rudra started crying.

We asked him gently why he was crying. He replied that he was afraid that she would come and take him away and he did not wish to leave us! We explained to him that she would never be able to do that.

After this incident for a week, Rudra appeared very frightened. He did not leave the house or even go to school. When we questioned him, he kept quiet. But we knew he believed his mother would kidnap him and he was feeling insecure. I went to see his class teacher and told her what had happened, and that Rudra would not come to school for a few days. By divine coincidence, it turned out that Rudra's class teacher had also adopted a girl, so she helped us. She rang up Rudra and talked to him on the phone and convinced him to return to school. This moment is very memorable in our lives.

After this Rudra never said anything concerning adoption but we advised him that it was our secret and it was not necessary to reveal it to anyone on his own. We told him that if anyone did come to know and asked him questions he should just tell them that he was adopted. There was nothing bad or untruthful about it and if anyone related any distorted things to him he should come and tell us about it or discuss it with us. Nothing should be kept hidden. A lot of time had to be given to this issue. We had to talk to him repeatedly to make Rudra strong and to face the world firmly. This exchange between us was very supportive of our child. Now Rudra has accepted and adjusted well to being adopted.

When I go as a guest speaker at a Pre-adoption workshop, I share my experiences. Before going I tell Rudra about my visit and ask him if he would like to give a message to the New parents to be. He asks me to tell them all good things about him and that he does not trouble me so that these parents would also adopt. At times, he wishes that he had hair like his father forgetting he is adopted. Then he asks me how he would have looked if he had been born to me. At times when he disagrees with his father, he says to himself why he smiled at us on that day? If he had not smiled his father would not have adopted him and then he would not have to be bothered by his father's discipline!

We were succeeding on one front, but we were still working with Rudra's learning incapability. Slowly Rudra was trying to overcome his challenges and Rudra's Remedial teacher was making great efforts to help Rudra with his remedial learning because it was arduous to manage his moods and get the sessions completed. That time the school was also pursuing us to change Rudra's school as students like Rudra would be detrimental in the school getting 100% result in the S. S. C. Board exams. To safeguard the reputation of the school, the school started to create pressure and fear in the minds of the parents that students like Rudra would not be able to learn properly in the school. It was another challenge but Rudra's counsellor informed us that according to the all-inclusive education law the school could not ask Rudra to change school. No matter what, Rudra's school would not be changed even if they had to fight with the school. They would have to find the GR and submit them to the school.

Slowly we began a campaign to collect all the information. Due to Rudra's counsellor, we started thinking if special concessions in the curriculum could be given to meet the challenges faced by students? Could a separate special pattern of examinations be brought into practice for their needs? With our help and with other parents like us, our counsellor made a documentary and met and presented it to the(then) Education Minister.. After discussion with him, a new GR was drawn for learning for incapacitated students who would now be able to study in mainstream schools with all the children. Separate rules for concessions in studies and examination patterns were drawn up. Then we had to make a few visits to the school and convince the school that Rudra can stay and study in the same school. Every year we have to meet his class teacher and inform her all about Rudra and how he should be handled. We have to tell this as Rudra has a high I. Q. and takes advantage. He tells the teachers that he has dyslexia and so is unable to write quickly or he cannot copy down in his notebook what is written on the Board. When we were made aware of it we firmly told Rudra that after his five years remediation he has been cured of dyslexia. Sometimes for the child's good one has to take recourse to falsehood. Rudra's counsellor and his remedial teacher too supported us as Rudra would not have believed us if they had not backed us.

Rudra is 14 now. He has entered the teens and his understanding, behaviour and development are suitable for his age. His questions have changed. His emotional needs from his parents are also changing. Though not easy, I repeat parenting is not difficult, but it is challenging. The challenges change at every stage of the Child's age and parents too have to change and adapt accordingly.

Nowadays, if I am invited to pre-adoption parent's workshops as a guest speaker Rudra wishes to accompany me to speak about himself. It is definitely a positive change in Rudra. Rudra is, as some knowledgeable artists have said, a born artist. His artistic talents are innate. In future, we wish Rudra may make a name in the artistic field. Rudra is musically (artistically sounds repeated) inclined too and has appeared for three exams of Tabla. Both painting and tabla have helped him in the development of motor skills and attention span.
Rudra is the captain of his school's volleyball team. Rudra is now in the 8th standard. To prepare for the SSC. Board exams he has to start some remedial sessions. According to Government G. R., he is allowed to have a writer. It is

necessary to prepare him for it so that he is ready for it when the time comes. I too will have to give him more time, so I left my school job and have taken up a part-time job. My office timing matches the time Rudra is in school. Rudra also desires that at least one parent is at home when he comes back from school.

Until now in all the problems we faced in our journey with Rudra, the cooperation and help of all our relatives, friends, or Social Worker, our counsellor and remedial teacher made our battles easier to face. If we firmly support our children at all times, Society also pays attention and accepts our viewpoint. Society does not look down upon or debase adopted children or adoptive parents, and members of our society gradually learn to understand and assimilate the differences.

Lastly, I only wish to say that allow the children their space. Let them grow up to fulfill their own unique potential. Just guide them and help them to differentiate between right and wrong. Do not impose anything on them. Be their support system and your child may be an Einstein or a Leonardo Da Vinci...or just be your remarkable Rudra himself!

BUILDING ON THE BLUEPRINT

Human beings have certain inborn capabilities. However, with what capabilities a child will come into this world, one cannot say so. Whether a child is your biological child or adopted makes no difference. So, feeling that your child is the best is true for both, a biological or an adopted child. In nature versus nurture, I firmly believe that nurture should play a larger part in bringing up a child. Nature is the blueprint. Building on the blueprint is the role of parenting. My daughter first asked me a question when she was two years old. It was at that time I started introducing the idea of adoption. It was a gradual process suitable for her age and understanding. A small child is dependent on the parent. Young children are not capable of understanding the meaning and implications of adoption. That is why they do not resort to rebellious extreme reactions. If the child is of an older age or in a difficult stage of development he/ she may be badly affected by poorly communicated information about the fact of adoption, especially, if the information comes as a shock to them without preparation. The worst situation is if they are informed about their adoption in words which are bad and hurtful by an outsider. In such situations, they run away or brood or become very aggressive. "You brought me and put me into this situation, so I am going to behave in this manner!". This is how they lash out at parents. This anger can also seriously affect their academics.

My daughter became aware of her adoption in stages by the time she was 13/14 years old. I always remained aware and explained to her as well, that except for the fact of adoption everything was normal in our relationship. For some time I accepted the risk involved, that she might think that certain things were being denied to her because she was adopted. Still, I would say 'no' to her for the wrong things. Later on, she admitted having thought that my discipline was due to the fact that she was adopted.Soon enough she realised that it was normal to be denied. (This has been shown beautifully in the movie 'Nal'.) She understood that boundaries and discipline are part of parenting.

People around us, according to their preconceived notions, have firm ideas regarding adoption. They spread their belief in society that adopted children are backward in their studies. Without bothering to understand any reasons behind their notions they just put a stamp of backwardness on them. Adoptees also conveniently believe that 'adopted children do not do well scholastically'. My daughter's school believed it and so did my daughter. A child may know that he/ she is adopted when just a child but the reality hits only at the age of 12/13. The mind is in turmoil and attention in academics gets distracted. An adolescent is also rebellious and has instability of mind. At that stage in the 5th/6th standard several new concepts begin and if they remain weak future education gets affected. For this reason, it is absolutely necessary for parents to be constantly aware of what is going on in their child's life and inculcate in their minds that adopted children are not inferior to other children. Parent's efforts may not always succeed. Some children are very quiet while some brood, some are happy- go-lucky while some are aggressive.

Many educationists are of the opinion that children should be educated in their Mother Tongue or the language spoken in the area they live in. I admitted my daughter in Marathi medium. Most of the children of our family or even children from the surrounding area went to English Medium school. For many years, my daughter complained about why I put her in Marathi Medium though later on, she realised that because she went to Marathi medium she was able to understand some concepts she had not understood before. The English language was something she was learning anyway. Not just my daughter but all the children in her school know the language well.

I always gave examples of intelligent, sensible, and versatile students as an ideal to pursue. However, I was aware that those highly accomplished and perfect children were just a handful. I realised that my daughter was ordinary like at least 95 % of the children are. All my friends talked about their children's faults and behaviour so even if I felt my daughter's behaviour was improper/ wrong, I realised it was actually quite normal and could also be attributed to the generation gap between us. Whenever I talked to her on behaviour issues, I used to tell her that though she was wrong she had the possibility to rectify and improve her conduct.

Formal education needs some special capabilities (especially without having any interest in it a student can learn and give the exam!). Each person/ student may not be as capable. Every person may not realise where his/her interests lie or even the time or pace of learning he/she will have. Constantly trying and exercising various options and choices may unexpectedly lead to the discovery of one's potential and inclination. I told my daughter that while searching for the right stream of education she also had to focus on becoming financially independent. It was my responsibility to help her to stand on her own feet. I would take on the educational expenses required for a suitable degree. However, if she kept on changing her tracks and searching for the other options she would have to pay for those expenses. After that whenever it was possible for me I would help her with her expenses but that would not be my responsibility.

The standard of our financial situation gives us certain advantages and our children naturally benefit from it. I made it clear to my daughter that it did not mean that my capability/capacity of earning should be her expenditure level. We had many tussles due to my attitude as a result of this view, but I wanted her to realise the value of every Rupee she spent (indirectly, I wanted her to feel the need to become financially independent which is very important in the modern world).

I repeatedly told her that it is a fact that man is a social animal but in reality, in our everyday life, there are very few people who are our well-wishers or are helpful when we are in crisis. That is why we should not pay heed to what others tell us but make our own decisions. By this personal independence, we do not fall in our own eyes. From her response and acceptance of this practical guidance, I gathered her thinking was the same.

Even if I had a biological child my policies/attitudes would have been the same. My daughter herself can state from her point of view if this was the right way to deal with the challenges of life.

Now a few details about my daughter. My daughter is a happy-go-lucky person. She had to face many problems in her school. I knew she had the capability, but she did not pay attention to her academics. In the 10th standard, I challenged her that in the last two months, "Study for two hours and show me how you fail", in that way I persuaded her to study. She cleared her 10th std. with 82% marks! She decided to take admission in the science stream. I told her if she went for science she would have to study hard for the first two years and also till she graduated. There was no option, she would have to study hard. I tried to dissuade her saying she should think 50 times before going for science. She just about managed to pass 11th and 12th standards. She selected architecture after her 12th standard exams. To my amazement, she changed drastically once she started her architecture education.

Her important capability was a vision for beauty and excellent visual memory. My mother always sided with her saying she is an artist, that I should permit her to do what she wants. Let her follow her own talent. In architecture, she found her direction. Besides always standing first throughout college, in the final year she ranked First in the university and got a gold medal. Then she got a job in Ahmedabad for a year and went to Germany for masters on a full scholarship. After completing her masters for the last two years she is working in Germany in a German firm as a landscape architect. She should at least be financially independent as my wish. I am so proud and content about her achievements.

In retrospect as I recall all her challenges, particularly in her educational journey. She was not alone in the challenges she faced, as many other adopted children have to confront similar issues. It is very important for schools to recognise those issues. My daughter's example could certainly be a learning experience. Hence I wrote a long letter to the school once she had made her way into her career.

Letter to the school's management sent by me

"

Letter to School Director and Trustees

In the year...My daughter....was admitted to the small nursery group of your school.

I was clear that the medium of instruction for her should be in our mother tongue, Marathi. As Marathi medium schools were limited the choice of school was not difficult. In this school being adopted and fatherless was accepted. She was treated like any other child and her life was made easy by the attitude of your teachers and other parents.

But when it was time for her to go to the seventh standard both of us got a shock as it had been almost decided that she would have to repeat the 6th standard. " Our School does not rely only on the examination report but also depends on other performances and merits of a student, and as I am good at singing why should I be left behind?" was her valid question. I had no answer to that. I was aware of her capabilities and where and why she falls short. That time the reply to her letter to the school was positive. Hence in June 2007, she was able to complete 10th standard. If she had been made to repeat 6th standard, her confidence would have received a great blow. I am grateful and thank the school for that positive decision.

The purpose of writing this letter today is that there are many children like my daughter in your school who have to overcome their 'difference' and mix with other mainstream children. To accept this fact, they have to adjust a lot mentally. Besides like any other child they may have to adjust with financial or other home problems. I have come to the conclusion that by observing such children from this and other schools, that around 6th /7th standard children undergo a lot of unease and mental turmoil which in turn makes it difficult for them to concentrate, to remain stable, focus only on their studies and do well in school. In the last few years, I have come across many students of my daughter's age (my daughter too had expressed the same) who are unable to bear academic failure. A general conclusion is drawn that, "adopted children are weak in studies", which is not the truth. Adopted children do face certain emotional and physical challenges which can be overcome with understanding and support.

With this background, I request that in future your reputed school should think about adopted children' performance in studies in a different manner. Maybe their base will remain weak but once they fail (without taking on board their wider capabilities), it will destroy their self-esteem and their future prospects of recovery and progress. Maybe as a result of a softer policy, there could be chances of failure in the 10th standard (in my daughter's case it was a possibility and I was prepared that she may fail in 10th standard), however, till that time the child would develop and with encouragement and support, the results could be surprisingly positive. Alongside other issues relating to the child's development would be effectively handled.

Whatever my daughter's result, I had decided to write this letter to the school as I felt it was necessary for the School to take note of this experience and observation. As she passed 10th with good marks it helped me to be certain of my observation. She benefited and scored good marks also because of the relaxation of the policy of the S. S. C. Board examination. She had also scored though more than 70% in the school's second prelims. This success may have made us happy but both of us are aware that she has to achieve a lot more and go a long way still. As the base is not strong she may have a lot of problems ahead in her education or may even have to face a great failure. There is a great change in her attitude now. Even if she is unsuccessful in future she will look for the reason of failure in herself and will not put the blame on circumstances. The school's good wishes will always support her.

Thank You.

”

My daughter surpassed all my expectations. Our teamwork as Mother and Daughter helped us fulfill all our aspirations and build on the blueprint of her genes.

THE MATERNAL WARRIOR

During the two decades of our adoption journey, the first eight years were spent in a small town and the remaining years were spent in the city. In both the settings, a small town and a big urban area, what I intensely experienced was that our Society, even today, does not accept a normal family with an adopted child. The only difference is that in a small-town people ask questions directly while in a city people are not open, but their attitude and their body language convey their social prejudice against adoption. Everywhere the attitude towards adoption was the same and we could not get away from it.

As Divya started growing older I always told her that in her life she will come across all kinds of people with all kinds of prejudices. Whenever she finds herself on one side and social attitudes on the other, she can remain assured that I will firmly stand by her and I will not give a damn about our Social circle. Whenever I had to stand in support of my daughter, I was blunt and gave people a piece of my own mind. At times I was aggressive in dealing with people. That is why I think people did not try to challenge me or my daughter. Some experiences though remain engraved in my mind forever.

Divya was about two and a half years old and a watchman and his wife stayed in the next house. They had a six months old daughter and Divya always wished to go and play with the baby. But the woman treated her a little differently as she was an adopted child. So, I never let Divya go there.

One day Divya was insistent so I allowed her to go but I was paying full attention to the woman to see if she said anything to Diva. After a little, while the woman came out for some work with the baby, I was watching from our upstairs window and the woman asked Divya, "What is your mother doing?", to which Divya replied, "She is doing some work". To this response, the woman again asked nastily, "Which is this mother of yours?" Little Divya did not know what to say. I was intensely angry. I rebuked her severely and retaliated by telling her that instead of questioning a child about their mothers she should find out how many 'Kept Women' her husband had. That shut her mouth.

The second incident occurred when Divya was four and a half years old and the town had a 'Healthy Child' competition. According to all the criteria Divya was undoubtedly the best choice. In the last round, some questions regarding the health of the child were going to be asked to the mother. A paediatrician from the town was the examiner. He was aware of our adoption. He asked me a few nonsensical questions like, 'This year where did you go for a holiday?' We were put out of the competition. Divya scored the best in all the other categories and elimination rounds. But we were denied our relationship as a daughter and mother because Divya was adopted. I was upset and sad. I called our Social Worker and let out my feelings of hurt.

We cannot argue with everyone everywhere and we cannot fight everybody as we also belong to the Society. Even today, well-educated people also regard adoption with an extreme viewpoint. On one hand, they look at the girl with pity. On the other hand, if an adopted girl does something wrong their reaction usually is 'Oh, she does not belong to our family line, so she is behaving in an unacceptable manner.' Some also acclaim, 'You have done a righteous deed'. These are the most often repeated reactions and remarks we hear from the people around us.

An adopted child's family is also like any other family and it is quite normal that we would have arguments, differences and stress at times as all families have. It does not mean that there is no natural bonding or love in the family. Many people do not have the understanding and maturity to accept this.

I also have to share my experience that a woman who has not given birth to a biological child is not invited by her society to functions like the naming ceremony, baby showers and other auspicious occasions. She is not looked upon as an auspicious presence or held in esteem at these functions. In fact, I have seen that other women cannot accept the fact that an adoptive mother is a mother at heart just like any other mother who has given birth. The real relationship of motherhood begins in the heart.

Before I adopted a child I had four abortions and my sister-in-law did not conceive either. Both of us understood the feelings of the other. Our mother-in-law, fortunately, did not hurt us by making adverse remarks. But other close relatives have shown their opinion by making remarks about our inability to give birth, or by their body language. They have never invited us to auspicious family functions. They have shown that they would not appreciate our shadow to fall on their new born or pregnant women. These women may be well-educated doctors, engineers and other professionals held in high social standing, but their attitude and their hearts are very negative. I have made it a practice to avoid going to such functions even if I am invited.

Divya will be twenty years old soon. I was not aware of how time passed. I have come across many types of experiences. People hiding behind masks. These experiences have taught me to accept the bitter truth.

I am indebted for life to the birth mother who gifted me this wonderful motherhood. The beautiful relationship with my daughter has brought love, happiness, and satisfaction in my life.

HONESTY IS THE BEST POLICY

We have two beautiful, intelligent, and different chalk and cheese children aged 13 (daughter) and 10 (son). We have adopted them from the same Childcare Institution. Over the years, their bond has further strengthened because they both know that we adopted them from the same Institution. And this was our reason to adopt from the same place, to give them both the same rooting, despite their differences and the difference in their birth stories.

The decision was after multiple failed IUI and IVF cycles that completely broke me. We were overseas and had a lot of time to heal and then reflect on the way forward. That is when we discussed adoption as being THE only alternative to us becoming parents on our return to India. Thus, our decision was made, or so I thought. While my husband was very clear in his head, it was I who had lots of questions, doubts swirling around in my head. For most of the time, I didn't have answers to all my questions and did not know where to look for answers either as there was no one in either of our families who had adopted a child. There were no adults that we could consult or seek advice from. So, it was a rather clinical and practical decision.

On returning to Mumbai, we got busy with our careers and adjusting to the pace of the city, and actual research took a back seat. One day, I read in the newspaper, that an open house on adoption was being conducted over the weekend. We both decided to attend the open house as a starting point in our journey. It was an interesting and little scary experience as the panel shared good and bad stories. I remember there was an official from one of the Institutions that gave a very rosy and happy picture of the entire process while another official gave a very devout religious picture. Neither helped in resolving our concerns. Luckily for us, a friend and her husband had recently adopted a daughter and I reached out to her. The couple gave us some very solid and practical advice for which we are eternally grateful. At the same time, my mother-in-law made a few inquiries in her city. Fortunately, she supported our decision to adopt.

We did not know anything about adoption. I started researching online and found very little information. My concerns related to issues like:
- *What is the Adoption Process?*
- *What are the documents required?*
- *How does one contact the institutions?*
- *While applying:*
- *How young a baby can we apply for?*
- *What should we look for when we do meet the babies?*
- *The health of the baby – both physical and mental.*
- *Will we be good parents? How will we know this is 'our' baby?*

Most of the questions were answered by our friends and paediatricians within the family, in free-flowing conversations. The more we sought answers, the more help we got and slowly we inched towards kickstarting the actual process of adoption.

Once we had filled and submitted all the forms and applications, the real challenge began. We also had to work on the backup family member to take over in case we both had some exigencies – a very important decision as well.

Preparing ourselves emotionally and mentally to become parents was an active part of the process. I was working for a large MNC and quit my job about 6 months (in retrospect) before we brought our daughter home. I had a very hectic and stressed job and wanted to calm down before becoming a mom. I am also a short-tempered person and went for an anger management workshop to learn how to control my anger. I also started yoga and meditation. Every day seemed very long. The wait for a call seemed distant and when we did get the call, we rushed to the Institution to be informed that there were two babies whom we could meet. We met both the babies on the same day. The first baby was in foster care and our daughter was at the institution. She was brought down to the office, while we were reading her medical file (as advised by our friends). My husband looked up and saw this beautiful, frail beauty. When he held her, she snuggled into his shoulder, like she always belonged there. I was still mid-way through her file when I looked up to watch them. I saw him admiring her long fingers and looking so lovingly at her. He caught me and just with his eyes he said, "She is ours!". I said, "If you have decided, can I hold our daughter now?" In response, she did the same thing to me, snuggled into my shoulder and I could not say no.

Once we had confirmed our decision to the institution, lots of things had to get done quickly. My father-in-law had to get an open heart surgery done and we wanted that over to have him back home in time for us to bring our daughter home. While he was recuperating post the operation, I had moved to Pune to get to know our daughter and familiarise myself with her routine. I used to go to the institution twice daily and spend as much time as they would allow me to be with her. In the evenings, we used to sit on the bench under a tree and look up at the sky with the sun playing down at her smiley face through the tree in the courtyard. Did I mention that she was six months old! For us, she was newly born.

My in-laws wanted us to bring our daughter home on Ashtami, as that is the day of Shanta Durga, the family deity. To this day, every year, we visit Durga Maa pandals for darshan on Ashtami and celebrate her homecoming on that day.

There was much excitement to bring our daughter home. All the elders from both our sides were present to bless our daughter at the beautiful, simple ceremony where the first adopted girl from the institution was given to us. Both I and my husband were over the moon. We could not believe that our wait was over. She was given a resounding welcome by my mother-in-law, a bigger welcome than I got when I came home as the daughter-in-law…(just kidding !)

She was accepted immediately by family. Her cousins could not wait to meet the little munchkin. Her older cousin sister went to a school near our house. Every alternate day she visited us straight from school to play with her. Her older cousin brother wore a pink t-shirt only for her. She loves both of them very much. She has friends with whom she has grown up in the building. Most of our friends came to meet the little one. We had a big grand celebration for her 1st birthday as this was also her 'coming out' to our extended families, professional colleagues and friends who had not met her yet.

Both my children study at a well-known school in Mumbai. they both have lots of friends and partake in various extracurricular activities and sports.

We call our daughter, 'Durga' because she has fought many obstacles very early in her life. She is inherently a strong girl and we are very proud of that. As mentioned earlier, she was the second child we met. She had more medical issues than the other child. In fact, our social worker sat us down to discuss the issues. However, we had decided she was our daughter and that was that. She was a seven month, premature baby, with very low birth weight and had suffered from pneumonia too. She was a very quiet baby. We were regular inpatients at her paediatric hospital as she fell ill very often for the first two years. Initially, we thought it was adjustment issues and she was reacting to the new environment but when it became a fortnightly event, we took her to the doctor. The brave little one underwent a battery of tests to rule out internal issues.... remember I said earlier she was our Durga !!

She went through an MRI machine to rule out GERD at eight months and was smiling throughout the test, while my sister and I were very anxious. We needn't have worried. She was poked with many needles to either put in a saline line or for a blood test, but she rarely cried, now she is 13 and she screams at the sight of a needle!!! She was finally diagnosed with Asthma and we started her treatment, we had to also find out her triggers for an Asthma attack and that meant exposing her to various stimuli. Now she and we are well aware of her triggers and know what we need to do should she have an attack.

She was a small baby and we wanted to increase her immunity and weight by feeding her immunity-boosting food. I remember asking my paediatrician when I could start feeding her eggs. She asked me to wait until she turned 1 year old and trust me when I say this, that I fed her eggs for breakfast on her first birthday! We were also told to handle her with kid gloves until the age of five.

We did that and when she turned three, she became an elder sister to a brother. He was adopted from the same institution and she was instrumental in meeting him and helping us decide her brother and our son. She was a part of every step of the process for her brother. In fact, we requested the institution to give him into her hands while she was happily perched on her father's lap. The photographic proof also helps in settling the ever eternal 'I hate you' amongst siblings :)

The second time around, we had applied for a full-term baby as the first addition to our family was still delicate and needed a lot of care. He was simply adorable and had THE naughtiest eyes, which thankfully he still has. Unfortunately, he fell ill while he was still in foster care with us, even before we got the official Adoption Birth Certificate. He was hospitalised and his elder sister made a small rakhi for him at home, as the commercial rakhi would be infectious. We did a small ceremony in the hospital and came back with tears of happiness.

Our son loves water. When my daughter turned five, we decided that teaching her to swim would improve and increase her lung capacity. Our son was only two years old when she started her swimming class and as I would sit alongside the pool with him, I found him always crawling to the edge of the pool and was scared that he would dive in without a thought. After about two months of constantly pulling or picking him away from the pool, I requested the swimming instructor if he could join too. They do not take children under five years for swimming, but they made an exception and took my son. This started their love for swimming and increased their sibling bonding. He is ten years old today and has learnt diving and can dive from ten feet above!

Our children have always known that they were 'Heart babies' (adopted). Our social worker, while counselling us, had mentioned that we should introduce the concept of adoption to the children from an early age. We followed her advice and were thankful to her, as when the time came to tell them, it was an extension of our many conversations. While researching for books on adoption to read to my daughter, I came across a very simple yet beautiful story, The Lonely King and Queen, published by Tulika. It is a bilingual book and the day we got our son home, we gifted the institution 100 copies of the book in Hindi and Marathi to help other parents tell their children their story and initiate the concept of adoption.

Our daughter was about ten years old when she wanted to know her story. Prior to verbalising her questions, she went through a week of anger, tantrums, crying and lack of sleep. We kept asking her and she would get angrier, so we let it pass until one school night, she refused to sleep and kept crying incessantly until I finally urged her into telling us what was bothering her. In response, she shouted and pushed me away. We both persisted and she finally said she wanted to know her story. Since we were putting both the kids to sleep, I told her that we should step out of the room and let her brother sleep. While my husband was putting him to sleep, I asked her to help me remove her official file from the storage. While doing that, I quietly told her that we have been waiting for her to ask her story. She seemed surprised. I guess she thought we would get angry, upset or feel hurt as she is a very sensitive child and does not like to upset or hurt anyone.

Once my husband joined us, we both took turns in telling her stories about her childhood. We also shared the detailed application form that we had filled individually. She didn't read it all but was surprised that we had each filled such a long-form!! She asked "Who am I?" to which my husband replied by showing her two certificates — the court given Adoption Birth Certificate and the PMC issued Birth Certificate. The first states Name of {adoptive} Father, Mother and Child while in the 2nd one states Name of Father, Mother and Child. He told her that she is our child irrespective of what the court certificate says and that the choice is hers to decide if she saw herself as described in the court certificate or the PMC issued certificate. She also wanted to know if we knew her birth mother and the reason why she gave her up for adoption. We told her that we did not know their details but were thankful to them as they gave us our opportunity to become parents. We also approached the school counsellor to meet with our daughter to help her through this phase, I was also counselled along with her. It really helped sensitise me to see her perspective.

In 2019, we shared my son's story with him. His story is different from his sister's but he wanted to know how they were in the same institution when their stories were different. I also took him to visit his home prior to coming home in 2019 and though he was a little scared and held my hand while we walked towards it, his natural confidence came through when he introduced himself to the nurses at the reception stating the name registered in their files. I was very happy and surprised at how well he understood. I have asked him on several occasions if he wants to know more he can always ask us. So far no more questions. Que Sera Sera.

During the 2019 summer holidays, while driving to a hobby

class, my daughter asked me why we changed her name, who named her while she was at the institution and who amongst us held her first? My son was in the car too and he was listening intently and quietly processing the questions. I answered my daughter truthfully and told her that when we decided to have children if we had a daughter I would name her 'XYZ' and if we had a son, then my husband would name him 'XYZ'. She had the broadest smile when I told her that her father held her first. She is totally a 'Daddy's Girl'. The next morning my son asked me the same question again while driving to the class.

This time I told him that his sister held him first. He refused to believe it! That evening they were quarrelling over something silly and he teased her by the name that we changed and she, in turn, teased him back with his name that we changed. That was so simple for them, we adults complicate it in our heads. I, however, told them that these names would be our family secret, as I am not sure if the society at large will understand. Both the children attend a prestigious school in Mumbai. In the admission form, we had to fill in if they were adopted and we ticked that box. While submitting the supporting documents we submitted the adoption birth certificate too. Since the children are aware, we saw no reason in hiding the fact from their school either. They have faced NO discrimination in school. They both have lots of friends in school and they are average students academically. It has been hard on me personally to accept it, as whenever we discuss Nature v/s Nurture, everyone advises that nurture is greater and more influential. My husband and I have excelled academically and studied at the most prestigious colleges and Education has been the root of our progression. It took me five years of my daughter's school years to accept 'being average' is okay.

Since my elder one is a fresh teenager (just turned 13), we are currently facing and dealing with regular teenage angst. Though once, during the COVID lockdown, she did throw the 'mom comparator' to me where she mentioned that a good friend of mine is a far better and more understanding mom than me and wished that she were her mother! It hurts like hell, but you bounce back as we have been advised that they will throw this all the time at you once they know their reality. It's how we react that will keep the relationship grounded. My response to her was, she was open to go and ask my friend to be her mother. She was stunned into silence with my response. However, I also realised my mistake. They both are always looking to see and ensure that either one of us is always around. Maybe it is their fear of being abandoned again. We can only assure and love them and help them realise that we are NOT going anywhere. What they don't realise is the fear we (more me) have about them wanting to search or get to know their biological parents. I honestly don't know how I will react.

There have been occasions when we have imagined what their biological parents must be like, especially when they display some actions, respond non-verbally which is unlike either my husband or me. My daughter tends to twirl her hair when she is concentrating on something, neither of us does it. When we first told our friends that they were adopted, some of them flatly refused to believe it as our daughter looks exactly like I and our son looks like his father. We both have never been conscious of our looks, what society thinks of us or enforcing religious practices (he is a Hindu and I am a Buddhist). This did confuse the children when they were much younger as we celebrate all festivals with equal fervour, and they know that they have the choice to follow any religion.

We have had our fair share of violent tantrums. Our son has always had a temper. He is extremely short-tempered and can fly into a tantrum at the slightest provocation. As a baby, he used to hit, pull our hair, bite on some occasions. For a long time, we didn't know how to handle him, but slowly we realised that since he is a very hyperactive child and does not want the fun to ever end, going to the washroom, eating when hungry or fighting sleep was his triggers for a full-blown tantrum and have learnt to control them. Once, when he threw a tantrum in public for the helium balloon which is not allowed in the car, I chose to walk away from the scene but kept a very close eye on him. When he saw me walk away with his sister, who was pleading with me to go back and get him, he quickly got up and ran after us and quietly came and held my hand. Maybe it was a harsh way to react, but it needed to be done. Did I think about his fear of abandonment, honestly NO because we do not think of them as adopted children. They are ours and we treat and discipline them as most normal biological parents do. On another occasion, he was so violent that we had to physically restrain him in the fear that he may harm himself. Not just us parents but even the elder sibling now create diversions for the little one to get over his tantrums and cajole him into being himself and restoring his equilibrium.

We introduced him to the drums when he was three years old. I called him 'my drummer boy' and never let it on to him that the reason he is learning to play the drums is a way to release his anger. Now he enjoys playing the drums and has cleared Level 2 of the Trinity Exams with distinction. A very proud moment indeed. He has a very high level of physical suppleness and picks up sports easily and moves on to newer high-speed sports - having moved from football, athletics to skateboarding currently.

Now, the latest threat is, this is not my family, I am going away. We don't react and that further increases their angst. They have opened the main door and gone out of the house as an act of defiance. But we know they are just hiding behind the door and waiting to see how long it will take us to come out and look for them. We open the door in 5 mins. We used to call our daughter the lull before the storm!

As they and we are growing up, a better understanding of their triggers has decreased the incidents. Have they totally gone? The response would be No.

We are very thankful that so far we have not had to deal with any rejection from the child, bodily or mental harm, stealing, emotional distancing, freezing out or any self - destructing behaviours. In fact, the Covid lockdown has substantially increased bonding between the two siblings, especially their games, music and dance, followed by long-winded discussions on life and secrets each night before they go off to sleep. The elder one has already started to take on more responsibilities towards her own studies and physical training and also the academic schedule for the younger sibling!! We, the parents, are eagerly waiting to see both grow up into majors and help them to stabilise their lives. In the meantime, we are enjoying each moment leading to those years. The parenting journey has its trials, but 'no pain- no gain' as they say!

Retrospectively, these lines from Sound of Music would describe our journey

I (we) must have done something good
cause nothing comes from nothing
Nothing ever could
So somewhere in my (our) miserable past
I (we) must have done something good.

LOST AND FOUND

Well, where do we begin? Adoption has been a great journey with both highs and lows.

After a long wait for a biological child, we decided to adopt and were supported by both sides of the family and friends too. We only wanted a child, caste and creed were of no importance to us as all babies enter the world devoid of any labels. Eventually, we were shown three kids and our child just smiled at us and that was that...or so we thought!

He brought a tremendous change in our lives...life suddenly became meaningful. More than him needing us WE needed him. He became the focus of our existence. From the beginning, we told him you came from our heart and not through mama's tummy. Maybe that did not make much sense to him, but he accepted it the way he accepted everything about us, his parents.

Things were great till I suddenly saw him change when he was nine years old. His father was out of the station and he started disobeying me, throwing things, and generally not listening. I was at my wit's end...

One night I went to his room and held him close.
He just looked at me, hugged me and asked, "Am I adopted?"
I very calmly said, "Yes", although my heart was racing
"Did you buy me or steal me?"
I said, "Are your parents like that? Thieves?"

He said, "My friend told me so…"
I finally told him everything, all that I had suppressed so far.
We talked for ages and he said, "Why did you lie to me?"
I said, "I will never ever lie to you, you are our child. So, what if you are adopted? Aren't we a family?" Do you love us less or do we not love you?"
He was somewhat convinced.

When his father came back we shared what we had discussed. To explain the situation further we took him to the adoption center. We noticed that he was uncomfortable, and he wanted to quickly go back home. We consulted counsellors and had sessions with them. After this, adoption was never discussed again. Then there were a couple of more adoptions in our family so the topic of adoption came up again. People still ask him about being adopted but he tackles it well.

Then another major setback happened. He turned out to have learning difficulties (LD), he was found to be dyslexic. This diagnosis came at a time when LD was not so well known but we got a great counsellor who guided him beautifully and restored his confidence. We can never thank her enough. Our son has overcome many obstacles and is a great guy. He has had anger issues but with professional help and full family support, he is out of it.

So, my firm advice to all parents is that if you adopt, please never try to hide it from your child. Only you can explain adoption to your child with sensitivity, understanding and love. No one else can. Fortunately, adoption has become more common in our society. Also, many well-known people are adopting; it helps in positive reinforcement of the concept and joy of adoption.

Whenever you feel the need please consult psychologists or psychiatrists. There is no need to feel isolated, worried, or scared about sharing the issues that you are facing. We all grow through the complexities of human relationships. Be open and share the adoption story sensitively with your child. Truth is the key to open all the locked doors and set your child's mind at rest.

P.S.: I hate it when newspapers say, 'an adopted child did this or that.'

A child is a child, due to certain circumstances the child may have been adopted.

Adoption is not a label or a status. It is a positive, optional route to family building.

WHERE DID I GO WRONG?

I was born into a secure and good family. After my education, I got a good job as a teacher in a government school. Somehow it was difficult for my parents to find a marriage partner for me from our socio-economic level, perhaps because I did not have some of the physical attributes that potential grooms were seeking. When a handsome man without much means came along to accept marriage with me, I made a compromise and decided to agree to this match.

We did not have a biological child, perhaps due to our incompatibility. But my husband agreed that we should adopt a child. So, thirty years ago we adopted a baby girl. As she was very weak, my private doctor suggested that we adopt another baby, but I was firm and decided that I would massage her legs and make her walk. I took leave for 3 months from school and gave her treatment. We enjoyed this phase.

Her childhood developments made me happy. We were happy to see her dancing in school gatherings, enjoying her birthdays, picnics etc. After she started kindergarten and Primary school education, I used to share enlightening, educative and informative stories with her at the time of breakfast. Suddenly my husband passed away when she was eight years old. He had not been playing an active role in parenting our daughter, still, he was a male figure in our home. After his passing, I raised my daughter with the strong support of my mother, father and brother.

I enrolled her name for sports coaching. We also had a teacher coming to our house to teach her harmonium. We enrolled her name in a swimming class as well. We made sure she participated in activities like holiday camps, visited book exhibitions etc. for her future development. I was personally taking care of her and making sure she studied for her exams. We also used to visit the children's home from where we adopted her. This was when she was young, about 7 years old. She played with the children as she did not have siblings. After a while, these visits discontinued when she got friends and got busy with school activities. We never really discussed anything about adoption.

Everything took a new turn when she entered adolescence. She started ignoring her studies. She was not doing any house chores. She has a bad habit of washing her face and gargling in the kitchen sink. Instead of going to school, she used to wander about and lie that she had not received her exam results. Her teacher asked me to withdraw her name from school or else threatened that she would have a 'failed' remark on her report cards. In agony, we changed her school, but she never changed.

She left my house and went to live with my mother next door. She sat in a room farthest away in her grandmother's house and secretly started writing love letters to somebody. She started going to the store across the street to talk via a paid telephone and continued to do so for a long period of time. She never bothered about the money she spent on such prolonged phone calls. She took money for her typing class but never attended them nor did she appear for the typing exam. She started coming home late at night while lying that she had gone to her girlfriend's house for studies. If anybody scolded her, she would argue with that person. She never called me 'Aai' (Mother), instead, she called me 'granny's daughter'. She spent hundreds of rupees on kulfi, etc. for her friends and on expensive dresses for herself.

Once, her grandfather's cupboard was locked and the key was missing. It came to our notice that she used to regularly steal Rs. 500/- notes with the duplicate key from his cupboard. I kept an eye on her and found the secret place where she kept all the stolen money as well as the keys. I took it from that place, but she feigned ignorance saying that she didn't know anything about it. Even after this incident, she kept stealing money.

She used to hang out with another boy in a room in our house. Both used to have lunch from one plate. At night she used to sleep on the veranda and lock the door from outside. During the day when she was alone in the house, she used to lock the door from inside and used to tell us that she was afraid to be alone. We came to know afterwards that she used to steal money with the duplicate keys during this time. She went out of town saying that her girl-friends and the boy were going to stay at a relative's house, but that was a lie. A few days later the boy admitted her to a hospital but disclosed this to us much later. He didn't give us the name of the hospital or why he had admitted her. But it must be for abortion purpose. A month later, she started arguing with me about giving her Rs. 2500/- for her medicines. She was not ready to tell me why she was taking these medicines nor the name of the doctor. In the end, frustrated, I gave her the money.

Around the time she had gone out of the station, my father was admitted to the hospital and kept in the ICU. She never used to help me out during the hospitalisation. She used to roam around with the boy but never went to the hospital.

The doctor said that the chances of recovery were slim and keeping him in the ICU would not help but she forced the doctor to extend the hospitalisation in the ICU. I was not able to pay the bills. I sold my gold bangles and encashed some fixed deposits to pay the bills.

She used to send notes and call someone to roam around with her. It was very painful and our life was becoming worse than hell. My left finger was permanently bent when she hit me in the brawl. She used to grab her grandfather's hair and hit him, she hit my brother also. At last, we spoke about it amongst ourselves and decided to hand her over to the police. Police Officers helped us with admission. She created a nuisance in her Remand Home also.

For her 10th grade, we admitted her to a residential educational Institution. Here as well, she used to send notes to another boy with the help of other girls and ask him to come to meet her. She threatened that if she is forcefully kept at the Institution after 10th standard she would commit suicide. The committee members, in their meeting, decided to send her back to us and asked us to take her home.

During vacations when she was at home, she never used to come back before midnight. We had to keep the door open for her and we stayed up because we were worried. One day she came late at night and without letting us know, went off to sleep. The next day unaware of this I told my mother and father that we would go to the police to look for her. She heard this and took many sleeping pills secretly. When the residential educational Institute came to know about this fact they came and asked us to take her to the concerned hospital for further investigation. The Police took a statement, but the case did not escalate. She hid something in her jacket. When

she was brought home from the hospital she was not ready
to go back to the Residential Educational Institute. Somehow
we talked her into it and sent her back there.

During her 11th standard, though we brought her home,
nothing changed. She started dating a third boy. There were
similar incidents once again. Finally, out of the three boys,
one boy agreed to marry her as he came to know that after me
and my brother, my daughter was the heir of our property.
We had a meeting with the authorities of the residential
educational Institute and the marriage was fixed. She argued
with me for jewellery and asked me to give her ten thousand
rupees. When I asked her the reason, she once again picked
a big fight with me. I gave some money to the boy for some
expenses and for purchasing jewellery for the wedding. They
purchased low-quality jewellery and pocketed the remaining
money. They never gave me an account of the money they
spent but instead told the authorities at the Institute some
things about me that painted me in a negative light.

After her marriage, she demanded money several times
and made me cry. After some months she came to reside at
my place with her husband. During the nine months of her
pregnancy, all expenses were borne by me and I did all the
work. Then they sold the flat and went somewhere else. They
took forty thousand from me for purchasing a vehicle but till
date has not paid a single penny back. Whenever she came
to see me, she used to complain about my jewellery, money
and home.

I am in my seventies now, unable to go out shopping even
for my basic household needs. I am not able to do much of
the daily house chores. Whenever she comes, she comments
on my weak health and gets upset about many things. I don't

want her to come to my place because of this. Now she is asking me to give my father's house to her. Whenever she comes my blood pressure shoots up and I feel frustrated and exhausted. I think that I will have to go to an old age home in the near future. It is really very miserable even to think about it.

In the meantime, my son-in-law called to tell me that my daughter is doing a job in a private place and that she does not do any household work, neither does she prepare food at home nor does she serve him properly. He came to a decision to divorce her, but their daughter is the reason why he is not going forward with it. He has shared that his wife takes out a lot of anger on their little daughter. She seems to be carrying forward her anger. The daughter adores her mother in spite of her violence towards her. The husband has sought the support and intervention of child protection authorities. The child wants no separation from her mother and is very loving to her.

At my stage in life, I am really very tired and unable to do anything for her. I do not know what to do about this situation, so I am keeping a distance. Where did I go wrong ?

BORN IN THE HEART

Our son Vinayak's journey of life is a very joyous one. He became a part of our family as our son twenty years ago. An adoption agency helped us to become parents of this wonderful son. When our friends adopted a daughter from an adoption agency they introduced her to us and we too wondered why we could not become parents by the same path they had followed.

So our friends informed us about the process. The Agency helped us tremendously. (The words - a lot - have been used multiple times throughout the book, maybe because it is in part of our spoken English. We can consider changing it) We submitted all the required documents including our medical reports. We spent six months eagerly waiting to see our baby. At last, we went to see the baby boy early into the new year. It was cold and the nurse brought a baby boy wrapped in a blue blanket. The baby was shivering and crying because of the cold. The baby was handed over to me. He stopped crying in my arms, and he looked at me and smiled sweetly. He had a dimple on his cheek. I looked at him in fascination and immediately experienced love and affection for this child who was not born to me but was undoubtedly my son. My eyes welled up and I fell in love with the baby. I did not wish to let go of the baby. With a heavy heart, I handed him back to the nurse. We had to wait for just a few more days.

Soon Vinayak arrived. We gave him a huge welcome. Our home which used to always be quiet was now full of our relatives. It resounded with laughter. There was happiness in the atmosphere. We lost track of the days and nights.

Our home had not known any celebrations and functions but with the arrival of our son all festivals and functions were celebrated with fervour. Vinayak's naming ceremony and other ceremonies and birthdays were celebrated with pomp. He had and still has a lot of friends.

As a child, he was not a cry baby, but he was not quiet. He loves to be amidst friends. He detests being alone. He loves to talk. He is quiet, cheerful and social. As a child he was mischievous. He is strong and healthy. He was ill only once in his childhood. If he does fall sick it's just with a mild cold or cough.

We wanted to put him in a particular Marathi medium school. We took him to the school for an interview and he answered all the questions in English. The teacher who interviewed him said this child is clever, and asked us to put him in an English medium school. So, we put him in an English medium school where he studied till the 10th standard.

He was good at studies in school. He was good at sports, but he was also mischievous. Not a day passed without complaints from the school and we were summoned to the school. He was energetic and full of energy. Teachers told us to engage him in sports so that his attention would be diverted, and he would use up his energy. We put him in a Taekwondo class when he was in the fourth standard. He performed well in the sport and every match, he earned either a silver or a gold medal and earned the trust of his teacher. He is now a national champion and has two black belts.

Vinayak is 20 years old and is good at studies and sports. He is energetic, very helpful by nature and always has a smile on his face. He is a loving person and both his father, and I are proud of him. In his future life, we wish him every success, acclaim and riches.

I did not give birth to Vinayak, but he is my son in the true sense of the word. I showered him with all my love and care. I was responsible for moulding him into the man he is now. I have realized two important things in life: motherhood pulsates in your heart and mind. It is nurturing that forms a child and not the blood relationship.

THE ETERNAL TRUTH

I was always the favourite cousin or aunt for the kids in my family. I enjoyed being around kids. Thus you can imagine the sadness in my heart when later in life it was concluded that I would not be able to bear my own child.

Yet this sadness was short lived. My gynaecologist not only advised me to consider adoption, but also shared information about a particular Agency which she was aware of, as the best setup to connect with. After a big family discussion we decided to pursue the adoption option. We reached the suggested Agency for our first interaction.

The conduct of each one at the Agency was heartwarming. We were counselled, guided and shown around the nursery. Unlike the other NGOs we had visited, this organization clearly knew they were dealing with sensitive matters and every action, gesture and communication was based on compassion and humanism. All our fears, doubts and apprehensions vanished. We enlisted for adoption and completed the process involved.

Eight months later we were called to see our baby girl. I personally was conscious of the fact that I do not wish to select or reject a baby. I was in a dilemma on how to deal with the final moment. Ms X, one of the founding members, laid a reassuring hand on my shoulder and said, "your labour pains begin now and you will know which baby is yours!".

That's exactly how it was…we walked in without looking left or right, through a passage where babies were lined in the arms of their foster parents. Suddenly this 8 month old baby turned around on her own and grabbed hold of us!!!! We had been selected !! Today it seems absolutely a deep karmic bond that connected us from that point onwards. Mystically, as she grew older her resemblance to me was uncanny. Even today, as she stands tall at 26 years of age, no one is ready to believe that she is adopted, because of our strong resemblance.

She truly converted our house into a home. Even the extended family showered her with love and with genuine acceptance as our own. And that grew deeper over her growing years. Cousins would happily babysit her and there were times I would carry her bassinet to work. And wow, my clients would abandon their work stations or household chores to spend time with her, while I supervised the workers (I am an interior designer).

She added value and joy to every facet of our lives. I remember being counselled that there may be awkward times - either via the outside world or may be from school mates. We also realised that her own progressive understanding about adoption related issues, will lead her to ask us sensitive questions.

All the above happened, but each time we had the liberty and direction to call the social workers at the Agency for guidance. Their experience was valuable and always showed us how to make our own path to address the matter. We had made up our minds to stay open about her adoption. The guidance was to wait for the right moment and of course with words of empathy and compassion rather than sympathy.

The date and month she was legally ours was a red letter day. We would mark that day each year by visiting an orphanage and distribute sweets and clothes. She may not have understood the reason, but her heart was so caring and connected that she would beg me to take two more kids home as siblings.

When she was around 3 years old, we were watching TV. In a commercial break there came clips where they were showing pregnant women and how babies grow in the stomach. Her instant question was, whether she too was born the same way? I took this as an opportunity to start the storytelling towards the truth. So I replied, "yes but not from my stomach but another mother's stomach".

The innocence of her age accepted this information as a matter of fact and not something unusual. Of course over the years we got more opportunities to add more to the dots. We left it for her to join the dots to arrive at the understanding of the reality. She was comfortable with it all. This was because the reality unfolded for her in gradual stages, as per her understanding.

For a short while I was posted in a different city and we visited the child care Agency on two occasions. She joyfully interacted with the staff and children. She offered to paint the walls (she is an artist). On the second occasion she witnessed a puja ceremony in which the child was placed in the lap of the new parents. On our return home I pointed out the pictures of her ceremony, in our own photo album when we had received her in our arms and our hearts.

By the time she reached the end of middle school she naturally began to share / talk about her adoption as a happy fact of life.

Here I would like to share the guidance we had received from the amazing team at the agency - The same senior founder at the agency gave us her view that, "In life we hide something when we know it's incorrect or wrong. Thus if we hide the fact of the adoption from the child, then we believe we have done something shameful or wrong. This message will transfer to the child. So if we are happy and comfortable with our decision then let's live that way too". This had a deep effect on me. Thus, from a very tender age of our child I would, through stories, talk about adoption, and I would use the Adoption word liberally.

At the age of 5 our daughter adopted her first pet, an abandoned dog (she is now on her third!). How mystic.

Over the years we gradually stopped visiting orphanages or marking her date of adoption as we used to. Again, we were guided by counsellors not to continue to make a big deal of the adoption by giving constant reminders since she was very much our child who had only come to us through the adoption route. We wanted her to form her new identity very purely by her own instincts without burdening her with her past. We left it to her to integrate her story into her identity as she experienced it.

Yet, as I have shared earlier, her heart knows her story, which has made her very empathetic towards others. In school, I often got feedback that whenever some kids would argue or fight, she would walk across calmly, arbitrate and help diffuse the situation.

Well after she turned 18, I took the opportunity to tell her that as and when and if she ever wished to search for her biological mother, I would be fine and accept her need to search for her lost roots. A few weeks later she went and got the family names tattooed on her wrist …our names, to say, "YOU are my family forever!"

When she turned 21, I waited for the right moment and brought out the beautiful hand made album that had been put together by the Agency, which was given to us during the final adoption process. It contained photos of her as a newborn, pictures of her foster parents and the team at the Agency. Some personal information too was mentioned. Then her diet chart and medical records while she was at the child care center of the Agency. She went through it all, while chattering away and asking questions. It was a great gift for her which showed how many people had taken part in her early life care.

Today she is an independent confident young working lady who carries herself with dignity and pride. She is working for a cross border organization promoting and guiding on issues related to mental health.

All of us in the family are truly blessed and feel we are the chosen ones, to have her as our daughter. Her name means, 'The Eternal Truth'. Indeed her presence in our lives through adoption, has taught us what all faiths teach...that Love is the eternal truth.

NEVER GIVE UP

Our adoption story began soon after my wife and I got married. My cousin brother adopted a baby girl and we too, after experiencing difficulty in conceiving, decided to adopt.

My wife always had a dream of having a daughter so we decided to have a baby girl. We adopted our daughter, Gauri, from an orphanage near Chennai. She was a very beautiful girl, fair-skinned with large eyes and curly hair. If I had to tell you the truth, she looked exactly like my wife and no one would think that she was not our biological child. It was important to have a child who resembled us, which would make for better integration in our extended family.

We were well settled in Chennai. Gauri went to a very good school; she was a skilled classical music singer as well as a very good artist. We were very proud of our daughter. Not a day went by when we didn't feel that having her was the best decision we made.

We had not informed her about her adoption, but one day when she came out of her art class on a Sunday, some girl told her that she was having a puja at her house, but her mom said not to bring Gauri because she was adopted.

Gauri came and asked us if this was true and we said yes, it was, but we never wanted to tell you because it meant nothing to us. You are our daughter no matter what the circumstances. But Gauri changed after this day. She was no longer the playful fun-loving daughter we had. She began to lock her door listening to sad music, shutting us out. She refused to eat, especially if my wife cooked. She would only eat if she knew the maid had cooked something.

My wife used to cry and cry. She felt heartbroken and rejected. And of course, worried about her daughter. So did I, but I had my business to keep me occupied all day. My wife worked at a bank but finished her work around lunchtime each day. To be greeted by a closed door and monosyllabic words from our daughter was unbearable.

One day we got a call from one of my business associates who was also a family friend. He said that he saw Gauri getting into the car with some strange looking fellow. He did not like what he saw and he called to warn us. I said it is not possible because Gauri was in school at that time. But the associate insisted it was her as he knew her since she was a little girl.

Soon the truth dawned on us when the school principal called and asked why Gauri was missing so much school. We realised that she was in very bad company and instead of going to school she was going out with some bad company. To God knows where and doing God knows what. We tried to confront her but she denied all knowledge of this, even said that her principal was lying. My wife and I wanted to believe her.

One day we got a phone call from one of her close friends telling us she was very worried about her. Some guy had some compromising photos of her and was blackmailing her. This was very hard for me to deal with. I come from a very orthodox family and I did not know whom to tell and who would help me in such a situation. But my wife and I didn't give up. We managed to catch the guy red-handed, meeting her. With the help of some business associates, we managed to delete the photos from his phone and warned him to stay away from our daughter. This experience was very disturbing. My wife was suspicious of everyone and we were very anxious when our daughter stepped out on her own.

To protect her we even hired a detective company to ensure her whereabouts and safety. We wanted to trust her but we did not trust the world around her which was ready to exploit her vulnerability. We were very worried because she had lost her appetite and lost a lot of weight. Sometimes we found scratch marks on her arms due to self-harming. It was very painful to watch her suffering. It was a long time before some of her cheerful personality began to resurface. I developed a very close bond with her at that time as she could see that I did not judge her promiscuous behaviour but that I understood it came from her emotional disturbance. We shared little jokes and secrets with each other and that too brought us into a close father-daughter bond...sometimes our little jokes were not even shared with her mother!

It was year 12 and our daughter was meant to be studying for her exams. It became her dream to become a CA like her mother's sister, her favourite relative. Sadly, she did not pass the exams. We went for a retest in September but once again we were among the parents whose child's name was not called out, as she had failed again. We appealed to the board of exams and someone known to us from the department of education said that she had not even written anything on the papers, just her name. It felt like she had given up on life.

It was a very sad time for us. But we told her that we loved her, and we knew that she was in some pain, and was trying to push us away. But no matter what, we will never be able to leave her. My wife said, "You may not have been born from my stomach but you have been born from my emotions, my tears. I knew the first time we saw you that you were mine and Appa's."

Slowly I think she began to understand that every time she would fall we would be there to catch her. If she tried pushing us away we would just pull her back harder. Well-wishers suggested putting her in a hostel, sending her to another city and various other "remedies." But my wife and I would never hear it. She was our daughter, our responsibility and we decided we were going to stand by her no matter what.

Slowly, our persistence made her realise that she was loved unconditionally. We showed her the adoption file which we had and we shared all the information with her. It was scary for us to do that. My wife especially thought she would run away and try to find her biological family, but that didn't happen. Paradoxically, opening the file closed that chapter of her life for her and opened our daughter's heart to us once again. She no longer felt that we were ashamed of her biological history and she understood our feelings and apprehensions about losing her. Gauri was finally at some peace with herself.

Today, years later, our adult Gauri is more stable. She did not fulfill her dream to become a CA but she pursued a creative path which was truly an expression of her own talent. She teaches various skills to young people and also teaches watercolour painting on weekends. She and I continue to be very close and we laugh a lot together. We still share secrets and jokes. But when you see her with her mom, my wife, you realise how great their mother-daughter bond really is, in spite of all the quarrels and disagreements between them.

They even share the same expression on their faces when they are happy, sad or angry. But most of all they...we...share the love of a family which did not give up on each other.

MOTHER COURAGE

THE DECISION TO ADOPT A CHILD
The idea of adopting a child was thought of when I was a little girl reading Enid Blyton in whose books the mention of orphanages came up pretty frequently. Being bookish, I looked up the meaning- from that came the idea, triggered by a childless couple who showered their love and attention on me, that why couldn't people with no kids take a child from orphanages to make them their own!!

The idea was at the back of the mind. Marriage happened, I broached the topic- we should have one child of our own and adopt another. A girl if we had a boy, a boy if it was a girl. I was convinced of having at least two children. My husband was initially taken aback but was never ever negative. He in fact kept on challenging me by questioning how deep my conviction about adoption was.

Before we could think of anything, our biological twins arrived early into the marriage, both boys. There was never any concern. Neither did it occur to us, how complex the process of adoption could be. It was only later, when the boys were in their 3rd year, we started the process of identifying NGOs which would give us a girl, did the reality hit us. We wanted them to grow up together.

Everywhere we went, we faced rejection. Since we were fertile and already had children, no one could comprehend the reason behind our desire to adopt, that too a girl. We were abroad, but every time we came to India, we would renew our efforts. It was 1986, we had just come back, permanently and it took awhile for us to settle down.

The parent class representative in our sons' school had become my friend. We got to talking and I shared my adoption issues by cursing the red-tapism, the obstacles, the mentality, all working negatively. The school representative said she knew of an NGO, which thought differently. She put us across to the right person and we went through the whole process, through to adoption.

BRINGING THE CHILD HOME

We got our daughter and our sons got their sister on December 15, an unforgettable date. We came back to Madhya Pradesh via Mumbai. Our baby spent the first night with us in a hotel in Mumbai, slept with her father and me and travelled back the sixteen hours long journey as though she had always been there with us.

The whole family, my in-laws and my parents were all there to welcome her. She had her Annaprashan, fed by her Mama, ate her first payesh, wearing a lehenga, stitched by my mother.

Her first Birthday was celebrated with a few girls her age from our neighbourhood and the whole family. Before that, her father had arranged for a huge get-together to celebrate her homecoming. In fact, as long as he was around, her birthday was celebrated twice, one her homecoming, the other her actual calendar Birthday. Our twice-born daughter!

CHILDHOOD

Though the beginning was full of fun, frolic and amusement filled activities, tragedy struck soon. When she was going to be 5 years old, her father passed away suddenly. All of us were distraught, fatigued, sad but her situation was really bad. Being hypersensitive and extremely attached to her father, this sudden turn of events led to chronic health problems for almost a year and this required frequent trips to the doctor. It also made us rearrange our priorities to focus on her rather than us and to try and renew living life as normally as possible.

We three (three or four? - mother, twins and daughter) were struggling with various issues, reorganising our priorities, financial, emotional and above all the fact that I had to become a working, single mother, so the 100% that I had been giving them physically had to be curtailed to a large extent.

This hit her too. Being too young, she could not understand the mechanics of it, she took it to heart, leading to a change in behavioural pattern. The biggest blessing under the circumstances was my mother's shifting in with me since my brother had moved abroad. That gave her an anchor for the whole day, the mornings, evenings, and weekends being ours.

INTRODUCTION TO THE CONCEPT OF ADOPTION
As soon as she could sit, around 6 months, we had storytelling or singing every afternoon. That is the time I chose to introduce her to the idea of adoption through the stories of The Cuckoo and the Crow, The Ugly Duckling, Karna, Krishna etc. All depicting different angles and aspects of adoption, mythological and fictional.

As she grew older it was mentioned in a zestful, fun way how she was different from her brothers. That though she was not born to me and her father, she was our daughter. Our sons, without saying anything ever, just by their behaviour, remained and still remain her pillars of strength.

As a child, she was never into discussing or asking questions about her background. Another thing unusual about her was that from early childhood, she showed signs of being empathetic towards the weak, especially children with disabilities. This was brought to our knowledge by her teacher in KG2. A new entrant had speech problems, which drove away most kids in class, except our daughter. She shared her lunch, got him help wherever, whenever needed. During the Annual Sports Day, our daughter was coming second in the 50-metre race, when this same boy fell down while running. Our daughter ran right back, helped him get up and finished the race last to the clapping of the audience. What a great moment in our lives!

THE PROBLEM YEARS

As she approached puberty, the boys left home to start their working life as I was unable to help them further to pursue their post-graduation. They agreed and one of them got a job in a large conglomerate, immediately after graduation. The other, a year after that. Her beloved brothers having left her alone with only me (working) and her grandmother at home, she was left alone with just TV for company. She stopped sharing much about her friends or school or studies. She veered towards her classmates/friends for comfort and advice and most of the time making wrong decisions. She would try to impress them by taking small things from home and gifting them.

TALENT

Since the time she had been a baby, the rhythm was something that was ingrained in her. She would play the dholak with my brother-in-law when she had just learnt to sit. She would listen to rhythmic music, sing and dance as soon as she could walk-11 months. Once we found her mimicking the famous dancer Shobhna Narayan, at an open-air performance so well that the audience was smiling and watching her. We decided that this was her special talent and we must put her to learn dance. So, her father had bought her a pair of ghungroos. The whole house was filled with music and the sound of her dancing with those ghungroos. In spite of her father's demise, financial troubles and my work, she was enrolled into the topmost Bharatnatyam Academy and she started performing on stage with her classmates, every year.

When loneliness took over her mind, she lost interest in studies and dance. She turned to draw all incomplete works and terrible, terrible brooding. Her 9th-grade final exams happened and though she was never good in Maths, always barely scraping through, this time she flunked. The school decided to push her through with grace marks. During this time, my Mother, my backbone, fell and fractured her femur. Unable to take such pressure, I discussed with my sons and with their support decided to chuck my job. The repercussions of leaving my job and concentrating on the daughter and mother paid off. But even then, things were not OK.

With her High school exams about to begin, she almost backed off from giving it. A lot of cajoling, counselling went on and she agreed. She flunked in Mathematics, again. We decided to get her to give a supplementary exam, she flunked again.

All the months of tuitions, down the drain. We had hit the wall. Not much information or help was available about handling a situation such as this, where a student, refusing to discuss, faced a scenario where she could not, would not do Maths. She, in those days, was like a trapped animal, many tears of anger and frustration, many violent scenes, but we bore each other with her brothers' and Grandmother's love and support in the background.

Racking my brains to find a solution to this unprecedented, never imagined turn of events, like a Godsend, saw a tiny advertisement in a National Newspaper, about enrollment for 10th-grade exams with NIOS- The National Open School. I checked deep into the system and realised this could be the via-media. I went to their office, first by myself, the second time, with our daughter. Once I got the picture, it was OK to not take Maths and still pass H.S. exam and be recognised. By then our daughter had comprehended that it had to be the last opportunity, or else there was practically nothing to look forward to in the future.

She worked hard, though there was a bit of a tug of war, initially, regarding the choice of subjects. She wanted to take subjects which would have been too much to handle, at that particular time. With almost no studying for almost three years, I felt she needed something lighter, giving her the chance to do well. She sailed through both her HS & HSS exams in two years, instead of the customary three, with no tuition.

The worst was over, Bharatnatyam started again. College enrollment, joining Bachelor HSc gave us a few things to smile about.

TRUST ISSUES
She had no one else to turn to, she did trust me but in turns hated and loved me. She was violent in her reactions,

always testing my resilience, my love, my perseverance by taking matters to the brink, but often, repentant too. I was the battering ram. Her being the non practical one, at that point of time, did not want to grow up and start taking responsibilities like an adult. I, on the other hand, insisted upon that.

My assertions that life was hard and would turn out to be harder if she continued acting like a child, loving to depend on us for even the smallest things, irked her to no end. This led to many rebellious scenes and actions. Thankfully, holding steady in a storm came naturally to me and was the need of the hour.

With her growing up, came the sexual urges and the desperate need to have the attention of members of the opposite sex. This combined with her simplicity in such matters, her vulnerability, and the urgent need to be loved resulted in many misadventures. Some in passing, some serious but all of them ended up hurting her, psychologically. Yes, there have been damaging incidents, one major one was when she craving affection and attention of the opposite sex, got used and ditched, making her life unbearable at that point of time. The family rallied behind her and helped her move forward with positivity. All these adversities made a happy go lucky, fun loving simple girl into one filled with anger, revenge, and mistrust.

College and good academic performance brought renewed energy, vigour and my continuous prodding made her learn to speak up for herself and to never hide the fact that she was adopted. She learnt to do that, it was tough, but it made her tougher. Academically, she has not looked back since.

To tackle the growing-up problems of a hypersensitive young girl unsure of her own identity,(which sorted out in her twenties) was a tough task. I never knew that I had it in me to solve such complicated emotional upheavals of my daughter, since the boys were not much of a problem, in their growing up years. It was the trauma of their Father's death at the age of 17, leading to innumerable financial, social, psychological assaults which could have seen them crumbling, but they are and always have been well sorted out, balanced persons.

What helped me support and communicate with her through her rebellions, was probably the fact that having been an amateur student of body language, human behaviour, genes and their effect on persons and psychology, I was able to analyse, understand, counsel and scold her as needed. Whenever any untoward utterance, action occurred, I was able to put things across to her from the family's perspective, not just mine. I am sure if I had not been fair, neutral, and empathetic in my dealings, it would have been almost impossible to bring her back from the negative environment she had built around herself.

One thing helped a lot, whatever she may have done, thought -- suicide was not one of them. Herself, being basically a simple, trusting, fun-loving girl, wanted to get back to that side of her desperately. She could not tackle her misfortunes, with humility and equanimity. So, the revolt, the anger, directed at her biological parents got redirected to me, funnily never to her brothers.

To try and sort out her anger issues, the hurt of abandonment, I guided and directed her towards first, the act of forgiving. We would sit together to pray and at the end of it, I would lead her to pray to forgive her parents, especially her mother, to whom she owed her life. Later I asked her to try regression, which I believe in, having gone through the process several times, after my husband's death, helps a lot in facing current problems, based on past life experiences.

Further, I guided her to Vipassana, which she voluntarily has gone through several times.

These activities helped a lot in changing her outlook towards life and it's hard-hitting lessons of rejection, adoption, love, family bonding etc.

She is now a far cry from the unsettled, whimsical, highly emotional young girl she was. She is now a far more controlled, steady woman, with a harder exterior but heart in the right place and a tremendous sense of right and wrong and fairness.

Her exposure to special children, whom she is now professionally trained to understand and handle, her Vipassana, meditation, Bharatnatyam (which she practises every day), higher studies, and taking care of a house full of dogs have kept her focused and more than occupied, in a positive way. After graduation, she spent 3 years in Delhi, learning Bharatanatyam under the tutelage of Padma Vibhushan Dr Saroja Vaidyanathan and has formed a lifelong bonding with their Institute Ganesha Natyalaya.

Career and marriage are non-happening areas still, which has no fault of hers or ours, but efforts are still going in that direction. We all enjoy each other's company, her being a huge support. We go out very often to eat and enjoy as all of us are foodies. We fight, share confidences, criticise, and support each other, including my daughter-in-law. She gets along very well with her cousins, who confide in her knowing she would be there to support them wherever, whenever needed. Same goes for her uncles and aunts. She is now confident enough to brook no nonsense from any quarter and speaks her mind.

Parenting alone, albeit with support of my sons (financial and familial), through so many turbulent years, has been a nerve-wracking, mind-boggling, uphill task, but love, fairness in dealing, perseverance, patience and straight talk, calling a spade a spade, has paid off.

As they say,

> "A mountain is not higher
> Than your confidence
> Because it will be
> under your feet
> If you reach the top!"

The Top is still many miles away, but God Willing, we will get there someday.

HAND IN HAND

We were waiting in the visitors' shed, a little apprehensive, a little restless, there was a kind of anticipation in the pit of my stomach. The minutes were ticking by.....and the wait was over… She came wrapped up in a baby pink colour, hardly visible in the arms of the foster parent. I peeked inside and could only see two shining, twinkling eyes. So delicate, so fragile I was almost scared to touch her, lest she breaks. But the pink bundle looked straight at me and gave a smile by just twitching her lips a little. I knew she was mine, she was born for me and no one else.

And the journey began. The quiet uncomplaining thin little baby, in a few weeks picked up weight, her cheeks puffed up and shone with light. She was growing up to be demanding, the quietness changed to a bawling for attention. She smiled more. When she turned one, we threw a huge party complete with 3 large cakes and 400 guests! We wanted to show her off to our friends and family!

Years passed by and it was a pleasure to see her grow into a beautiful, intelligent girl, who was so observant that she amazed us.

As a child she learnt gymnastics and also enjoyed playing games on jungle gym and parallel bars. But unfortunately she didn't pursue this passion later on.

From her early days she was choosy about her clothes and her looks. It never stopped amusing me to see her trying clothes on in the shops and knowing too well what she wanted.

In school, she was always good in studies. When she was in primary school we moved away to another town. But she could not adjust there as she was a victim of bullying and soon we returned home.

Then I decided that I would not leave my city until she completes her schooling.

 She grew up to be a graceful little lady.

Life was peaceful.

After her 10th standard, we moved to another big city as I got a job there. She stood first in the college with a distinction in 11th Standard but we were not too happy with the college and the bustling city life didn't suit us so we were back home. Though we faced many challenges in our personal life, our bond was intact.

There was a particularly challenging time for us when my daughter was in her late teens. For some years then my husband was going through his own set of problems. As time went by he was unable to take on any responsibilities towards us-my daughter and I. I could not depend on him either emotionally, psychologically or financially. I found out that he was into financial malpractices and fraud. This was a very unfortunate situation for my daughter to experience. She spent some time with her father and seems to have had some negative experiences. She understood that her father was a man without values which impacted her foundation.

Under the circumstances I was forced to take up jobs in various cities to support us as a family. At one point I got a good career opportunity in an educational institution in another State at a senior position. I decided to keep my daughter with my parents till I had settled down in the new place. Sadly it was also the time when I was separating from my husband. My daughter was understandably undergoing a lot of emotional turmoil-- her parents were separating. She was going to have to live far away from either of us. This was all probably leading to a sense of abandonment for her. It was like a re-enactment of her birth story.

Unfortunately all this was happening to her when she was a teenager. As a consequence she made a lot of bad choices in her relationships with the opposite sex. She got involved with boys who had a bad influence on her. It was difficult for my parents to cope with her behavior. It was a very difficult time for me too, staying so far from her. It was then that I resolved that she should be with me where I was living. so I decided to take the year off. During this time, she worked voluntarily with special needs children. This helped her decide her career- she wanted to be a special educator. And she is now working as well as studying with a determination to be successful in her career.

If I have to sum up my daughter in short, I would say she is a loving child who is gifted in recognizing people within a short span of time. She has a strong character- her ideas of right and wrong are quite well-formed. She cannot bear to see injustice and voices the same uninhibitedly. She shares a strong bond with her mother. And I, her mother, am very proud of her; we are a team- we argue, get angry with each other, but at the end we are inseparable.

A JOURNEY OF LOVE, LEARNING, EVOLVING AND REWARDS

Nurture: Have you ever thought how the need to nurture gets ingrained in the human psyche? Where and when did it start surfacing and becoming a part of our natural instincts? As the mother and the extended family fusses over a newborn child I'm sure even its wee little brain understands and responds to the touch, the warmth and attention. As they keep growing, children then show their need to nurture something they love. It could be an inanimate object like their favourite toy, a certain pillow, a pet or a younger sibling.

As we grow into adults most of us then find ourselves wanting to nurture a new life amongst us. I, for example, remember with crystal clarity always enacting the role of motherhood towards my dolls, the new seedlings of various plants I would put in pots, my pets and my little younger brother who to a four-year-old me looked like a living doll. As an adult even before I chose my life partner I would choose lovely storybooks I would wish to read to my children of the future. My work also involved being around children, so there were secret yearnings of having a child with the attitude of the confident little girl, or the giggly laughter of the curly-haired boy, the dimpled cheeks of the Punjabi kid or the raven-black tresses of the lovely south Indian girl with her twinkling eyes. With these aspirations tucked deep inside my heart, life was kind to help me choose a life partner and companion, and it was indeed a step closer to think of starting a family.

Then life throws you a curveball, you realise that the way

hundreds of couples start their family with what looks like ease will not be your story. This was difficult to accept even though rationally you knew it didn't mean you couldn't get a child home, my family suggested I try IVF. I half-heartedly spoke to professionals who gave you all the scientific information and some glimmer of hope. I also met and interacted with someone who was expecting twins after her third IVF attempt. Just listening to her narrate the experience was my penny drop moment! I realised I couldn't identify with the process of IVF to experience motherhood. My husband, who otherwise wasn't the one feeling the void of a child in our lives, helped me realise that if nurturing a child is what my heart desired, why was adoption not my first choice?

Adoption, the concept as such was always appealing and when we were dating my husband and I had spoken about at least adopting one child. Fortunately for us, a few of our close friends had already adopted and seeing them and the way their children so quickly adopted the ways of their family, much convincing wasn't required. However, I realised one crucial aspect and have henceforth always shared it with whoever I speak to about my experience; we need to cross our own thresholds to accept that this is the way forward. For the longest time even though adoption was never far from my mind, my maternal instincts had a stronger hold with a yearning for bearing a child. I needed to cross that threshold to be open to the process without regrets.

Once our minds were made with support from our families and close friends we went to meet the person heading the CARA in our city. I will always be indebted to the wonderful lady for beautifully counselling us with wit, real-life examples, non-sugar coated truths and wisdom. Two things she said have remained with me in these last 8+ years and I know will stay for as long as I live. One: Don't ever think you are doing a noble deed by adopting a child, it's a mutual need, you need a child, and the child needs a home, it's a symbiotic relationship. I think this is very important as I have people telling me I have done a very charitable and good deed and I, in turn, tell them that it's not so, I have fulfilled my need. Two: Children need to be told that they are adopted, and how you explain this will vary at different stages of their life and their reactions too will change with age. However, she mentioned that it was important to stress that their parents wished for a better life for them which they could probably not provide hence they were given up for adoption. Surely, they are not to negatively think that they were unwanted or unloved.

Her counselling helped us a great deal in looking at our approach to adoption and I have always shared this with others whom we have encouraged to adopt too. Having officially filled an adoption form that day and having understood regarding the documents we had to prepare about our health profiles, incomes, our expectation of the child's age and gender, our expression of interest and how we plan to care for the child; a burden and sadness lifted off my heart. I knew that a journey had begun and there would be no looking back.

Patience, yes, you will need to have lots of it when you are waiting for the child to come into your life. Back then when the whole process was not online and on a single portal as it is today, we had the option of individually visiting the childcare homes once we had applied. Since my closest friend who was my mentor had adopted both her daughters from one of the child care homes, we applied there as we were familiar with the people and the environment. I was part of the joyous occasion for both her daughters' homecoming. Every now and then we would ask them the status of our application and they would patiently tell us where we were in the waitlist, how they would have to find us a child who would match our needs and us. CARA would ensure we were part of the annual programs hosted for adoptive parents and families and it was always enlightening to see and hear from the wonderful families and people we met, about their experiences. This is important as many times during the close to two years of waiting, our enthusiasm would flag at times, doubts would creep up and also we would feel comfortable as we were and wondered if life needed the hustle-bustle of a child.

A phone call and voila our lives were set to change!! I remember the evening on a cold day in February that I had returned home and was waiting for my husband. He came home and shared that he had been busy, and towards the evening had noticed four missed calls from a particular number. Upon calling, he was informed it was from the childcare home and they had a child who matched our requirements. The child was a year and a half old and if we were interested we could start the process. After a lull of two years, there was suddenly a storm of emotions of excitement, nervousness, incredulity that we had finally received a call! Next morning we went over to confirm our interest and they told us that they would formally come for the home visit and on a particular day in the week we would be allowed to take the child for a detailed health check-up if we wished. Even till then, we were neither shown a photograph or the child, so our suspenseful state of animation continued. A day for the health check-up was fixed and we landed up a nervous pair of prospective parents and then we saw her for the first time!

Once again, this is something I tell parents looking to adopt, we have so many versions of the child we wish to have in our minds that we expect that the moment we see the child we will feel a bond. Some people claim that happened, I don't think I felt so. However, that should definitely not be a decisive factor. Also, there are some misconceptions that you will be allowed to "choose" from a few children, that doesn't happen either. You may choose not to go ahead once you have seen the child, that's the choice you have. The day out with our chosen child gave us a chance to observe her and learn a few things about her. We noticed she was very observant of her surroundings, loved the car ride, happily ate the fruits and food we were carrying and was happy to explore the various clinics we went to. All the doctors and specialists we met that day were very encouraging and supportive of our decision. It was definitely a big boost to our morale.

That night, as we slept we couldn't help but feel how strange destiny was, the child who could be our daughter based on our willingness to go ahead was at that moment away in a home sleeping in a crib oblivious of her destiny. We realised how life-changing a decision it would be for both us and her if we said the final yes.

A 'Yes' it was! We were literally going to undertake the most important and life-changing project of our lives till date. A detailed home visit followed and we began to prepare our home for our little daughter. The week running up to bring her home was tizzy with activities, both of us had to tie up loose ends at work, a list of things we would require for a one and a half-year-old was prepared, support systems were lined up to help with child care. Most of the week went in a daze as it was difficult to comprehend how this was going to change our lives.

The most amazing part was the outpouring of help we got from all quarters, some completely unexpected. We got useful things from bottle sterilisers, a beautiful baby cot, a baby feeding table and chair, bedding, clothes and toys and of course tons of useful tips from our well-wishers, as we did not have any immediate family around. We were more or less all set to bring our little daughter home....of course, we had already chosen a name from a beautiful book we had read.

Learning with a child around you who needs you for everything, every parent is bound to learn. When we got her home we had a fair idea of her daily routine and her diet as shared by her home caregivers. I was fortunate to have my younger brother and his wife around who were visiting with my four-month-old nephew. So basic stuff as to what diaper size, how to effectively change a diaper, the signs that the child is sleepy, hungry or uncomfortable, foodstuff that was good for in between meals, all such information was readily lapped up by our new parent minds. To be honest, the first week was very overwhelming as it took a while to create a routine and reorient ourselves and our lives to the change. The most humbling realisation was how easily the little one had adopted us as her parents. We realised how children are like sponges ready to soak up and learn from every experience. In no time she would follow our mother tongue, she loved people around and easily mingled with all the visitors dropping in to meet her, a lot of new foods were introduced and she ate with a healthy appetite, outdoors and indoors play were enjoyed thoroughly.

Of course, everything was not smooth sailing and there were a lot of things we also learnt after making mistakes. New food needs to be gradually introduced as sometimes the child may be allergic or intolerant of some foods. However, mostly from the beginning, we gave her most food that was cooked for us rather than preparing entire meals separately for her. When she came to us she was still feeding from a milk bottle for her milk, our paediatrician told us not to buy one even and nip the habit right away. It meant she barely drank any water or milk the first two days and we bravely persisted, by the third day with a little help, she drank from a sipper. So we were spared the later struggle of weaning her off a bottle habit.

My neighbour, a speech therapist, cleared the confusion when I asked her if I should continue speaking in Hindi, she told me to speak in the mother tongue as that was what came naturally to most people who were spending time with her. It was one of the best things as today she speaks fluently in our mother tongue though we have never stayed in our home state. Her bonding with the extended family has been seamless partly because she can communicate in our mother tongue.

Inbuilt immunity, among the first things I realised, is that having spent almost a year in the home where children were not necessarily mollycoddled it made them stronger and adaptive. So I refrained from trying to overly sanitise her environment, continued to give her the water we drank at home without boiling, allowed her to taste the food we ate outside, let her play with mud and sand as well as explore her environment without too many restrictions. Though there were two schools of thought that had views about the time spent as a mother with her, I knew that the reality of life is that I was a working parent. Hence in the initial month itself, I would step out for periods of work for 2 to 3 hours, while she spent time at home with either of our mothers who had come to visit and help or with caregivers in our home. We created a pattern of saying bye and then having a welcome home ritual too. In the long run, this has made her a very independent child and she can stay with either of us not around. Creating a routine, though it may be difficult to develop initially one must have a routine in place for when the child wakes up, eats breakfast, has her bath, plays, nap time, meals and goes to sleep. In the home, it was a very early start to the day as they had so many children to look after, so it took us a while to re-establish a routine that was easy for us to implement. Also, we have realised that each one of us has our own parenting styles and there isn't one size that fits all, hence though there were suggestions and advice coming from all quarters, it's best to adapt what works for you in your given circumstances and means.

Health issues, as any parent, will share it is really important to have the first level of common medicines most children need at home. Even more important is to have a doctor who will be able to communicate with you if a case of emergency crops up. We had both a homoeopath and an allopathic doctor for her needs, if it looked mild we usually went to the homoeopath and in cases where it seemed it could go out of hand, we went to our allopath. After the first few times, we were able to notice a pattern to what were the triggers that caused the onset of illness and were better equipped to shorten her misery.

At age two and a half, we enrolled her in a play school. Some concerns were that since she didn't know much of Hindi and only a smattering of English how would she communicate. Interestingly as she was eager to communicate with her peers in a matter of a fortnight she understood and could communicate her basic needs both in English and Hindi. Here again, we encouraged the use of school transport so that there would be no expectations of picking up and dropping by us. Her school experience is something she has enjoyed and looked forward to. Later when she joined a formal school, we did mention to the teachers regarding her adoption. In the early year class activities are done where they are supposed to bring their baby pictures, this is when the child may realise that her baby pictures look different from the rest. Hence, the school was sensitised about this aspect.

"Did I come from your tummy?", that's a question which will surely come up once the child sees someone in the close circle of family and friends going the family way. Even schools with their stress on Mother's Day and Father's Day celebration and exposure to various media, will all fuel the curiosity of the child. So how did we deal with it back then and even now? I for one was never comfortable with lying to her about it so I would say that yes, she came from her mama's tummy. We always told her we got her, especially from a home. There were times she would ask if we 'bought' her as one goes and buys stuff, we explained that the people from the home came and first checked if we would be good parents and then gave her to us. We luckily had other children in our friends circle who were adopted and she witnessed it so it helped in the narration. Though it is now when she is closer to adolescence we can feel that the questions will be more complex and her urge to know more of her background will crop up. We still keep it as close to the truth as possible and deal with her heartache over this with love and attention.

As mentioned earlier it's a journey, we as parents, as individuals are growing, learning and hopefully evolving too. There are so many children out there who need a home and though we wished to add on a sibling for her, various life circumstances made us miss the bus for a second time.

The fact that we were instrumental in helping other people undertake the adoption journey made us feel we were part of a larger family reaching out to encompass the children who need our love and who complete the void in our hearts.

LONELINESS TO HAPPINESS

I was single, working and had already made my decision to stay unmarried. I was busy working overtime so that I could buy a house. Soon my financial condition improved and I bought a house of my own. I had some extra time now since I was no longer required to work overtime but I felt lonely after coming home from work. During that time one of my acquaintances had adopted a child. Although she was married (and I was single), the thought of adoption and the joy of parenting a child gave hope to me. I discussed adopting a child with my mother, sister and brother in law and upon further enquiry, I learnt that it was possible for a single mother to legally adopt a child. I was extremely overjoyed.

I decided to adopt a girl child since I thought it was easier to raise a girl for a single mother and also because a girl is more attached to her parents. One of my friends suggested that being raised by a single mother could create potential problems for the girl child but I got tremendous support and encouragement from my sister and brother-in-law and they willingly submitted a written undertaking on my behest promising to look after the child in my absence or the unfortunate event of my death or disability, hence I was able to complete the adoption process smoothly.

I was now the proud mother of a girl. My mother welcomed her home and she was very well received by all my neighbours. She was lucky to get the company of girls her age in our neighbourhood and all my neighbours were very supportive of her. I had taken 2 months leave from work and bonded very well with her. I was extremely happy pampering her and playing with her. As she grew up and watched her friends with their father, she started asking me about her father. I had to begin the process of explaining her life story.

When she turned four years old, I told her about her adoption from an orphanage. I also told her about the death of her birth parents in an unfortunate car accident and the reason she was sent to an orphanage. I celebrated her birthday in the orphanage from where she had been adopted. This made her realize the plight of the children there who did not have parents at all and explained that she at least has the care and love of her mother. She stopped asking about her absent father after that incident.

She faced many health challenges as she grew, with childhood asthma and a kidney stone.

She went through an operation for the stone which was very frightening. She required a lot of hands-on care which I gave her through many sleepless nights. Eventually, she grew stronger.

She got admitted to a good school, but her classmates constantly pestered her with questions about her father. She was repeatedly teased with questions about not having a father and this traumatized her so much that it reflected on her marksheet. Her performance in studies deteriorated and she was soon branded a slow learner by her teachers. I was even advised to enrol her in a school for children with special needs, but I did not give up. I enrolled her at another regular school where things seemed quite normal until she went to class 7 when she started behaving differently with me. She started arguing with me over petty things and her concentration in studies also suffered due to her erratic behaviour.

One night she argued bitterly with me and even asked me to drop her back to the orphanage from where I had brought her home. This shocked me very much. However, since I had attended adoption seminars and was made aware of how children emotionally blackmail their parents, I kept my calm and convinced her that since it was late in the night and the orphanage must be closed, and I would pack her toys and clothes and drop her there in the morning. She never asked me to drop her back to the orphanage again.

She was average in her studies and she managed to finish her schooling. I had my doubts about her completing her Higher Secondary Examination (12th Class), but she was able to clear her exams and she got enrolled in college for her commerce graduation. She got good teachers in her college and she completed her graduation in commerce. I was proud that my daughter who was branded a slow learner, was able to complete her graduation with good grades.

It was during this time that she started opening up to me once again. She shared her childhood experiences in school where some of her classmates used to tell her that I was her stepmother and not her real mother and hence I will torture her and mistreat her. It was this thought that caused her immense trauma. Perhaps this explained her indifferent behaviour and her childhood tantrums. The fact that she did not have a father had also caused her a lot of trauma. Sometimes I was forced to think if my decision to adopt her as a single mother was proper as she might have felt more secure and perhaps raised better by a couple rather than a single parent. I, however, decided not to overemphasize on the need of a father and hoped that she would grow stronger and realize that the absence of a father (though traumatic) will not affect her life or childhood experiences. Eventually, she managed to cope with the limitation of being raised by a single mother. She was able to tell everyone that she was raised by a single mother and that she does not have a father.

She had a boyfriend since high school and when she broke the news to me, though surprised, I responded very patiently suggesting to both of them to prioritize their studies and career and settle down first before getting married. She was perhaps more comfortable in the company of her male friends and thought girls are too reserved to be friends. I had a tough time during her courtship with her boyfriend till her marriage with him. Her late-night outings with her boyfriend made me very uncomfortable, despite having raised her properly with the right values, I always dreaded that she may end up making the wrong choices.

Her fiancé completed his graduation in Mechanical Engineering. His family never objected to her being adopted and they readily accepted her into their family. Although there was slight hesitation from his grandmother she very soon became a part of their family. She was a very nice girl and they all appreciated that. She got married at the age of 24 and I am blessed with a grandson. She stays very close to my home and looks after me.

From my perspective, I never ever felt that she was not my biological child. I am nearly 70 years old now and I thank god for helping me make the decision to adopt a child. Even though my initial years were challenging, they were very rewarding as we could both surmount the challenges we faced because we cared so deeply for each other. My daughter's presence, along with my son-in-law and grandson, has filled my life with joy.

I am glad God made me take this decision to adopt a child otherwise my life would have been terribly empty and lonely. Life has a way of compensating us with something good for the losses we may have had to suffer.

BONDING: LOVE IN THE TIME OF COVID!

STAGE I: DECISION TO ADOPT A CHILD

Since I became 21 years old, an adult, I was keen to adopt a child. After my marriage did not work out, I knew that was the way to go. I worked in a Library where a lot of doctors visited, and they often mentioned abandoned babies (especially girls) who were given to childless couples. So, I requested two such Gynaecologists who ran their own private Nursing Homes about my desire to adopt. In those days, the city where I lived did not have any agency who handled adoption unlike the agency from the city I was originally from. I also met with a friend who had adopted from the same city and learnt about the exact process. Unfortunately, the Agency in that city could not accept my application as there was no trained social worker where I lived currently, who could do my interviewing and assessment. I also researched and read a lot of books about raising a child. I planned the event by first moving my Dad to come to stay with me as I used to be his major caregiver after my Mom's death. I also bought an apartment and informed the library of my decision to adopt. HR said they would give me half the maternity leave and I began saving my annual leave so that I could be there for the child during the first few months.

My elder sister had some concerns about how the child would feel in a single mother set up and also how I would manage my Dad, a full-time job and a baby. After she saw how keen I was, the next discussion was on what the last name the baby would have. She offered her name, but I could not accept that, and we decided that the baby would have my name i.e. my Dad's last name as I used my maiden name.

The next decision was whether to accept a baby boy that had been left behind in a local nursing home. The Doctor told me to come to look at the baby and then make my final decision. I visited the hospital and then went back to work. I called two of my girlfriends who had little kids of their own to help me take the baby home in one of their cars. So, I left my scooter at work and shopped on the way for essentials and took the baby to my friend's nursing home for a health check-up. My friend, a paediatrician, mentioned that the baby had been born prematurely and demonstrated how to feed a baby using a stainless-steel spoon and bowl so that there would be less chance of an infection.

STAGE II: TAKING THE BABY HOME

Since I am an extrovert and very social, most of my neighbours knew when the baby came home, and they all came to admire this bundle of joy. One neighbour stitched his diapers; another kanthas/swaddling clothes from my Mom's saris; another stitched clothes for my son while yet another lent me the oilcloth that was used in most homes in those days. My son got a lot of hand-me-downs and many gifts from day one.

I went on leave and started the process of bonding with my son over nightly feeds, baths and playtime. Sometimes, I would ask for help from an elderly lady in my building, not only for advice but sometimes also for babysitting. My Dad also read up all the books like Benjamin Spock, Miriam Stoppard, Desmond Morris, and we marvelled at how generalizations work and how accurate the books were in their guidance. Most of the time, I was sleep-deprived and overworked. But the sheer joy in this entire experience more than compensated for the difficulties involved in raising my child.

In the 5th or 6th month, I hosted a big party where family and friends came over for the first rice Ceremony or the first time he was given solid food. Again, a friend lent me her silverware, another cooked the fish, while my sister from Mumbai who had come down with her kids, had cooked up a storm for the baby's first meal. We were flooded with gifts and some were also from the library (ex-Chief Secretary came down bearing gifts as did others).

STAGE 3: CHILDHOOD
The baby was healthy despite being a premature baby and other than the seasonal flu was not sick as a toddler. He was very fond of his Nanny and she was the one who was responsible for his potty training and other habits while I was away at work. My Dad supervised and cooked all sorts of delicacies for him so he grew up to be quite a foodie. Then after his Nanny left to have her own baby, we had a rough time as the city did not have quality Day Care Centres. I decided to move abroad. The idea had been growing in my mind for some time, and I was convinced that we would have a better life there.

The new country was great for him and he loved his school and day care. When he was five years old, I used the example of the movie, Tarzan, and many books from the public library to tell him about the adoption. When he was 7, I went back to school for my MBA. He accepted my classes and assignments quite well, only questioning me on why my homework took so long while his was just half an hour. Again, I received a lot of help - a babysitter who pitched in when daycare was closed for the day and who had a little one of similar age. She took him for apple picking, Disney World, etc while I got busy with my GRE/GMAT and applications to Universities while working full time.

We moved twice more to two different cities. In the last city we moved, he was able to join French Immersion and became fluent in French. When he was 9, we moved back to India to a large city and that was when he had problems adjusting to school and the methods of teaching in Indian schools. I taught him multiplication and division at home, but the fear of Math had started creeping in. Then came languages like Hindi and Marathi. He got an exemption in Marathi but had to do Hindi for a few years. We moved to a city in North India for a year where he joined ICSE with French. He continued that when we moved back to the city of my origin so that he did not have to study the local language. He enjoyed living in apartment complexes and had a huge circle of friends in both cities. When we finally moved to our own place in my city of origin, he left behind a lot of friends and made me promise never to move again. Subsequently, he asked for a pet as that had been promised when we got our own house, so we ended up acquiring 4 cats.

STAGE 4: ADOLESCENCE

Adolescence was the most difficult period though he adjusted well to ICSE and without tuitions did OK in his 10th boards. Then after a lot of discussions, he opted for HSC with Science from the local State board. Upon my suggestion, he took up Math/Physics/Chemistry which in hindsight was a mistake (these subjects came naturally to me). He struggled with 12th standard and then just gave up on self -studies. It was only with the help of many tuitions that after three attempts he could clear the 12th. He worked during his summer vacations in order to fund his gadgets and also to make an informed decision about his career. He then selected BA (Arts) with Psychology/Economics/etc. As he could not get a place in Psychology, he finally took Economics. Even in BA, he did not do particularly well and refused to work hard to get good grades. His argument was that he was well-read, could defend his views, wrote well but hated the factory style of teaching in college. Then, he wanted to learn the German language and it was at Goethe Institute that he liked their style of teaching. Small classrooms and learner-centred teaching were good for him. He started to excel in the course and moved from A1 to B2 very easily. Then after graduation, he opted to move to South India to join the Indo German Training Center for their MBA. Again, he liked his teachers and even topped the first semester.

He eventually joined Mercedes Benz as an Intern and has been there with them now for 3+ years. He was able to overcome his problems with academics and other growing pains due to a very good Counsellor. I had observed many of my friends struggling with their adolescent kids (both own & adopted) and right from 10th standard, had put them in touch with a Counsellor. We also did a lot of psychometric tests - Career choices/Math ability/IQ/etc. so that he could use self-awareness to overcome his fear of Math. He finally chose Finance as a career and is happy to take that forward. There were a few trust issues between us. Once he said he did not want to celebrate his birthday with family and friends as he missed his birth Mother. So, we started having intimate lunches/dinners at his favourite restaurant Mainland China. The gifts continue till this date— the first one a month ahead and then every week, with the main birthday finale on the actual day. (He has since mentioned in an Adoption circle that he accepted me as his only Mom --quite unconditionally).

STAGE 5: ADULTHOOD

He seems to have grown up into a well-adjusted adult except that he has very few friends and most of his relationships are one-on-one (just like mine). He has had two serious relationships with very strong girls with both beauty & brains. The last break up was a bit shattering, so he had to spend that Valentine Day vacationing as he could not bear to be around all the marketing that happens at that time of the year. He still has lovely memories of the places that they visited as a couple. So now Mainland China in our city is off limits as they used to hang around there. He has helped her get a job in his own organization which shows that he is not the vindictive type. I am so proud!

For me, it's now time to learn from him and it has been great to spend 3 months of the Covid lockdown with him in such close proximity. We are similar in personality traits like extraversion and empathy. But we are also different as I am a long-term planner while he is spontaneous. We have common habits like our interest in Food, Reading and Travel. So, all in all, it has been a great parenting journey!

ACCEPTANCE

I grew up in the garden city of Bangalore, where my father was the head of a renowned organisation. We always lived in beautiful homes and had a very charming life. When the right time came, my parents were flooded with proposals for me from other renowned families. But my father had a firm set of morals and values. Education was a priority in his view..this was why he chose a husband for me who came from a very modest background but was very well educated. Of course, we were both from the same community and had quite a lot in common when it came to our shared values.

Even though he had started out modestly, my husband became a success through his hard work and sincerity. We had a happy life together, but years went by, and it became a painful fact that I was not able to conceive.

I had always been a deeply respected girl from a very good home and been very proud of always doing the right thing. But now I faced a lot of stigma, from my in-laws, from relatives, and family friends. We tried going for fertility treatment but it was not the accepted fact that it is today. It was a shameful thing for me to go and get the treatment. I felt angry and resentful. My husband, on the other hand, was very calm and supportive throughout.

I had to reluctantly accept that fertility treatment too wasn't working for me and we went in for adoption, first adopting a girl and then a boy.

It was not easy at first for me to bond with my daughter. However, gradually the maternal feelings came and I stopped seeing her as a sign of my own inability to conceive. Soon I began feeling a good bonding with her. This gave us the confidence to adopt our son as well. Our family was complete.

In accordance with my strict upbringing, I also was very particular about imparting the right values to my children. I expected them to grow up according to our ' samskaras' which were passed on from one generation to the next so that our family was known for its code of moral behaviour. Our children did not have our genes but they were certainly expected to imbibe our values and conduct themselves accordingly in our society.

I had also volunteered at a childcare home in my city and had some understanding of children who had lost their birth parents. I believed adoption could remould them in the tradition and upbringing of adoptive families. A 'good' family was needed for every child. With my care and attention to both my children I expected them to follow our ways without question. So it was very disturbing when my children made their own choices.

During her junior college years, my daughter formed a friendship with a boy who was very unsuitable in my eyes. I came to know of their relationship from my son, who was very worried about her. He felt the boy was no good. In fact, my son had a big fight with that boy and told him to stay away from his sister. Nonetheless, they continued to see each other. It was very hurtful for me to see what was going on. I had poured all my energy into caring for my daughter but she seemed to be hell-bent on bringing shame to our family. As I mentioned before, I was from a very distinguished family of Bangalore, and my husband too was now the Director of a well-known IT multinational. The embarrassment of my daughter's association with this disreputable boy became too much for me to bear and I decided to get her married as soon as possible to put a stop to her wild ways.

We selected a groom for her from our community. He too was from a very cultured family and well placed in the corporate world himself. I felt I had been able to remedy the offences of my daughter by getting her married off to a distinguished person. This would elevate our status in society. But alas, despite being married, she refused to break off with her boyfriend. This was a double blow to our dignity. The same sweet and compliant daughter became such a defiant daughter.

At the same time, my son too refused to study Engineering, which was also very important, not only for him but for our social standing. He had not got the marks to get admission on his own merit, but through influence, we got him admission into a very good college in Mangalore. However, he dropped out after his first year of Engineering and told us that he wants to study photography.

The actions of my children hurt me to the core. I was very upset. Where had my upbringing gone wrong? At this point, I began questioning myself deeply. Was I so prejudiced that I had created this situation in which my children are not happy at all? Is my pride greater than my love as a mother? These were two big questions I posed to myself.

After a lot of soul searching, I realised that I need to move past my ego and my perfectionism. I had to realise that part of loving my children was allowing them to be their own person...who they really are and not just a product of my unrealistic expectations.

For the first time in my life, I understood that part of the journey of being a parent is acceptance. Especially as an adoptive parent, acceptance is doubly important as one comes with a burden of genetic loss in this relationship and it is the acceptance of that genetic loss that one must accept along with seeing one's children as individuals.

My daughter ultimately resolved matters with her husband and has made me a proud grandmother of two boys. My son is also happily married and pursuing his creative dreams.

I finally understood that my pride was preventing me from living life. Today along with being a fulfilled mother and grandmother, I am living my own life, I have joined a book club, taken up golf with my husband, enjoy going on Treks with a ladies group.. I have also discovered my own true nature and my potential. I feel truly free.

FROM A RAILWAY TRACK: GOD'S GIFT

Our decision to adopt a child was neither a prolonged affair nor very difficult to make.

We had visited a famous IVF hospital in Mumbai to discuss the process and the cost involved in taking the treatment. The probability of success being even less than 15% over two cycles and the mental agony involved in the process deterred us from going for it even though financially we could have managed. During this trip, we also met a senior Gynaecologist who explained the success rate by explaining that it is either 0% or 100% for the couple under treatment. Another gynaecologist, a motherly figure, was the first to suggest and convince us to go for adoption. Once it became clear that the only way to have our child was not to go through the IVF method, we opted to adopt rather than going through the agonising procedures. Her words of wisdom and experience made our resolve stronger. She was the one who also suggested an Adoption Agency and gave us the contact details. We had always thought of adopting a child even after having a biological child. So taking a prompt decision was never a problem.

That we wanted a girl child only was an inner call for both of us. We knew that this decision of ours may not be very welcome by our parents but our resolve paved the way forward without much ado from our near and dear ones.

Our major concerns with adoption were only two: firstly the

child should be physically healthy and mentally alert and secondly preferably the whereabouts of the biological parents should be unknown. A known history would complicate matters for our child...so we felt.

It was a God- gifted opportunity for us that a newly born baby left on the railway tracks was referred for adoption to us.

BONDING WITH OUR CHILD:

We were shown the baby when she was only a few days old and we immediately decided to take her home. But the procedures involved did not permit us to do so. We had to wait for three months as the biological mother, in case she was found, held the legal rights to the child until then. Then the case would be tried by the judicial process for adoption which takes some time. Finally, after a long wait, we could bring her home.

Every weekend we used to drive to the child care center of the Adoption Agency and request the staff to show us the baby, for which they cheerfully obliged. The process of completing the documentation also gave us a chance to get to know and to bond with the baby. Holding her in my lap and speaking to her was a blissful experience. The longing to bring her home grew stronger as each day went by.

The weekends were also utilised to do the shopping for the baby with a lot of discussions and thought behind it. It included soft cotton dresses, baby cotton mattresses, baby soft blankets, wraps, nappies, different feeding bottles, different types of baby food and lots of toys for a three-month-old.

Many nights we spent talking about how we will organise and manage to give her the best and be the best parents for her!

ACCEPTANCE OF OUR CHILD BY OUR FAMILY AND NEIGHBOURHOOD:
The decision of adopting a child was taken by just the two of us. Only after having brought our daughter home, we informed our parents and other relatives. We took lovely photos and posted them. Nana-Nani (maternal grandparents) came promptly to see and bless the new arrival. After a few days, Dada-Dadi (paternal grandparents) came and blessed the baby as well.

The day we had brought her home all our colleagues came to our house in the evening bearing many gifts. The decision was appreciated by all without any exceptions. The baby stole the show with her twinkling eyes and pretty face.

CHILDHOOD HEALTH ISSUES:
When we took her for a normal health check-up to a Neonatologist, he was concerned that the baby was hard of hearing and had a lower brain circumference than expected for a 4 months old baby. We were taken aback but kept our cool and had full confidence that she could hear. However, despite many attempts by the doctor she had not responded in front of him. After a few weeks we had gone back and this time she responded to all tests and the same doctor declared cheerfully- "Baby fit hai" (baby is fit).

When she was 5-6 years old she used to have severe asthmatic problems and had to be nebulised. We decided to improve her strength and immunity and put her in Karate classes. The coach did an excellent job and in a year she got a green belt and her asthma was cured for good.

INTRODUCTION TO THE CONCEPT OF ADOPTION:
We made sure that the bedtime storytelling always had

stories of Krishna, Sita, Karna and other fictional stories as the main hero. At the age of 5years, we had taken her to the same Adoption Agency and their child care center from where we had adopted her.

As such we never raised the issue because everything was known to her and she had accepted the issue positively.

EARLY SCHOOL:
Like any other child, she had the best of schooling and faced no issues related to this.

ADOPTION ISSUES:
We have never faced any issue related to adoption as we share a very strong bond and neither she nor we ever thought that she is our adopted daughter. Our relationship is strong and secure. Anyway, we had no birth parent history to share with her, so nothing was concealed from her. She was our God-sent daughter.

ADULTHOOD:
She was not able to make a career choice. She was selected for BDS from a reputed college. Though she completed the course somehow but never enjoyed the profession of a dental surgeon. She switched over to her passion for writing and completed her post-graduation in Mass Communication and Journalism and got the 2nd rank in the University. Now she is pursuing her career as a scriptwriter after studying at the best institute for visual arts in the country. We are now looking for a marriage partner for her.

ADOPTION JOURNEY:
We look at our journey as most satisfying and rewarding and are fully content with life. We can't even imagine our lives

without it. The decision to adopt was the best decision we ever took. We also took this decision without hesitation at the right time of our life, and at the right place, by virtue of the opportunity bestowed on us by the Almighty.

Never ever, not even for a moment, have we had any regrets or any doubts in our minds related to the decision. We have enjoyed parenting at each stage with complete fulfilment and now looking back at times we spent as a family makes us envious of ourselves. We would encourage all prospective couples to go for adoption and consider it as a God gifted opportunity that they will never regret even though parenthood can be challenging at times.

TO BE CONTINUED

It all started when my family started pressuring me to get married and marriage was never on my cards. My mother then casually told me to at least have a baby. I started my search for organisations in the city I live but did not get much or good response. During those days there was no CARA. Coincidently a colleague in office was also planning to adopt a baby and so I received all the help required for the process.

When I first saw my baby, I saw a fear in her eyes when she was brought to me. When I held her, I whispered into her ears "I am your mom and I have come to take you home". Although I spoke to her in English I do not know how she understood it; she looked into my eyes and that was it. I know it sounds dramatic but that is what happens when your hearts connect. Yes, that day she was born from my heart.

My baby was almost a year old with just 5 days remaining to turn 1 when I brought her home. She just hopped into the kangaroo bag and came along. I thought she would cry during the flight upon seeing unknown people and not able to see known faces but maybe she knew she was with her Mom and there is nothing to worry. Today when I sit back and look at the pictures clicked with my family just the next day after homecoming I see all the miracle as there are only happy faces as though the baby had been with us since she was born.

Next two years were difficult as she used to constantly fall sick. She was born with Tuberculosis and a small hole in her heart, so her immunity was very weak. Luckily, this was limited only to fever with no major illness. By the time she was 3, we got her 2D Echo to check the status of the hole in the heart which had completely healed by then.

I started introducing her to the concept of being born from the heart when she was 4 years old as by this time she started attending Kindergarten school. Being a single mother and her not having a father would be a big question in front of her when she meets other children with their father. By the age of 7, I told her about her background and whatever information I had about her biological family. Today she is 11 years old and asks me a lot of questions about her biological family. Being introduced to computers and the power of Google she has even asked me to Google about their names and addresses.

Her mother died during her birth and I told her this as I wanted her to know that her mother loved her. The night before her 11th birthday she asked me "Maa is my birthday a good day or a bad day?" I said "It is your Birthday it is a very very good day. The best day of my life." She asked "How can it be a good day? The day I was born my mother died. So how can my birthday be a good day?" I did give her an answer of which she was not much satisfied. But I leave it to the readers as what one should answer to this question. She has now started writing letters to her father and mother and even writes to her to rest in peace. Frankly, my heart aches both ways. She wants to meet them and is eagerly trying to search for her roots.

Having a single parent is more challenging than being a single parent and when it comes to school this must be handled properly. From Kindergarten to standard 4th I made it a point to meet her teachers and give them a background and avoid the question about her father. Primary section tends to teach children about family values and talk about their parents and have days with fathers in the school. Her 5th standard was quite challenging as now children do understand the missing parent and ask whereabouts. My daughter is straightforward in answering that she does not have a father and her mother brought her home through adoption. But I can make out that somewhere within she feels the pain that her father gave her away. Recently she has started becoming vocal that she hates her father for giving her away.

It is important to inculcate respect for their biological parents and I keep justifying through various examples that it was a right decision and for her wellbeing that her father took the decision to give her up for adoption. I also show her my selfishness that if he would have not done so, she would have not been with me and for that, I am so thankful. Sometimes she is very adamant that she wants to meet her family and I do not deny the meeting but just tell her that she must have patience. Since she has waited for eleven years, she should wait for just seven more years and then she can meet her biological family when she turns eighteen.

Her 10th birthday present was a visit to the child care organisation to see the place where she was before coming home. Our social worker left the organisation, but we are still in touch and my daughter has a special connection with her. I should say I am very lucky, although she knows everything, she has never distanced herself from me or from our family. Her love for them is the same. She writes beautiful letters to her grandmother and both her Cousin sisters. They bond so much that she prefers to study with them. Thanks to online studies in the new normal.

I could not find a closure to this article because there is not one. There are more beautiful years and memories pending to collect so….this is 'To be continued…'.

BLOSSOMING LOVE

It is said that marriages are made in heaven. I did not believe in this typical 'filmy' quote until I got married myself, but when I got married I was convinced. As I did not wish to pass on some genetic defects to my next generation, I did not wish to become a biological father. I wished to share this with my future wife and her family members and get married only with her and the family's consent. Now in an arranged marriage, this was rather an impossibility don't you think? But that is where the impossible happened!. God created such a girl who accepted my condition. We then got married with a lot of pomp and ceremony.

It had already been decided that we would adopt and so there were no objections from either side of our families, but my wife felt a bit pressurised. I had thought of adopting for a long time but that was not the case with her. She started preparing herself after she got married to me. Approximately a year into our marriage we enquired about registration for adoption and were informed that we could not register until we had completed two years of marriage.

We then decided to prepare ourselves further for another year. We attended two or three Pre-adoption workshops. There we met some parents and their adopted babies. We also took the guidance of people who had worked in this field for many years. Just after two years of our marriage, we registered for adoption.

By then we had realised that it would take about two years for our baby to come home. I had wished to adopt a girl. In fact, I had decided to marry because a single male cannot adopt a girl! But the Social worker who did our home study posed a question to us, "When you give birth to a child you have no idea of the gender. Then why are you opting for a girl beforehand just because you have the choice to do so?" We were convinced since as of now this was my first baby. So, I scratched the option for a girl and prayed to God to make me a father of a girl!

The saddest day of my life was the day my beloved maternal uncle expired and a couple of days later was the happiest day of my life when after a wait of 23 months, I received a message and an email that we had received a child referral. My wife had gone out for some work. I called her to inform her. I was impatient to open the mail but since we had decided to read the mail together I waited for her. She came home after about 50 long minutes and we opened the laptop.

The very first thing we read was that she was a girl! Wonderful! Life had become meaningful. Then we saw her photo. We had tears in our eyes. She had a smiling face and a slight dimple on one cheek. She was four and a half months old. When we saw her, we were sure she was our daughter. She had a dimple identical to my wife's dimple. We announced the news to our family. My father had just retired, and it was as though he was waiting for this day. It was an indication of how strong the bond was going to be between my father and daughter. After completing all the formalities, we got our daughter, our Blossom home about a year and a half ago and our home turned into a paradise.

She started by turning on her stomach, then crawling, then

standing by holding on to a support, then taking a few steps and continuing the development, running, sitting on the bike, lisping at first and now she has learnt to repeat words after us. Following her progressive development graph was exhausting but double the fun. Blossom is deeply attached to her mother, then the next person is her grandfather ' Aba'! I have never seen this side of my father before in my entire life. He takes utmost care of Blossom and she too delights in his company. It's absolutely necessary for a family to accept a baby first before Society does so. Both of us are blessed in this respect. We enjoyed all the festivals in the year, Holi, Bhaubij, Rakshabandhan, Diwali. With our little daughter, every celebration was joyful and meaningful.

We have travelled with Blossom everywhere. Since my childhood, I love travelling and exploring and so naturally my expectation was that my daughter should also pick up this quality. Blossom loves to travel and does not trouble us even a bit during travel. We have used all modes of transport like car, bus, railway, air and she enjoys all of those equally.

As she is growing older she has started becoming a little wilful and demanding but it is a lot of fun to give in to her demands. She loves to hum songs and she has a photographic memory. She sits with her grandfather and looks at the pictures of fruits and flowers and is able to recall their names. She recognizes the birds like crows, sparrow, pigeon when she sits on our balcony. She eats all the things that are prepared at home and or bought from outside. She is not at all fussy about her food. She is lovable! If one talks with her for five minutes one automatically falls in love with her. The residents of our housing society miss her if they do not meet her in the evening. She is very social. She can talk to even people she does not know.

The purpose behind writing this today is, in my experience, that once your baby comes home 'adoption' disappears from your dictionary and that baby is totally yours! Without any preconceptions, if your whole family accepts the baby as your own, then the baby not only becomes perfect but the whole family becomes enriched.

In our lives, a time will come when we will have to share with Blossom the story of her adoption, but we expect that such a moment will come so naturally that our daughter will ask us, "Baba, why are you pulling my leg"? Our love will help her understand and accept the reality.

~Blossom's Dada

THE PARENTING JOURNEY: JUST KEEP GOING

Hii! This is about adopting an older child, and this is my journey through adoption so far.

Before I start, I would like to give you a short background.

Ever since I was young, I have been very fond of kids and I had decided that I would adopt a child since I was a teenager. Mine was a love marriage and before our marriage, I had informed my husband about my wish. To my surprise, not only him but his whole family welcomed the idea wholeheartedly! Earlier we had decided not to have our 'own' child, but our parents wanted us to have our birth child too. And we wanted to have that experience also. So, we decided that if a boy is born we would adopt a girl and vice versa and we had a baby boy!

We had some financial problems back then so we couldn't adopt immediately and almost five years passed. Now we were both past 35, so if we had gone for the adoption of a 0-2-year-old child....considering the waiting period of 2-3yrs and the time it takes for a child to be independent i.e. 20-25 years we would be in our 60s...and considering the average healthy life of a person there was less probability of us giving our child full support till that time. So, we decided to go for an older child.

Our social workers advised us that if you already have a child you should go for an age difference of 0-3 years since the siblings can adjust easily with each other. So, we decided to adopt a child between 4-6 years old, but the waiting period was almost a year. We did not want to wait that long, so we decided to change our preference to the adoption of a 6-8-year-old child for whom the waiting period was just 3-4months! The social workers warned us that it may be difficult for an older child to adjust to our family.. However, I had been working as a volunteer in an orphanage for young girls, so I knew some of the problems and was not afraid of that. So, we decided to go for it!

While we were waiting we started talking to our son about getting a sister soon. We started to incorporate an imaginary sister in his daily routine. We would tell him that Gudia is going to share everything he has, including us, his parents. Gudia would always live with us and will never leave like his friends or cousins do when they go back to their families. So, he was getting more and more excited to have her in his life!

HER INTRODUCTION BY THE WARDEN OF THE ORPHANAGE

After roughly three months we got a message and a photo of an eight-year-old girl. We went through her medical and general history then called the orphanage.

Gudia had been found only a year back and at that time she hardly spoke, so they didn't admit her to school. Gudia did not have any education before she was found, she had no education whatsoever! As her parents were never found, they did not have her exact date of birth, so her age was approximate.

The warden there was not aware of the procedure of adoption and told us that the girl we are asking for is dusky in colour and they have other light coloured more beautiful girls who can be adopted! She also told us that the girl is somewhat different from other kids, maybe owing to her past trauma, and she is very quiet and withdrawn. But the looks or colour was never a priority for us, and our son is also a very shy, simple, and introverted boy. So, we thought she would fit in just fine.

FIRST MEETING

When we went to the orphanage and met her we asked her a few questions like...how was she feeling, what is her name, what does she like to eat and lastly, would she like to come with us to be our daughter and our son's sister. Gudia answered all the questions in monosyllables like 'good', 'Gudia', 'puri-bhaji' and 'Yes!!'. The social worker told us that was the maximum that Gudia had said in any conversation so far!!! There! That was our clue, Gudia was the one for us and we for her, decision taken!

FIRST TIME SPENT TOGETHER AS A FAMILY

While we were there for the process of foster care Gudia was allowed to stay in the hotel room with us through the day but was not allowed at night. The couple of days when we had to take her back to the orphanage at night, both our kids cried a lot and did not want to part, and we both felt helpless.

Gudia really spoke very little. She always listened to what we told her to do. Gudia played very nicely with our son. Our son also accepted her very well. There were some things I would like to tell you here.

Gudia had shoulder-length hair and there were thousands (and I am not exaggerating here) of lice in her hair! When we took her for a bath to clean her lice, her underwear was soiled, which we then threw away. Gudia also told us that she had a habit of wetting her bed in her sleep. Gudia had a large pustule on her cheek near her ear which was very painful and even caused a fever. When asked about it, Gudia said that she had many like that since she came to live in the orphanage, even showed us the marks on her body which were nearly one cm each (again not exaggerating, she still has those).

Gudia had these fresh and old scratch marks on her hands from nails. When we inquired about it she told us that she gets beaten and scratched by her fellow orphans! It was really painful for me to even hear about it, and I swore that I would never let anyone harm her like that ever again.

AT HOME

We took her home after completing the foster care formalities. Gudia was very happy, so were we and our son seemed to be unable to contain his happiness.

THE FIRST THING WE DID

We had already talked to different schools for her admission. Since Gudia was almost 8 years old and still had no education at all, reputed schools in our area were not ready to take her in the first standard. So, we had approached a small school, which was not on the list of our preferred schools. That school had agreed to take her in the first standard.

So, the first thing we did after Gudia got home was to get her admitted to that school. Gudia was very excited to study. She even sat in the school for the rest of the day and enjoyed it and till date she has never complained about going to school. But there is a little hiccup which I will discuss later.

DEFICIENCIES

At first, we got her pustule treated and started her on some general multivitamins.

After a few days, we started to notice a squint in her right eye. But it was not always noticeable. So, we took her to an eye specialist. He checked her eye-sight and it was perfect. So, he started her on some vitamin A and iron tablets and told us that the squint is most probably due to the nutrition deficiency and may correct itself by the time she was the age of 12. If it doesn't, we will have to operate later. But the healthy food and the tablets started to work, and her squint is almost completely gone.

Also, there were some white patches on her skin, and the doctor said those were also due to nutrition deficiency. And they vanished after only a few days of medication.

CURIOSITY

On her second day home Gudia started to show a little curiosity about the things that we had in our cupboards. So, we told her to open them and have a look for herself and we let her see everything unsupervised. Gudia seemed very happy and satisfied after doing that. On our way home, we had asked her what she would like to do after she got home. Gudia told us that she would like to decorate the house! And it really has been her practice since she got home. She is always tidying things lying around the house. She really likes to help with doing or organising different things. My son who is really the messy one learned a lot from her.

SOCIAL BEHAVIOUR

After we brought her home, our friends and family members came to meet her, and many invited us home. All of them brought gifts and made her feel special. Even we bought many things for her. Because of all this, she felt wanted and loved and happy. At the same time, our son felt neglected but to our surprise, he never felt jealous and never misbehaved with her because of that. He just envied her. It made us feel proud and even a little sad for him. So, we started to buy things for him too, even made people do the same. Finally, it made both of them, and hence us parents, very happy!

In all this, we also observed that Gudia behaved the same way with all the people visiting her as she did with us. She started to do more and more silly things in front of others to gain more attention which sometimes felt inappropriate. Gudia also started roaming around people's homes unattended. Sometimes she just looked and sometimes even brought things out from their cupboard which was unacceptable and a bit shameful for us. She could not understand the boundaries.

We tried telling her that our house is her own where she can do whatever she wants, but the houses that we visit are different. But Gudia failed to understand the point since for her they were giving her the same kind of attention as us. So, for a long time, we avoided going to people's houses and let her observe other kids in our society and differentiate the relations for herself. Gudia gradually got the point!

LICE

We cut her hair short to deal with the lice. Thousands of lice were not easy to deal with. Shampoos didn't work much. I used to sit with her hair daily for about 15-30 minutes to take them out manually. I even thought about cutting off all her hair but could not go through with it, as I thought it would have a negative impact on her because Gudia very much wanted to have long hair and did not like cutting her hair.

So, in the meantime, we all had lice in our hair too! It took us almost a month to finally get rid of all of the lice.

HUNGER AND HEALTH

Gudia still has quite an insatiable hunger like most adopted kids! She is always ready to try different things though her stomach does not always accept everything. Since we always give her as much as she wants to eat and can digest, Gudia put on weight very quickly.

DATE OF BIRTH

As her date of birth was not confirmed and Gudia didn't appear to be 8 years old, we did her bone age test and found that Gudia was 7. We got it updated in her birth certificate as well.

ADJUSTING WITH THE SIBLING

My son and Gudia got along very quickly as they were both nearly the same age. Soon they both started to like and care for each other deeply. He showed absolutely no problem in sharing anything with her. He even made sure that we gave her everything he had. And if we scolded her he started scolding us back! And that was really very sweet! He only seemed to have a problem while sharing the bed with her, although it was absolutely acceptable considering he was the first child and that was his special space. Gudia never complained.

In the beginning, Gudia was reluctant to share things / toys that we had bought for her or were gifted to her. Gudia even made a scene in the family court on the day of her legal adoption! She suddenly stopped talking to all of us, even refused to eat all day. We tried different things but no response. Even people at court started to notice and we became worried. She finally spoke when we informed her that we could not take her home with us and she will have to return to the orphanage. At that point, Gudia held our hands and started crying and said that she did not want to go back to the orphanage. She had this tantrum just because I let my son handle a bag which was gifted to her from my friend. Gudia was ready to share it now!

BEDWETTING

We all were sleeping together on one single big bed in the beginning. Gudia had a bedwetting habit. So, we started to wake her up at night and take her to the toilet. Initially, we took her 2-3 times. Eventually, that came down to only once. But then it became tedious because often Gudia would wet the bed before we could take her to the toilet. So, we made both our kids sleep in separate beds. And we encouraged her to wake up on her own if she wanted to pee, or at least after she wet the bed. But Gudia couldn't. We started to scold her for that. But then Gudia started hiding her bedwetting and would come out and sit on the sofa in her wet pants! It was really unhygienic! So, we had to check her pants on a daily basis after she woke up. Eventually, after she put on some weight and improved in her health and her sense of security, Gudia stopped wetting her bed altogether. Now we all sleep in the same bed again hassle-free and happily!

COMMUNICATION PROBLEM

Gudia used to say some incomprehensible words from her original place of residence, including some words which Gudia could not pronounce correctly. But simultaneously, while correcting them, we started to use her words ourselves! And it was just like when a baby starts to talk for the first time and everyone at home talks his language!

Her mother tongue is Hindi while ours is Marathi but as we could speak Hindi fluently that never created any problem. Now Gudia understands Marathi completely and even tries to speak a few things.

Even though Gudia can speak normally, when someone asks her a question, Gudia freezes. It has nothing to do with whether or not Gudia knows the answer. The questions can be as simple as what is her name or what is Gudia doing? But being asked a question just blocked her mind! Gudia could not frame a sentence! So, we started to give her options from which she could choose her answer. We still practice it. But that doesn't always work. We have tried comforting her, hugging her, making her understand that she can always talk freely etc. But Gudia just simply freezes.

This happens in two ways, one is when Gudia cannot answer and second is when she does not want to. Earlier when she did not want to answer, Gudia would stand in one place and would not move for as long as 4-5 hours! Twice Gudia even peed in her pants while she was standing. This was a matter of concern, but we knew she would go past this challenge once she gained confidence. Now her response time has come down to 5-15mins. Usually, when we know that Gudia is blocked we just let it be, we let her progress at her own pace. So, I can say we are making progress!

STUDIES

When Gudia came home we observed that she lacks the most basic knowledge of our surroundings which most kids normally learn on their own. Words as simple as clouds, sun, sky, moon, river, sea, birds, animals, horn, bike, truck, mixer, fridge etc. were unknown to her. It was very strange for us too. But it was amazing to see her learn all those and many more words in just a few months.

Even though Gudia does not always answer, she is very eager to study and even good at her studies. As she never ever went to pre-primary I started to teach her at home in order to help her cope with the first standard. Earlier Gudia used to go to school and just sit and talk to her peers because she couldn't read or write.

But after almost 4 months of home-schooling when I observed that Gudia was still not studying in school I got concerned. I told her that school is for studying and what we were doing at home was just temporary. But still, Gudia didn't start studying. Her books and copies came home incomplete. We sat her down and told her about the education system and what she could become after completing studies, and what would be the situation if Gudia didn't study. While going to school she always said she would study and yet she never actually did. I asked her the reason and Gudia told me that she liked talking to her peers more. It was as simple as that.

I talked to her teachers but could not get much help. I tried positive scoring, bribing, scolding, taking away her privileges and eventually strong punishments, but there was no change. Gudia always seemed to have understood the situation at home, but in school, she simply refused to study! I even tried not teaching her at home but in vain. Moreover, I had to work doubly in order to complete her backlog. The resulting irony was that Gudia studied with me happily at home, even if I made her study the whole day! I suppose it was the one on one equation which she really needed.

I started getting more and more unhappy and short-tempered with her. I started becoming rough with her, more and more (even though I always regretted doing it). My son who had never seen me become out of control said that I spanked her because I wanted to kill her (he didn't even know what killing means, just thought it's too harsh a treatment). So, I had to make him understand that even if Gudia follows everything I said at home, if she does not study at school she would suffer in the future and blame me for not making her understand.

I eventually observed that the spanking made her scared of me, but I still could not make her study in school. Now the schools are closed due to Corona. And I have taught her the entire 1st standard syllabus at home. After this is over we are going to get her admitted to the second standard in a better school. We are hoping that teachers will pay more attention to her there and Gudia will start studying in the school itself and stop this dependence on me. But if she does not, then we may have to seek professional help.

It wouldn't have bothered me at all if Gudia were an average kid. But after watching her complete the syllabus of almost four years (3 years of Pre-primary and first standard) in just a few months, I most certainly believe that Gudia is a brilliant kid! We are trying our best to educate her according to her calibre.

I am very proud to say that the girl who could not read or write even an alphabet or number is reading lessons from her book, writing the answers, and even doing calculations on her own. My Gudia is giving tough competition to my son!

PHYSICAL STRENGTH
While working on the stubborn behaviour of the kids, spanking is the last resort of any mother which she obviously hates doing! Our son occasionally requires the same. But he behaves with just a single spanking from either one of us!

In her case, it never worked. Gudia would tell us that she doesn't simply feel the pain.

On asking different questions about her past we found out that her birth father had the habit of hitting her with thick bamboo after he got drunk and no one in the family dared or were too scared to stop him. It made us hate him and the whole family to the core. We wanted to punish him badly for messing up with our daughter.

Now we found out that Gudia had emotional injuries which were not visible to anyone but us! Similarly, we found out an extraordinary thing about her, that even though her birth father did all that to her countless times, Gudia never showed any interest in payback! She just wanted to stay away from him and never see him again. Not only him, but Gudia had the same feelings about the girls in the orphanage. She even did not want us to hurt them on her behalf. Hurting anyone is the worst thing in the world for her. Gudia can't even bear to watch fights on the TV till date.

Even though we consider it as the best thing about her, we do not want her to be that soft. So, we always encourage her to feel angry as well and to express her anger and her other locked up feelings. We rarely interfere in the fights of our kids and we always encourage her to hit our son if he hurts her. We even make her do a few bodybuilding exercises. Also, we ask her to punch the bed 50 times daily and express anger while doing so.

We also observed that when we spanked her for doing something wrong Gudia gets blocked even more. So, we started talking about it whenever we did so. We explain it to her again and again that even if we disciplined her in this way, we do not intend to hurt her! We simply want her to do better and that too is for her own good. We try not to push her too much. Now her block seems to have a lesser and lesser effect on her!

But her pain bearing capacity is tremendous, we observed the extent of it recently. When she had a small accident, the doctor was amazed by her capacity to bear the pain. She fell off a kid's scooter and hurt her elbows, when the swelling didn't go down we did further tests and found out there was a minute fracture. The doctor was amazed that she was so calm while suffering from a fracture! She had to go through a minor surgery for the fracture as the cast was not done immediately. Throughout the process, doctors checked and tried to move her hand multiple times. And they admired her pain endurance again and again. But all we could think of was of the emotional injuries which made her immune to pain!

She had to put on a cast for almost 6 weeks and did all of her daily activities including school and studies without any complaint. It made me sad sometimes to see that she was not dependent on me. But at the same time, I am happy that she has tremendous inner strength and she is self-reliant.

Interacting with her was not a normal or easy experience for us. We understand better now that there is always more to a person than meets the eye, even to a young child. I know that I have made countless mistakes while dealing with her. But I have made many mistakes with my biological child too and I regret all my mistakes from the bottom of my heart. But I know that no parent can say that they haven't made any mistake while raising their child.

The future is always unpredictable but looking back at the

past I can say that I am happy in every way possible for a mother. We have made tremendous progress so far on this unique journey. I hope that sooner rather than later we will all reach a state of equilibrium and I can lay to rest some of the battles of parenthood!

TO ALL THOSE WHO WANT TO GO FOR AN OLDER CHILD

Bringing up any child, be it a baby or an older child is always difficult. Yes, the problems are different. You may fail again and again in your efforts, but never fail to try again and do better the next time, just keep going!

You must have heard your parents say to you countless times, "When you become a parent you will understand better, how we feel about you!"

That, my friends, is a hundred percent true!

THICKER THAN BLOOD

Our journey into parenthood began almost thirty years ago. I really don't know where to begin, but we had the desire to adopt after six years of marriage. We shared this with my brother-in-law and with his wife, who is my best friend. My brother-in-law himself was adopted by some relatives. They welcomed our decision.

Some people advised us to adopt from our relatives so that we would share common genes with our child. But we were firm in our decision to adopt a child from an institution. A supportive friend helped us to find all the information we needed about a child care institution in another State. Everything moved so fast after that and within three months, our baby was in our arms.

Our baby daughter came into our lives on our wedding anniversary. We renamed her Tanvi. She was one and a half years old. Our first halt with baby Tanvi was at my birthplace. All our family members were so happy. They graciously welcomed Tanvi. All the relatives accepted her. Back home we arranged a small Puja for our relatives to welcome our baby girl.

Tanvi studied until her graduation in our city. I had great moral support from my parents and other family members. I also found a job in due course. Life went on smoothly for us. There were six girls and one boy, including Tanvi, in our family. She was very attached to her sisters and brother. They share a very strong bond and help each other whenever required. As a family, we loved to spend our free time together.

Around the age of nine or ten, I had told my daughter that we had adopted her from this particular city. I told her, "It is better that you know the reality from me, not from other sources. No one will tell you but every relative knows the fact. But there are some in our society who may try to give you misinformation".

I didn't see any reaction from her at the time. Both of us continued with our lives the way things were before. There was absolutely no change in our behaviour-- neither her nor mine. Gradually she passed her secondary, higher secondary school, and then graduated. I never burdened her with my expectations where her education and other things were concerned. She represented her school in state-level matches.

Her life changed after she completed her school education. She had a lot of friends. I had no problem with her friends being girls or boys. Her friends came home whenever they were free. She was very popular in her group. I also enjoyed the company of her friends whenever I was at home. She enjoyed her college days on her own terms. I put no restrictions on her as to where she could go or not go.

From her college days, I started sharing my life stories with her. There was no secrecy about what I was doing and what my plans were. I think she always understood whatever I shared with her. I never wanted either of us to lie while sharing things. I had taken my life as it came my way and I wished that she did the same. I wanted her to stand on her own feet from the beginning and to earn a living whether it was necessary or not. No one knows what sort of situations would come up in life. It would not be good to be unprepared and start to look for a solution at that time. Instead, one must be prepared with strategies and solutions beforehand. This is what I taught her, based on my own experiences.

One day she told me about Rohit and his family and his intention to marry her. I told her to take her own decision while taking into consideration as to whether he would adjust to our family's free atmosphere. Also, whether his family would accept her adoption, and their age difference as he was younger than her. I had no objection to whatever decision she took. He was from a good family. I felt that she should take her time to consider all possibilities that might affect her later in life. I wanted her to have the decision-making capacity with regard to her own life.

Finally, she took her decision which I gratefully accepted. The wedding date was for the convenience of even for relatives living abroad, to enable them to attend. All local and outstation relatives from both my husband's and my side were present at all the wedding functions. She is very well-loved by all our relatives.

I missed her a lot after her marriage. I really enjoy her company, just being around her. We are mother and daughter and we are also best friends with each other. We used to speak to each other at night whenever we wanted to share something. Just her presence at home gave me great comfort whether we spoke or not. Once she left the house to go to her in-laws, the house felt empty and automatically a feeling of loneliness enveloped me. Not a single day goes by when we don't call each other. I want to hear her voice at least once a day.

She is very caring towards me and gives instructions over the phone as to what I should do on my sixtieth Birthday, she called up at midnight and wished me and asked me to check her WhatsApp status immediately. It was "Aai" (Mother), my face that shone from her number.

I am so proud of my caring daughter. I have no words to express the deep connection and feelings I have for her... my beloved daughter Tanvi. **Who said blood is thicker than water?**

THE TRIUMPH OF FAITH

The decision to adopt a child came to our mind when I lost my baby in the eighth month of pregnancy. It was a deep and painful loss. It was very difficult for me to come out of depression. It took me two long years. With the support of my husband and my family, I came to terms with my loss.

I was fortunate enough to have my great Gurus beside me. In the light of their wisdom, I realised there were other roads to motherhood. Under their guidance, I took the decision to adopt a child and they opened up this avenue for me and held on to me every step of the way to give me the strength to deal with the challenges.

Basically, my husband and I did not have any sort of expectations and concerns. At that time, our only concern was whether we would be able to take care of a baby? We both just wanted a baby who would change our empty and monotonous lives. On this path, I had two angels who helped me in the journey of the adoption and how to go about the whole procedure.

The wonderful day when we went to meet our little boy along with my father in law, we knew that he was the special one who was chosen for us by our Guru. We brought him home to a great welcome where he received abundant blessings. But after a few days, he was quite unwell, and we had to admit him to the hospital. We were always there to take care of him and grab the chance to bond with him. Due to his acute illness, we became completely involved in his care and a deep relationship formed between us.

His health condition became critical. We were not sure whether he would survive. But we did not leave his side and stayed up day and night for a long time of uncertainty. We were anxious and exhausted but by God's grace and our Guru's blessings, we kept our hopes alive. We took all possible care of him with lots of love. We never thought even once that he is so sick and what the impact of this serious ailment could be. Whatever the outcome we loved him and would never leave him. We gave him all our love and care and after many months of struggle, his health improved. For better or for worse he was our own child, and we had a strong biological link to him.

He was accepted very well in my family and my husband's family. He was more attached to his father and grandfather. Neighbours were very sweet and accepted him very well. As my father in law had seen him first, our son had a great bond with this wonderful grandfather.

Introduction to the concept of adoption was of course challenging. We were told that it is better to share the story of adoption with our child at a very early age before he or she hears it from some outsider. We started telling him through the stories of Krishna when he was 6 or 7 years old. Finally, he told us one day, "Yes, now I know that I am adopted please do not repeat it again." After that, we have never told him about adoption. We also completely forgot that he is our 'adopted' child. He was our child and we gave all our love to him. He never asked any sort of questions related to adoption.

We faced umpteen problems in his early schooling. He was

good in his class when he was in his playschool and nursery school. Problems started when we shifted his school to a new one because the school he attended had classes only till Upper KG.

He refused to go from day one to his new school. We did not know what happened to him suddenly. We were bewildered. He used to cry the whole day. The teachers started complaining from the first day. Thereafter, his interest in studies got lost. He started fighting with his friends, making excuses to come back home, like vomiting, stomach-ache and many such issues. Obviously, he was very distressed.

One day his principal called us and told us to shift him to another school because they were not able to handle him. Then started his journey to a new Open school where his life took a drastic turn in a negative way. His nature changed to a violent child filled with anger.

There were obviously many issues which he was dealing with in his young mind. He was keeping quiet and wasn't talking about whatever was bothering him. He was maintaining silence with us about adoption. Maybe he wanted to talk about it, but he never opened up. We used to ask him, but he refused to say anything. He said I have nothing to say, nothing to ask. But we could sense that he was bottled up and wanted to ask questions. Added to that it turned out that he was dyslexic, and his issues were not well understood.

After our sharing of an adoption story during his childhood, we never brought up adoption again in our communication. He kept us at bay regarding his adoption. He never asked us anything nor allowed us to ask him. He was getting more difficult for us. By God's grace, we both have lots of patience and have complete faith in God. That is what kept us going as he tested us to our extreme limits. At times we felt unsafe when he lost control. Sometimes I broke down and shattered into pieces. We were feeling guilty about where we went wrong.

His behaviour was very rude to us in his adolescent years. He used to talk back very rudely to us and kept fighting for small things and demanding gratification by material things. He was bottling up his anger and would burst like a volcano sometimes, which we had never expected.

As we knew that something was bothering him, I met my friend who is a very good child counsellor. She started counselling us, and later on our son as well. It was very difficult to take him to her and get him counselled. But gradually he was getting friendly with her and started going for counselling quite willingly. These sessions were very helpful through very troubled times. We never had any trust issues with him, but he had some doubts and kept hiding his emotions and other things from us. But believe me, we had full faith in him, that he will be fine someday with our love and support.

At this critical time, we also had so many questions about his birth family which we wanted to know, to understand his needs better. We were told by the agency that they had no idea where his parents were now, but both his parents had been healthy when he was born. We had to leave this matter then and there, but we knew that these were the questions which were bothering him, and he was wanting to know something about his birth story. He went to his childcare center on his own once and tried to find out about his biological parents, but he was not able to find out much. He came back again

with sadness in him.

We never came to know much about his friendship with girls as he was not very vocal about it, but we never heard anything regarding sexual misbehaviour with the opposite sex. He fell into bad company at some stage and kept a distance from us. He never indulged in vices like stealing, though he went into habits like smoking and drinking

When he was 12 years old we saw his exploding anger and violence for the first time. It was unimaginable, never seen before. We were all shattered. Thereafter so many times we have experienced his massive anger issues. We were advised that he should see a psychiatrist. It was a very difficult situation to take him to the psychiatrist, but I think he also must have realised that he needs to seek professional help. So, we visited a highly reputed psychiatrist. He was getting a little better with the therapy and we were with him to give him the support he needed from us. Us both, his parents, were also disturbed. Our lives were lived like zombies. We did not know what had hit us. We were sitting on the edge; anything could happen at any time.

One day he came home drunk and started banging doors and glass windows and hurt himself very badly on his hand. It was the scariest day of our life. After this incident, he had an attack. We rushed him immediately to the hospital and the doctor informed us that he had a heart attack and immediate surgery has to be performed. We were shocked completely out of our wits and really did not know what to do. The next day the surgery was done, and we were told that his heart condition was not good. The doctors were not sure of the outcome and told us that anything can happen to him. That was it! We were shattered completely and started praying for him day and night. He was crying for us and other family members. For the first time, he expressed his love and need for us. All the bottled-up feelings finally spilt out. All we knew was that he was our child and we loved and needed him as much as he too loved and needed us. Miraculously, after fifteen days he came back home.

Our lives became completely challenged as parents of our unusual son. We had to face so many challenges from the family too, as we were in a joint family there was lots of criticism, questions, and opposition. Our young son was often very hurt by comparisons to his cousin. We felt so sad for our child, how much he must be suffering to behave so violently? He was confused about himself; issues of identity and self-esteem were obviously bothering him. He felt different. He perceived himself differently and must have struggled a great deal inside himself. In the end, we have overcome all sorts of challenges on our own with very little help from other family members.

On this parenting journey, we have forgotten ourselves, our pleasures and other priorities, our only goal is to look after him and to see him as a good citizen and a kind person. Yes, after all this churning, his anger and violence are under control. He is trying his best to keep himself calm and polite too. It is not easy, but he is making a great effort. After all these years and the hard experiences, he has changed a lot. He has become quite calm and got into a business. He is very intelligent but sometimes over-confident and into risk-taking ventures.

It has been a tough ride for all of us, truly a trial by fire. We have come so far only with our strong faith and trust, our will power, love, and patience. Our son has also suffered.

We never ever harboured any thoughts about turning away from him. We remain completely committed to him and feel responsible for him. We have a connection to each other which is much deeper than biology. It is the unbreakable bond of divine love.

BIG SURPRISES COME IN BABY BLANKETS

My husband and I decided to adopt our second child even before we were married! This came as a frivolous thought at a time when we were sitting on the beach and were looking around to see so many children. We felt why should we bring another child to this world?

A few years later, we got married. Four years after our marriage I was pregnant with my first child. I was the only child growing up and I always wanted to have 2 children. But then, I also wanted to have one biological child so that I could go through the process of giving birth to a child! So that's how we decided to adopt our second child.

It was not an easy decision. This was 18 years ago; my parents were not ok about adopting the second child. They felt that I had one child and I can have the second one as well. Why adopt? Also, my dad felt it would cause issues between the siblings when they grow up. But my husband and I were very convinced that I need not go through the second pregnancy to bring another child into our home.

We went ahead, filed our papers in the adoption agency that was recommended by my paediatrician. Thus, the process began, and our daughter was then 4 years of age. Once we got ourselves registered, we used to take our daughter almost every few months to the adoption home to show her that her brother would be coming from that home. We wanted to have another girl but then those days in a Hindu Marriage

Family Act, if we had a biological daughter then we could only adopt a boy baby! So, we were waiting for our son to come home! We waited for around 15 long months.

I clearly remember that day! I had just come from work and kept my bag on the table and my phone rang. This was the agency telling me that they have 2 boys in the same age group, and we could come over to choose one. We were very excited and planned our trip the next day to visit the agency. The fact that we could "choose" one baby kept bothering us. Then we got the clarity, why should we choose based on how they look? Let us just see one baby and bring that baby home! So, the agency showed us two files, and we picked one baby without seeing the child! We had requested that we show the files to our doctor to seek his opinion.

We had taken both the files to show our doctor, who pointed out that one file showed more details than the other. He told us the pros and cons of both the babies. Here again, we were confused! Should we go with more details so that It will be useful in future or should we just go with fewer details and take it as it comes? Doctors gave us their opinion and as we walked out of the clinic, we decided. You know what? From today he is our son! Let's go with fewer details and with no details make it fresh and start our lives! So, without seeing our son, based on our file with fewer details we said we will go with it! Quite brave to have done that 18 years back! But I firmly believe if it is in my destiny and there for me, the world conspires to make it happen for me.

Our son came home when he was 5 months of age and bonded very well with my daughter who was then 6 years of age. When we decided to adopt, we had so many questions and fears. What if the child had any health issues? What if the family does not welcome him?

How would he look? Will my children bond well together? I must say these fears were real at that point and our conviction told us that we will take it as it comes and face the consequences as required.

With a strong belief that what we were doing was absolutely right, we brought our son home. Then we moved between various countries and had many paediatricians. My children both bonded well right from the beginning and our families welcomed both of them equally.

As parents, we never ever once felt anything different between our children. Since she was involved from day 1 of bringing my son home, my daughter never ever fought much with him and she is protective of him up until today. They grew up well together and had a fairly smooth and happy childhood.

When my son was around 4, we told him that he was from another tummy! He didn't understand much but heard us. From then on, almost once a year, I would bring up this topic to let him know and later on he became comfortable with it. When we met someone and if they asked where they were born, he would immediately tell the adoption agency's name and we as a family were very comfortable with it. We never kept this away from our families and friends and never thought this information is not to be shared.

When my son was around 10/12 years of age, he asked us again about his mother - Who was she? How was he born? Why did he land up in this agency? and etc. All I had to tell him was that there are difficult circumstances because of which his mother could not bring him up and gave him to a safe place from where he could find his new parents. But I kept telling him, how does that matter today? Now, we are your parents. But still, every time I would wait with bated breath to hear his thoughts!

When he turned 16 or so, once when we were out for dinner at a restaurant, I asked him at this unusual time: Do you ever think of your background or does being adopted ever raise any questions. He replied, "How does that matter now?" And I must say, I was pleased to hear that. He said it doesn't bother him anymore and moved on to talking about something else.

I think what worked for our family was to have been completely transparent about this process and sharing it openly with our family and friends. It was definitely not a secret we wanted to keep. That brought confidence in all of us that we were doing the right thing. People around us also took a cue from our confidence and did not provoke us in any way.

In terms of growing up, like all children, like my daughter, my son too had anger and manifested some behaviour issues related to adolescence issues. How does it differ between a biological and an adopted child? As I said at the beginning, we really found no difference from day 1. If I had to deal with some issues with my biological child, it was no different for my adopted child.

We are so glad we took that decision that day, probably the best decision of our lives. He may still have questions/ thoughts as he grows up to be an adult but we will deal with that as and when it comes, in the same way, that we have dealt with things till now - with truth, sensitivity and openness. That is the best way to deal with relationships.

SPACE AND TIME TO GROW

We had decided we would adopt even before we got married. Our first attempt did not materialise because we were not financially stable. After three years we had a son, Saurav. Even so we had decided to adopt a child. My in-laws were the first to support this decision. About eight years back when we were financially secure, we went ahead and registered at the Adoption Agency.

Since we had a son we decided to adopt a girl. Basically there were no issues regarding the child's caste or religion. The only thing we wanted was that the birth mother's medical history should be available.

Would we be able to raise her well? How would the relatives behave with her? How would the baby be? All these thoughts would go through our heads.

We were also a little worried because there was a seven year age gap between Saurav and the baby. Would we be able to take care of a baby once again after a gap of seven years? We had these trepidations. But sometimes we would also have doubts whether the child would accept us as parents? Would the child love us? At the same time we also had to take care that Saurav did not feel that we loved him any less or that our behaviour towards him had changed because so far he had been the only child and as a result the center of attention. But now that was about to change.

At the same time there was joy and enthusiasm that another baby was going to come home.

It was necessary to mentally prepare ourselves for all this. To do that we were talking to our relatives and friends about the arrival of the baby. We were updating them from time to time about how long before the baby would come home.

We had involved Saurav in this whole process right from the beginning. That is why he was aware of each step. It was he who would ask, "Did you fill up the form? Ask the aunty (social worker at the Agency) when is the baby coming home," etc and that is how he was also getting mentally prepared that a child younger than him would be coming home. As a result he saved money to buy a dress for the baby. The waiting time gave us time to prepare our family for a new addition.

We were also speaking to a friend who lived close to us and had also adopted a child. Along with this we also read books on this topic and issues related to adoption. We read Developmental Psychology and "*Adgul Mudgul, Aapli Mule*" one more time so that we could refresh our understanding of all the issues around a baby's development.

Also we found the workshop conducted by the Agency to be useful. We were counselled about how to behave with children. How important it is to share the fact of adoption with the children and how the information could be shared, were very important issues which were discussed at the workshop.

It was rather a prolonged 'pregnancy'....but finally after a long wait of nearly two years, Suruchi, our daughter, came home. She was three and a half months old.

A big ceremony took place at the Agency. All of our close friends and relatives and both of our parents - nearly 50 to 60 people were present for the ceremony. We were very happy with all the good wishes and love showered on us. We felt so blessed.

The question was whether Suruchi would accept us as her parents. It took some time for her to really get close to us. She did not like to be cuddled while going to sleep at night. She did not like being held close. It took her seven months to accept a cuddle. We had to give her that much of time. Then we realised that she takes her time to adjust and trust. Until she feels comfortable she does not give any response.

At the same time it was a lot of fun to watch her laugh and play. My in-laws were paying close attention to her when she woke up from her sleep and her activities thereafter. Her coming home had brought a lot of joy. Everybody was interested in her daily progress.

Overtime we became familiar with her likes and dislikes. She particularly enjoyed food that was savory or had Jeera in it. If she was hungry or scared she would take her hand close to her mouth. We started understanding these small things. We started understanding her signals and her baby language through her gestures.

Saurav used to play with her after coming back from school. All our relatives and friends would ask about Suruchi. It was enjoyable to watch her every step of development. I started writing a diary about her.

We had informed all our relatives and neighbours about her arrival so everyone was very happy since she came home. We would take her outdoors everyday. Everyone would come to meet her. Saurav had taken her to school to meet his teachers.

HEALTH ISSUES

Suruchi was very delicate as she was a premature baby born in the 7th month and weighed only 1.4 kgs. So she would fall sick with every weather change. The place where we live is quite cold and she had to be admitted to the hospital twice for pneumonia.

The doctor informed us it was important that we took care of her health till she was 6 years old. We realised gradually that we had to reduce her frequency of falling sick brought on by weather changes. So we started to put her in warm clothes and give her warm water as advised.

We also noticed that when Suruchi was 8-9 months old she was not crawling. She could comprehend everything around her but she was not able to express herself in a manner appropriate for her age. With the help of a psychologist we started occupational therapy for her. We had to take her every week. We also had to do the exercises at home. This led to an improvement in her development.

We kept in mind that there was a difference between Saurav and Suruchi. Gender differences, the environment she was in while in the womb, the environment before she arrived home- - all of this had definitely had an effect on her! And that is the reason we would never make any comparisons between them.

INTRODUCTION TO THE CONCEPT OF ADOPTION

The workshop organised by the Agency had stressed the importance and necessity of sharing the fact of adoption with the children. So we had decided that we would share this fact when the baby came home. I started talking about adoption in small ways with Suruchi from the time she was seven months old. I think as a mother it is difficult to cross this stage. But it is always ideal that the child finds out from us rather than from someone else.

Gradually I started telling her the story that was appropriate for her age. The story was about her journey to her home- - about her coming from her home to our home.

In the beginning when I told her the story she would just listen without apparent understanding. Then gradually I began to give her details. She would enjoy listening to her story. Now she is seven years old. She asks to be told her story.

We shifted to a smaller place in another district.
One day as he was passing by, a teacher remarked- "Is she the one you adopted?"
It took me a moment to realise that he was talking about Suruchi.
I said "yes!"
He said "Good thing that you got her. Otherwise what would have happened to her. Poor thing!"
I replied "I don't know what would have happened to her but we would have been deprived of this joy. She is not a poor thing, she is a fighter!"

QUESTIONS ASKED BY SURUCHI REGARDING HER ADOPTION

"Why wasn't I in your stomach?" Suruchi has asked me this question two to three times.

"Because your elder brother was in my stomach. You were at

home."

"But I wanted to come into your stomach."

"That doesn't make a difference. I still love you. You are my baby."

"Then whose stomach was I in?"

"You were in the stomach of another mother (the adoptive mother has written Tai). She was worried about you."

"Why?"

"Every mother worries about their child. Like I worry about you."

"Then?"

Then she met aunty (social worker at the Agency). She told her-"I cannot take care of my baby. Would you look after her and find parents for her ?" Aunty said 'yes'.

Aunty then called up your father and told him that your baby is with us. Then your father brought you home.

EARLY SCHOOL

We decided to put Suruchi in a Marathi medium school. We admitted her to anganwadi. But she didn't like school so used to go for three to four days in a month. We did not push her to go to school. We waited until the time she felt the need for a friend.

But we would take her to street plays and meetings with us. So her non-formal education was continuing. As a result wherever she goes, she mixes with people very easily. This is equally important for us.

Suruchi is now seven. She feels the need for friends and wants to go to school on her own accord.

She has to sit down to study because school is now online. We realise that it will take her time to comprehend and learn. Suruchi is very possessive. She always has some toy in her hand. She always needs that to be with her. Even when she wakes up, she first holds the toy in her hand. She decides whose house she would like to go and play. She likes to play sitting down games. She likes story books. She likes old songs more.

She takes time to learn. It is difficult for her to sit in one place. She avoids doing things that are difficult. She is more drawn towards music and dance. She really loves chapati/ bhakri and vegetables that are not dry. She has just started eating mangoes and raw mangoes.

Overall she takes her time to do everything and she has to be given that time. We understand her very well and give her the space she needs to grow at her own pace. She took her time to accept us but now we are inseparable.

FROM PAIN TO GAIN
THE ADOPTION JOURNEY

I was a topper in my medical college in Kanpur. It was here that I met my husband. He was a batch senior to me and after graduation, we got married and moved to Delhi.

Years went by and we were both immersed in our careers, during which time I also pursued a Ph.D. After six years of marriage, we both decided that perhaps it was the right time to have a child. However, unlike our careers, we were no winners in this part of life. Several unsuccessful attempts to get pregnant and several failed IVF rounds gave me a feeling I had never had before. The feeling of being a failure. My husband didn't feel that sense of failure. He was not the one who was not able to do what he had to. Medically he was fit and fine. The problems lay with me. This is a feeling I had never known, being a high achiever all my life.

My husband and his family convinced me that adoption was the route we had to take towards parenthood. The day came when we went to the orphanage to see the child that had been matched with us. However, a slightly older child with big eyes insisted on holding onto my dupatta and insisted, "You are my Mama Papa".

Both of our hearts melted and we knew we had found our daughter. The years went by peacefully and we had a happy life together. We named her Nidhi. For the first few years of her life, my mother in law cared for her, I did not take any leave. I was still very focused on my career. After my mother in law passed away we put her into a crèche and this is where we started facing certain issues. When we informed people that she was adopted people would ask the strangest things. Everyone from the manager at her crèche to other parents had questions to me about her. "What was wrong with her that she was abandoned?" "Who is her mother?". My husband dealt well with all these people. But I could not. It hurt me a lot and made me very angry. Because I wanted to be her mother. Why didn't people just accept that? However, these feelings tormented me too. That's why they made me so angry. I feared the day she would grow up and tell me that I was not her mother and go off to find her real mother. Who was I then? I was just a failure who couldn't conceive a child. A big biological failure. That was my secret.

As she entered adolescence my daughter, Nidhi, went through a storm of issues. Telling her she was adopted was something I was very nervous about but we did tell her on her 11 th birthday. She was stoic about it and we didn't talk about it. She was now in year 8 when slowly she started faltering in academics and began spending a lot of time in the company of unsavory boys in our neighborhood. My husband and I were both busy at the hospital. Patients took up most of our time till 8pm, sometimes we returned home even at 9 pm. She would come home from school and then if she was not hanging around with her friends, she would just be online chatting with various people. She would make Maggi Noodles for herself to eat. She should have been studying, but she was just not interested in academics. At this point, things started getting from bad to worse. We came to know that she was not attending school and this angered me no end.

We saw a family therapist at the school, who suggested that either my husband or I should drop her to school or one of us should be there when she gets home from school and sit with her and do her homework etc. My husband needed to keep working all hours, as he had invested in a new clinic and it was a significant sum, which meant it was important for him to keep his practice steady. But I said it was just not possible for me either., I had patients who depended on me. I could not just stay at home suddenly. I now realize I was subconsciously distancing myself from my daughter, both emotionally and physically. I was afraid of the day I would lose her when she would also feel what I felt. That horrible feeling of not being her mother.

I was so angry during this session with the counsellor, and heard myself say the words "The reason she is doing so badly in school is that she has bad genes. She was discarded by a woman who frankly, only cared about her pleasure and she is now repeating history". I was shocked when I said this. But it made me realize that somewhere inside me I had not allowed myself to be a proper mother because I didn't deserve to have a child. And even that woman who only cared about her fun, could do so much better than me... she could conceive. I could not.

The teenage years were traumatic for us. Nidhi tested us in every way possible. There were days when I would tell my husband I couldn't go on taking care of this child. But you know what, I did go on, and ultimately I realized that is what motherhood is. Never giving up. And it made me realize that I am not a failure. I would have failed if I had let go. But I never did. I always held onto Nidhi, each time, tighter than the next. Challenge after challenge.

When we thought the challenges were behind us we confronted another situation where we found that our daughter was single and pregnant. Accepting this pregnancy went past all our social standards but somehow we tried. In the final months of pregnancy she had a miscarriage and gave birth to a still born child. She was in an immeasurable amount of grief and anguish and I stood by her more than ever and shared her pain. I realised that she had no other birth connection in the world, as her parentage was entirely unknown, I realised just how deep this trauma was. Perhaps in this moment of loss we came together as never before... both of us coming from a deep sense of loss to a beautiful relationship like no other relationship in the world.

Today she is a grown-up independent young woman. Yes, she is not academic like my husband and I but she has found her own creative path. I have completely accepted her uniqueness and stopped trying to stamp myself on toher. Because she is my baby, no matter what. It took me a long time to get here.

But I have finally accepted who I am... I am Nidhi's true mother.

TRIAL BY FIRE

Before we finally decided to adopt a child, the topic was discussed in some detail in our family. Many areas of concern were discussed. Our main concerns were mostly of the practical, financial nature. I was in service and as the adoptive father, I had to consider down-to-earth issues.

With my logical brain I calculated that by the time I would retire, the adopted child would, at the most be in the Ninth grade (i.e. the boy/girl would not have completed even Secondary school.) The second concern I had was about the genetics and the nature of the child whom we proposed to adopt. What if he or she had criminal traits of the biological parents? What if he or she was violent or carrying any undesirable traits? Thirdly, did we have the required parenting abilities to bring up a child properly (given that the child was otherwise perfectly normal)?

Relating to all these issues, the discussions with family members and friends from both the sides helped us a lot. Finally, since we felt we were also supporting a noble cause, we decided to go ahead in the hope and expectation that things would eventually work out without any complications. Once this big decision was taken, both of us went with an open mind in search of the child we hoped to adopt. A mature friend of ours who was teaching at a school told us that a few children from a local child care center attended this school. Among them was a girl whom she was particularly fond of. This girl had been through turbulence in her young life, but she was charming and intelligent. As far as she knew the child care home was seeking parents for her. She introduced us to the center and we told them about our interest in this little girl.

Due to her disrupted personal history the center was being very cautious about prospective parents. We started meeting her in a friendly manner and taking her out to get to know her. She did not need time to get to know us. She knew we were her parents and she clung to us. Each time we dropped her back to the center was like an abandonment for. She used to become hysterical with anxiety and cling to us.

Finally the day did come when we could take her home as our daughter. We accepted our adopted child whole heartedly with the feeling that the child was now our own.

The child was accepted by all members of our family and also warmly welcomed by the neighbourhood. The child was also very happy by the welcome shown by the neighbourhood and this supported us tremendously in building a relationship with the child in the initial days.

We had been given all details by the child care center about our daughter's complex history. She had previously been placed in adoption to two different adoptive families. For their own reasons they did not want to continue with the adoption and both times she was brought back to her institution. So she had experienced the disrupted relationship with different caregivers, added to the loss of her birth parents.

As time went by she even shared with us what her experience was with the two families who had adopted and left her back to the institution. One of the families had a son close to her age. However he was not as intelligent or even good looking as she was. There were lots of comparisons being made about the two children and unfortunately the biological child felt threatened. So the family members put the adopted girl down and started degrading her in ways, such as making her sleep on the floor while their son slept on the bed, and so on. Finally they brought her back to the institution and she was relieved. She was not at all happy with them.

By the time the next family came to take her far away to their home for adoption, she felt the need to test their commitment to adopting her. When they took her to their place of stay she performed every kind of disruptive behaviour and gave them hell. They could not go through the trials she was putting them through and decided to let go of their decision to adopt this five year old girl. She was no baby !

In the early years of her life our daughter had been raised by her birth parents, so she understood her own emotional need to be nurtured in a family. But she could not trust adults at all, given her experiences. In her child- like manner she gave out very tough tests to prospective parents.

When we went to adopt her we were aware of the traumas she had experienced and we were willing to take on the challenges we would face with this grown up daughter who had accepted us as her parents. She seemed determined to come to us and we were determined to do our best as her parents.

Her experiences had made her well aware of her background as an 'adopted' child. Hence it did not need any special effort on our part to introduce the fact that we were not her biological parents and that she was our adopted daughter.

She knew the story better than us. The story was traumatic.

She told us that one day her birth mother stealthily took out some of her father's money, gave it to her to go and out and buy a popular children's snack called Bobbies. Her father was furious when he found out that his money had been taken. A violent fight broke out between her mother and her very hot tempered father. They often had such fights. Trying to leave this frightening experience, she went out to buy the Bobbies from the shop outside their home. She even put those Bobby rings around each of her fingers, eager to show her mother how cute they looked on her hands.

As she turned home she saw her house on fire. Somehow her mother was caught in this fire, her clothes were burning and her husband was trying desperately to rescue her. Both got severely burnt in front of her terrified eyes. Her mother was charred by the flames. They were rushed to hospital. Her mother died first, then her father. The picture of her burnt parents was imprinted in her mind, a picture that she has never been able to wipe out of her consciousness. She remembers the details of their funeral which followed. That burning scene is forever tattooed in her psyche. She remembers the funeral that followed, where once again their remaining physical bodies were consigned to the burning flames of their funeral pyres.

She was taken into a care home where she was taken care of with love. In the company of so many cheerful little children eventually she began to feel secure and settled down. Her anxieties were reduced as she realised she was in a place of safety and harmony. But she had been brought up in a family, and an institution was no substitute for parents. She watched her younger friends being adopted and waited for her turn to be accepted by a family. With two families she had unfortunate experiences. She could not accept them. With us she felt a sense of belonging. Sequentially we were the Fourth family she had...

We took her home in an auto rickshaw to begin a new life with us. The bonding with me, her father, was easy for her. But she had some initial barriers with her mother. It was a new beginning for her with us, but certainly it was not possible for her to close the chapter of her early childhood. Fortunately she could share her story with us, once she learned to trust us.

Her transition into our family through adoption was not very difficult as she accepted us as her parents. During her childhood days, she did not ask us any questions about adoption.. Her early schooling years were pleasant as she was an intelligent girl, academically inclined and would also participate in other extra curricular activities. Thus her schooling part was not difficult for us.

As she reached adolescence she became more concerned about her identity. She was troubled by questions like : Why did we adopt her? Was it because she was a fair skinned, good looking girl? Was it for her smartness or her all-round performance at the adoption home? Why was she rejected by two prospective families before we took her in? With such questions she was always evaluating a situation relating to her self esteem.

Understandably, she has very deep rooted and hidden insecurities and fears. There are many things in her mind which she does not want to share even with us. Whenever, we try to drive a conversation to try to address her fears, she catches the drift quickly. She then starts giving vague or evasive replies like, "I don't know".

Many-a-times she has openly said that she does not trust anybody, not even us. How can she?

She is physically quite strong for a girl and therefore she relates more easily with the boys in her class. There is a child-like innocence in her interactions with boys. We discuss the changes that happen to a girl as she approaches adolescence and how to cope with them. Sometimes these fall on deaf ears. There is a been-there-done-that kind of an attitude in her.

Definitely there are anger issues lingering within her. She likes spicy and hot non-veg foods. This may be aggravating her short temper. She is very adamant and has fixed ideas about many things. She is a perfectionist and is therefore unyielding or unbending. She refuses to concede a defeat and will continue to defend an argument tooth and nail no matter how incorrect it may be. Initially, we would find it very difficult to tackle her when she would be in one of her foul moods. Gradually, we realized that ignoring her for that moment or merely "letting things be" for the time being was a good way of tackling the situation. After a couple of days, when she would be in a better mood, we would try and explain to her the right way but again there would be no assurance of acceptance of our suggestion.

We had received a CD with a film of her childhood at the child care center. We kept it very carefully. Due to several postings and changes of homes and cities a lot of our possessions were misplaced. This CD was one such item. It became a matter of great conflict for nearly a year as she accused us of destroying the only piece of her lost past that existed in that

CD. She was quite distraught. She accused us of burning it because we did not care for her feelings. Burning was always symbolic of her horrific past. Fortunately the missing CD was found and she was comforted. But she attributed it to her grandmother, that grandmother had kept the CD safely. In fact her grandmother— my mother— had passed away some years ago and it was us who had stored the precious CD. But in her teenage rebellion she did not want to give us that credit.

We are fortunate that, despite her insecurities and anger issues, there have been no instances of stealing, lying or any other physically destructive behaviour. We are aware that many children have indulged in those patterns to deal with their personal crisis. But now in her teens her turmoil has surfaced in other ways. She is always listening to songs with very sad lyrics. She is in a state of grief and this grief manifests in rage. Her past life seems to haunt her and vivid memories have re surfaced inside her. There are so many unanswered questions and so many ghosts. At times it is hard for us to deal with her emotions and we fear that she may be slipping into depression. We are looking for new avenues of help through this phase.

She is a talented child and if she applies her energies constructively, she can certainly go places. We are trying to channelize her energies in that direction so that she can grow up to be self confident and secure. We now understand and accept that she cannot erase her past experiences and memories. They were literally a trial by fire.

Considering her haunting past, we feel that our parenting journey has been rather positive. The trust we share in our relationship has given her a solid foundation on which to rebuild her life, and enabled her to keep going forward even as she continues to reflect on the traumatic experiences of her childhood. One day we hope that she can extinguish the fire that burnt her childhood, and emerge like the Phoenix from the ashes.

QUESTIONS AND ANSWERS

When little Parth entered our lives, our whole universe changed, and it acquired a beautiful new meaning.But he still does not know the secret of his adoption. We have tried to give him an indirect, rough idea and we assume that it could have seeped in a little. He has started asking some specific questions now. Questions such as, 'Did it hurt when I was in your tummy?' or 'I was born in which hospital?'. Once my husband mentioned that we should celebrate his real birthday in August, that was the day he came home. He immediately did the calculations in his mind and asked, "I was born in October, then where was I for 10 months? Was I in the hospital?" It is getting a little trickier day by day to answer his inquisitive questions. I was caught between the effect of the truth on his mind and my reluctance to lie.

When Parth turned 7-years old, we arranged his thread ceremony. I felt that now he had become truly ours and this would be a good time to tell him about his past, but my husband insisted on waiting till he was older and calmer. Parth had a quick temperament and my husband was worried about his possible outburst. Finally, we decided to get some consultation from an experienced paediatrician. He solved our worries and gave us the contact details of a counsellor for further guidance. We immediately reached out to the counsellor to clear our doubts and were advised about how to start the conversation and to not wait any longer as his acceptance level would decrease with his growing age. We were also warned about the threats in telling him when he became independent.

Then it was decided, and we started preparing ourselves for the conversation. We read the recommended book, discussed, and decided how to answer all the possible questions. Our relatives were more tense than us and questioned, "Is this even necessary? He's gelled in so well with the family, why do you want to tell him?" But we had decided to follow the 'earlier the better' technique and decided to talk to him at the earliest.

On a relaxed Saturday, when the three of us were home, we decided to approach the topic. His old medical file still had the name the adoption agency had given him. We used that connection and showed him the photos from his handing over ceremony at the adoption agency on our computer. Then we told him many stories about how he came home, how he was observing everything with his curious eyes, how he finished the kheer and how he pooped on his father at night and many such incidents. We also told him about how we had a wonderful naming ceremony in the presence of both his grandparents and his beloved sister. After a few days we showed his photographs and videos from a few months after his adoption and meanwhile answered all his questions. We didn't realise how we spent 2-3 hours reminiscing in all those memories. On the outside, it looked like he accepted everything very coolly, but I am sure it created some chaos in his little mind. Later that evening, his cousins visited, and he was quick to tell them – "Did you know that I didn't come from my mother's tummy?" Even they took it casually and asked, "What happened then?", he simply replied, "Nothing". In the next 2 days because of some urgent matter he had to stay with my sister. I had given her an idea about our recent confessions, but he did not talk about it again.

We felt like we were tense over nothing and thought everything went smoothly. In the following week we asked him if he had shared the news with anyone and he said, "Yes, I told 2-3 of my close friends". When we asked him for their reaction, he said, "Very normal" and sighed.

However, we have all noticed a change in him. He's become more mature now and his progress in his studies is also very satisfactory. Sometimes we used to get complaints about his mischiefs in our society and about him hiding someone else's belongings. We told him sternly just once that he shouldn't bring anyone's belongings for free.

We kept thinking everything was okay on the surface but once he randomly asked me, "Mumma, where are my first mother and father? I want to meet them. Did they have twins? Is that why they gave me to you?" Sometimes he also asks us to tell him his story from the beginning....Perhaps he is looking for further clues to his identity. We understand that many more questions will follow. Our concern is: will we have answers?

LIKE SHATTERED GLASS

I was nearly thirty years old when my parents arranged my marriage to a man very much older than me. My parents did not have money for dowry to find me a husband earlier in my life. The man I married was much older than me. He had left his first wife because she could not bear him a child. His family came from a reputed line of priests who were custodians of a shrine to Krishna. A male heir was essential to carry forward the priestly lineage.

Unfortunately even from our union no child was conceived. Our footsteps, perhaps our family deity himself (Sri Krishna), led us to the local general hospital in Nagpur. A young unwed girl had given birth to a male child whom she could not take care of. This child was destined to come to us. That was more than forty years ago.

We brought him home soon after that. There was a great celebration of his arrival and our Lord Krishna blessed the baby I held in my arms. That night very renowned classical music artists came and sang bhajans to celebrate his arrival. My husband too sang in gratitude and joy.

We lived in a joint family who inhabited different parts of our traditional home. At the center was the temple where everyone assembled. The new born baby Krishna was mostly in my arms. I pampered him and gave him all that a mother could give to express her love for her baby. Money was not a problem though our needs were rather simple.

Our son grew up and with each passing year he looked more handsome and very much a part of our family. He was intelligent and caring. He was doing well in school and life was good for us all.

I spent a lot also on myself. I used to project myself as a very confident person. But really inside me I was rather insecure and very possessive, especially over my son. He did not like my controlling behaviour and instead loved to be with his father. They had a very close relationship.

Then tragedy struck. One day when my son was in school he was called home to be told that his father had a serious heart attack. A short while later he left the world. Our adolescent son was struck by grief and despair, totally unprepared for this terrible loss.

Somehow we carried on with our lives. But life became complicated. My son started rebellious behaviour. One day he ran away from school. He was often in fights with students. He was tall and muscular and projected himself as a tough guy. He became very resentful of my control. He started indulging in unacceptable habits like smoking and drinking.

I could not understand this change in him. Was it due to grief and loss ? Later I came to know that he accidentally found papers relating to his adoption in his late Father's documents. He felt shocked and betrayed and went wild. None of the uncles or cousins could control him. He was always out of the house in what is called Bad Company. I blamed his friends.

Somehow he made his way back to the place he was born,

which he found in his papers. He ordered the staff there to give him all information relating to his birth parents. He assumed his birth mother was an immoral woman who had given birth to him for pleasure and then abandoned him. He wanted to find and kill his birth father.

Due to the violent thoughts, the staff member he spoke to tried to calm him and counsel him. She advised him to volunteer at any institution for children to better understand their circumstances.

He gradually accepted this wise advice and started volunteering at a small orphanage and a women's shelter home. Gradually he began to understand their circumstances. He realised women were not abandoning their child but seeking a better life than they could offer. That is why they gave up custody of their baby. This was his story too. He also saw that the women were not so-called immoral but rather innocent and vulnerable.

He developed a different view about his own situation, particularly with counselling he was receiving from staff members. He became Big Brother and peer counsellor and everyone turned to him for support.

However at home with me he remained very angry and rebellious. He felt we had broken his trust, shaken his foundation and shattered his self esteem.He could not recover from this. He made himself an outsider by anti-social behaviours... smoking, drinking, staying up all night and waking at noon.

He had good friends who loved and cared about him but could not control him. A mature woman friend spent a lot of time talking to him about his life with empathy and insight. Over a period of time he became emotionally dependent on her and married her in secrecy. She was older and gentle and somehow she fitted his missing birth mother s image that he had formed in his mind. I became the outsider and I was angry and very hurt.He took his wife to live in another city because he knew I would not accept her.

After a couple of years someone informed him that I was very sick, and that was when he returned home with his wife. I just could not accept this unconventional marriage and the fact that he was committed to this woman although I had brought him up. So they lived in another part of the house. I took care of the needs of my son, his food and everything but this daughter in law was left to take care of her own needs.I could not forgive her for taking away my innocent son.

All the while my son continued to smoke and drink and inflict violence on his wife. It was obvious he was really fond of her but he used her to express his rage. Our domestic maid used to create further politics and conflicts between us. He became like an erupting volcano. Whatever upset him outside or inside his mind, he used to take out on the wife. He used to shout at me but was never physically violent.

After one serious violent episode his wife walked out without telling him. He nearly lost his mind and tried self harm to get her back. She did come back. But he could not alter his behaviour and life was very difficult for us all. Good friends really supported us.

Even as his mother it is hard for me to understand why he changed from a loving teenager to a violent unreasonable man, only because we did not share the truth about his birth with him? Love and trust have to go together to form a secure parent -child relationship....so I have learnt the hard way.

OURS BY CHOICE

Adoption was our first choice so we were excited and looking forward to it. We did not have any concerns or expectations when we decided to adopt. We talked to a family friend, who is an adoptive parent, about the adoption process. She was very helpful in guiding us step-by-step through this special process leading to parenthood.

We have adopted two girls. When our elder daughter came home, it was all about taking care of her physical health and mental anxiety initially. Children go through a lot before being adopted, so in the initial months, we were busy making sure that she felt safe, she picked up her health, and she got the medical care that she needed. After about one or two months, we noticed our daughter preferred being with us instead of going to other people. She clearly enjoyed her time with her immediate family. Gradually she started hugging and showing affection. We bonded organically and it was a gradual process. When I look back I see changes in both her and us for over a year.

Our child was openly accepted by our family and neighbourhood. Most were welcoming and continue to make our daughters feel loved. Our neighbours and friends have been kind, normal, and accept our daughters the way they accept every child.

A few relatives were cold towards our daughters. They didn't say or do anything, but their overall discomfort was noticeable. In that case, I made the choice of distancing myself and my daughters from those relatives.

I believe we are fortunate to have thoughtful family, friends, and neighbours. Over time we have consciously decided to associate with people who tend to be positive minded and are supportive of adoption. We have also made it very clear that we expect people to treat our daughters fairly and properly, and we will not tolerate even the slightest wrong or insensitive behaviour towards them.

One of our daughters has a moderate special need. We knew about it at the time of adoption, and we chose to adopt a child with special needs because we believed we could support her and provide the appropriate resources for her to thrive. We manage the special need through regular physiotherapy sessions and a physical aid provided by her physiotherapist. These two things have been phenomenal in helping her gain strength and manage the special need. She is a kind, generous, smart, and happy kid, and through proper planning, her treatment plan is easy to manage.

SHARING THE FACT OF ADOPTION

The adoption conversation in case of our older daughter started within the first few weeks of her coming home, because she was old enough to understand adoption when she came to us. With our younger daughter, we started reading adoption story books to her since she was a toddler. My daughters have had evolving reactions to the adoption conversation as they grow older. Sometimes they are very interested, and sometimes they are not interested at all. Sometimes they want to hear other people's stories, sometimes they want to hear their own. We bring up the subject and let it go in whichever direction they want to take it. Many times the conversation around adoption comes up in an unexpected manner, such as when my daughters see a pregnant woman. In those cases, we continue to talk to them honestly and positively about adoption. Of course our answers tend to change over time based on their ages.

Question: *Why did you take so long to find me*
Answer: *We had to take many flights and stay in many hotels to reach you. You were so far away. I am so glad we were finally able to meet you.*

Question: *Do you know the woman who gave birth to me?*
Answer: *Sorry, I don't. But once you grow up and if you want to meet her, we will go find her together.*

Question: *Were you adopted by Nani (maternal grandmother)?*
Answer: *No sweetie, I wasn't. Some children stay with the parents who gave birth to them, and some children have two families and they go to their new family sometime after being born.*

Question: *Why did you adopt us?*
Answer: *Because I wanted to raise awesome kids and God/ destiny told me that you were my awesome kids. I am so fortunate to have you.*

We sent our kids to a small local school initially, so they don't get overwhelmed and get proper attention. The principal and teacher knew about their adoptions. Our younger one had a tough time assimilating into school, not because of adoption, but because she doesn't warm up to new situations easily. Eventually she settled down because of a kind teacher. Our older daughter was okay with school but she had some catch-up to do. Her teacher was excellent and paid extra attention to help her come up to speed with other kids. Both the teachers and the School went out of their way to be supportive.

Looking back we couldn't have asked for a better route to parenting, we love it!! It has been extremely rewarding every step of the way. To see our children transform and thrive has been the best experience of our lives.

TRULY BLESSED BY ADOPTION

My husband and I had been childless for 7 years after marriage and we were not getting any younger. Pressure was building up from our extended family on when we would bring them some 'good news'. We had tried quite a few fertility treatments, which were invasive and difficult treatments to go through, especially for the woman. I was a working woman and very dedicated to my profession as a Design Manager in an exciting digital media company.

In the year 1999, me and my husband shifted to Pune. By some co-incidence or serendipity, we had found a place that was earlier occupied by a couple who were very well associated with the cause of adoption. I was always open to the idea of adopting a baby. But was unsure how my in-laws would react. Surprisingly, the suggestion to adopt came from my father in law. I think he sensed the vacuum in our lives and took the brave step of suggesting this option to us.

We registered with a local organization. We had to answer a few questions and we specified that we wanted a healthy, baby girl. In a few months, we got a call to visit the orphanage and that a baby had been selected for us! We went to meet the baby with some trepidation in our hearts- would the baby like us? How would she be? Would we bond?

When we met her, the baby girl was lovely, but did not smile at us even once. This worried us and we spoke about our concern to the staff. They mentioned that they had noticed this too. Perhaps she was unwell or perhaps we had not bonded together? We returned a bit unsure. I had almost forgotten about this entire episode, when we got another call, asking us if we wanted to see the baby again. Since my father-in-law was around, we agreed immediately. On the given date, the staff called us up to tell us that the baby had a chest infection and had to be moved into a hospital, but we could visit her there if we wanted to.

We decided to go and see her again. When I saw her in the hospital, she looked so frail in her cot. She was asleep and with little needles pinned into her for saline. Tears filled up my eyes and I knew that I could never walk away from this baby. We gave our decision the next day. We brought her home in a week's time as foster parents. The process of adoption started and we filed for her adoption in the family court. A few months later our baby was legally ours.

There was such a change in her, the moment our baby had come home. She could not stop smiling the entire way and to our delight she became a plump, healthy baby soon. Her round face, little bald head and big eyes drew admirers everywhere. We were proud parents, though a bit unprepared at first. I remember, I had only one bottle for her feed and that we were constantly running out of supplies. But we got our act together pretty soon.

Every stage of her growth – her starting to crawl, her first steps, her first words have been etched in our memory. From about the age of 3, I would keep showing her baby pics of her orphanage- and tell her how she had come from a loving place, where she had many friends. I would tell her stories of Krishna and Karna to get her used to the idea of adoption- as being different from other children growing up with biological parents. But at no stage was it associated with being an unfortunate difference. I always told her that her birth mother had loved her and that she had given her to us, because it was so difficult for her to care for her baby, as she had many problems. As a result, I feel, our daughter has had less anxiety and feelings of rejection about her birth parents.

There were however, two challenges we faced with her- for one she started to bed wet at the age of 3 and secondly, she started stammering at the age of 5. We took her to a couple of wonderful speech therapists who worked with her very patiently and also told us how to cope with this. For her bed wetting, we had no solutions except to remain very patient with her. It finally went away, when she turned 11 years old. She was and continues to be in good health today.

Our daughter went through a great childhood and some wonderful schools. She was great at sports in school and very popular. She always had friends around her and has been very independent. She is very creative, and even when she was small, she used to make great little stories and sketches in her doodle book.

Our experience was so good that we went ahead and adopted a second time. We adopted a beautiful baby boy 3 years younger than our daughter. Our son had a hole in his heart and we were informed about this before we adopted him. We went ahead nevertheless, as we felt that we could help him when the need arose. Fortunately, the hole healed itself and he is totally fine today.

With my daughter, bringing her up was easy. With our son, we did face a few behavioral challenges. Even as a baby he had a lot of anger in him. He was extremely fussy about clothes, food and his own preferences. He would throw huge tantrums, if we did not act as per his wishes. We thought he was being stubborn and getting a bit spoiled by us. We also discovered that he was dyslexic and had eyesight problems that required strong lenses even at a young age.

We consulted a family therapist and she put things in a framework. She made us understand that some kids are just differently wired. We would have to deal with him with a lot of patience and understanding. He was not getting spoiled, but had issues that needed careful handling. She gave us a different way to think about him, and set up tools on how to address the issues of extreme obstinate behavior, anger, etc. And to our pleasant surprise, as we changed our methods, his behavior too changed. His temper calmed down and his acceptance of someone saying 'no' to him, improved. He also received a lot of help from a special needs teacher to help with his dyslexia. Today, he has overcome most of these challenges. I shudder to think that if we had to treat him harshly or in a very authoritative way, how it may have impacted him.

Today, my daughter is 20 and my son is 17. I can quite happily say that they are both confident, good human beings and very loving too. I feel so proud of them as they continue to do well in their academics and pursue their other interests. My daughter is studying a creative professional course abroad, perhaps following my footsteps, while my son pursues the interests of his dad- computer science and economics. It's as if, their being born in another mum's tummy was a programming error! They were and are totally meant to be with us. We feel blessed to have received the gift of our wonderful children.

KIDS ARE WIRED DIFFERENTLY

We relive our "Own Happy Childhood" when we become parents. We really see our own childhood in our child, and we enjoy every moment!

The happiest and luckiest moment of our life is when we get a lifetime companion of our own choice and liking. From that happily married moment and along with the new journey of life; the next couple of years we come closer to our partner and through our extreme intimacy we expect a newcomer in our family. That anticipation takes us to extreme happiness. Then we, along with our family members, start waiting impatiently for the arrival of our new family member and we start guessing about the gender: HIM or HER!! Isn't it!? It's just obvious as the natural outcome of our marital relationship. But when things go wrong and do NOT happen as per our expectations of time and situation, the mind game begins of Hope and Despair, and ultimately we reach a stage of grief. A door seems to have closed in our face as our dreams die out.

Then a moment comes when we may be forced to walk on a different path which is a deviation from the normal when we find ourselves in an abnormal situation. And here the "Mental War" begins, which really tests our entire relationship with our spouse and family.

We, unfortunately, faced a similar situation in our lives.

In this war-like situation we, my husband and I, took a bold and beautiful, and aggressive decision to conquer the huge challenge that we suddenly confronted in our lives. It was a difficult decision at first. The person who encouraged me was my Gynecologist and her social worker friend who is involved in the "Child Adoption" field. They put forward the adoption option as a path to parenthood. By that time, I was mentally prepared as I had undergone a difficult situation during my pregnancy period earlier. I had been through enormous pains at that time. I gave birth to a baby girl in just seven months, and since it was a premature delivery, her lungs were very weak and within one day she left for her eternal journey demolishing all our dreams.

After this disaster, I told my hubby firmly that I will not become a biological mother of any child in future as it is not in our destiny at all. I was also not ready to undergo those pains once again; instead, we should adopt a child from a renowned and guaranteed organization. I tried to convince my husband from June to September for three months, after forcing him to read a book on adoption by Mangala Godbole, he made up his mind and said "Yes" for this decision to apply for adoption.

That day I became the Happiest Person in the world. I communicated this with my mother only. As my In-Laws were not alive, there was no question of taking anybody else into confidence from my in-law's relatives. Due to my job my father and mother were going to raise this child in future, so their consent gave me more confidence and assurance for the same. In due course of time, we completed all the formalities. We both selected a girl child, and after three month's procedure, a cute little angel entered our life and our home.

On the auspicious day of "Ganesh Janma Divas", she got her new name with the blessings of all relatives, friends, and office staff. We all were in seventh heaven and extremely happy.

The decision which we took felt extremely right and we could enjoy her childhood, her growth, her activities and her infectious happiness. She reciprocated our care and nurturing by giving us her love and affection all the time. We both got the energy to lead our new journey of life with this beautiful angel. With my own sacrament (samsara) and a good upbringing, I could also raise my little girl giving her the same values which she imbibed as she grew up. And now my angel is a married adult enjoying her "Motherhood".

One thing I have noticed is that kids learn from our sacrament, upbringing, traditions, behaviour, and by association with others. However, we have to keep our eyes open from the view of attentiveness, consciousness, timely guidance, and quality time with our child. This is our sole responsibility. Otherwise, our kids keep on growing by their own observations, experiences, involved with other social activities. Our duty is to stand like a stalwart behind them and give them the right direction when needed.

Unfortunately, our angel had to face very unhappy incidents in her life from the age of nine. My life partner, my husband, with whom I had such a happy relationship, developed multiple sclerosis. He had to stop work and all physical activity ceased as he became increasingly paralyzed. It was a very sad time. I took all care of him till he finally passed away. But he left us a legacy of happiness, warmth, humour and kindness. Even in our grief we both, mother and daughter, felt supported by all that he had given us in his lifetime. And our angel had been the source of so much joy to him, with her cheerful and happy nature. While he was sick she spent long hours with my mother, in her grandmother's care. She became very close to her grandmother and did not feel neglected although I had my hands full with the care of my husband along with a full-time job to meet our expenses.

With my parents' support, we explained adoption to our angel only when she entered adulthood and we were seeking a marriage partner for her. She was upset and went to her room and cried. Later she asked many questions. Did other people know she was adopted? Why was she the last to know? She asked questions about her birth mother, if we could ever meet her, if we would help her in case she needed any support. I said, of course, we would meet her if ever possible and help her within our means. We informed the prospective marriage partner's family about her adoption. They had no objection to marriage on that issue and their marriage was settled. The whole village turned out at her marriage as our angel was so popular and loved by all. The village too was aware of our adoption and celebrated this beautiful union with full acceptance and joy.

I feel very proud to say that even in the worst situations, without any prejudice, with her balanced thoughts and behaviour she gave her best to me and my husband —her father. Now as a married woman she remains a great support for me and her grandmother. She is taking extreme care of us all. She still handles the worst situations of insult or defeat in a very balanced manner. Sometimes she becomes a mother to me and sometimes like the living vein of her wonderful father.

Overcoming so many challenges she has grown into a strong young woman. She has also attended workshops on adoption for future parents who are thinking about adoption. She attends these workshops with great positivity and without any self-pity because she is an adopted child. Apart from telling her about her adoption, in every way she was our very own child. We just fully loved and cherished her and she did not have any inferiority complexes relating to her adoption factor. Even in the case of unhappy situations, she knows how to ignore the moment, wisely. We are very proud of her fighting and conquering spirit, which she manages without creating conflict.

In this throwback of twenty-eight to twenty-nine years, I would say we have had a very successful, satisfied and happy family life. We were truly blessed the day this little angel flew into our lives through the womb of a woman whom we do not know.

WHEN AN ANGEL KNOCKED ON THE DOOR

A little angel knocked on my door more than a decade ago in early October. What a wonderful day that was!! My lovely and pretty adopted daughter, Sai, came into my life and changed it completely. My house was now a home. I was so blessed!!

I took the decision to adopt around the age of 40. After my divorce at 25, I focused on getting a masters' degree and establishing my food enterprise which kept me busy for the next 15 years. After I had settled down, I felt the need for a family of my own. I was always fond of children, right from my childhood and had strong maternal instincts. This led to my decision to adopt. Also, while I was in college I was very inspired by the actor Sushmita Sen's decision to adopt as a single parent. So, I decided to go ahead with my wish and will.

My sister and my parents supported me a lot and the people at the adoption agency helped clarify my thoughts about my motivation to adopt, my expectations from the adoption etc. I think in my mind I had no expectations but wondered just that whether society would accept her and whether she would have a sense of belongingness with my family, whether she would accept me and my family as her own.

Single parent adoption was a bit challenging at that time, but I was fortunate to overcome it. I did not face major issues from my family as adoption was not a new concept for us. My (need to clarify, might be "cousin sisters and brother) cousin's sister's brother had adopted children by choice. All my friends welcomed my decision and supported me. The housing society I belong to mostly has educated & cultured people. As a result I did not face many issues on this front.

My father is a doctor so I was confident that if the child had any health issues they would be taken care of by him. I think my approach towards life is that of problem solving which helped me overcome issues in this aspect too.

The main challenge according to me in the adoption process is sharing the fact of adoption with Sai. Being a single parent, I decided to disclose the fact at an early age to avoid any confusion regarding the father. I had expected my daughter to ask me this question around the age of five. But on her 3rd birthday Sai's friend from our housing society had come home with her mom and dad and before going to bed Sai asked me, "where is my father"? I was not prepared with a proper answer, so I told her that I was both her father and her mother. But I realized that I need to address this matter carefully and my response needs to be age appropriate. After all she was only 3years old!

I consulted my adoption case worker, counsellors, parents, friends, practically everyone! And I got tips from everyone. They helped put me on the right path. They advised me to give examples from Nature like plants, birds, animals where the father and mother are not distinguished by their physical appearances. So, I showed her a bird's nest in our balcony where the mother would fly out and bring seeds to feed her baby. I compared myself to that. I told her when I go out, I am the father and when I come home, I am the mother.

Also one of her close friends had lost her grandfather and

had only a grandmother. So I explained to her that every person has a different set of family members. You have a grandfather and a grandmother but in case of your friend her grandmother is now both her grandfather and grandmother. One of my friends, a well-known writer, also helped me. She wrote my daughter's story which goes like this, 'I was praying to God for a child and he told me to go to a place where you were waiting for me. The aunty who was taking care of you asked me to promise her that I would give you the love and care of both a mother and a father. I was allowed to bring you home only after I had made that promise". My daughter liked the story so much that she used to relate her story with pride. I faced a major problem when I went for her school admission. The entire process was online. When I was filling the form, it was mandatory to write the father's name. I wrote my name down but I felt that the school might disqualify the form assuming it was a wrongly filled form. At that moment I felt really very sad. I gave it a deep thought. I took a printout of the form and attached a letter stating my details and also that this was a single parent adoption. I requested the Principal not to disqualify my form as a wrongly filled form. I went to the school and handed over the form and letter to the clerk as the form clearly mentioned that neither the Principal nor the authorities should be contacted for any admission related work as the process was to be fully computerized and by a lottery method. The clerk read my letter and asked me to wait while he took the letter to the Principal. Imagine my surprise when the Principal herself came out and said, "Admission granted" and wrote that down on the form!! What an experience!!

My daughter has over time accepted both single parenting and adoption with great understanding. There was a lesson in her 2nd standard EVS textbook which included single parent as a type of family and yet till her 8th standard she was uncomfortable when asked why her mother's name was her middle name. So I gave her the example of a film director Sanjay Leela Bhansali who proudly wrote his mother's name as his middle name out of great respect for her efforts in bringing him up. Somehow she overcame her discomfort and was able to answer such questions confidently after that.

I REALLY FEEL THAT ADOPTED CHILD CONCEPT SHOULD BE CHANGED TO ACCEPTED PARENT by the Constitution. In real life also the child collects wombs or parents. It will become easy for the child to face society.

I would like to share a bonding experience here. When Sai was about 7/8 years old, I was facing a very challenging time with regard to my business. It became essential for me to tour. Though my parents were with me, it was not possible for them to look after her in my absence especially at night. Until that time Sai had never slept without me at night. During the day I was the 'father' so I was allowed to go out but after I came home in the evenings and until I left in the morning I was the 'mother' so I had to be home. So, my friends suggested that I keep her in boarding school for a couple of years. But I thought to myself, "She has come to be with me, at home and not to live separately. Why did I bring her home in the first place? Just to send her away to an institution again? It would be injustice to her. I have to choose either my 'brain child' (my business/my brand) or 'my child'. Of course 'my child' won and I went on to collaborate with another food company, became a consultant and lived happily with my dear Sai. Due to the challenges in my business I could not devote enough time to her studies. When she was in the 8th standard, she was facing difficulties in Maths and Science. Individual tuition did not prove successful. But after I understood what the issues were and how to go about solving them, I started teaching her and there was progress. So in the 9th standard Sai requested me to teach her most of the subjects. So once again, it was a tough decision for me. If I was to give her more time, it would affect my earnings. I am proud to tell you that when I explained to her that this would affect our lifestyle, for e.g. we may not be able to spend on her favourite pizza and coffee very often, she said she will not ask for it and indeed she did not ask for months! Instead she started asking before spending, "Can we afford this, mom"? How understanding she was! How wonderful!! Then I told her that if I stop working for two years, I may not be able to get any work after that since I would be 58 years old by then. She said, "No issues. I will study hard and earn for both of us". What maturity!!! I had tears in my eyes, literally! She was so understanding! And I am very happy to tell you that in her school boards exam she scored above 90%. I am very proud of my daughter! She also draws well. Sai and I speak openly about adoption if the topic comes up. But in our everyday life adoption is forgotten. We are living a happy and normal life.

I am not interested in knowing about her biological parents, but if she wants to know I will support her. I will insist on her higher education and financial independence before she gets married. I am sure she will proudly disclose the truth about adoption to her better half and their married life will be based on faith and great understanding.

CONFRONTING CHALLENGES

We are a family of doctors with well established roots in Akola. I am a well-known pediatrician and my wife Vaishali is a gynecologist. We used to practice in the family hospital that my parents started. After getting married to Vaishali, we were engrossed in settling down and succeeding in our own careers. We faced constant questions about having a child and starting our family, but we dodged them as our priorities were different.

After 8 years of marriage, our attention shifted, and we finally gave a serious thought to starting our own family. After some unfruitful time, we decided to get medical opinion and got diagnosed with 'Unexplained Infertility', a condition that 10% of the population faces. Our doctor friends suggested umpteen solutions and treatments but Vaishali and I discussed adoption and were firm about our decision.

During my education years in Nagpur, I had come to know of a hospital-based institution in Nagpur who had an adoption facility. I went back to my college and enrolled after enquiring about the procedure. In just about 2 months we were contacted by the hospital to come and meet a 6-month old baby. The baby was born premature, with low birth weight and delayed milestones but we instantly fell in love with his sparkling eyes and sharp nose. Vaishali and I took a bold decision and took this big challenge to develop him and raise him as our own child; our son Kushal.

In his first 6 months home, he quickly developed and started showing growth milestones like an average 1-year old baby. As he started going to school, we understood Kushal had trouble seeing things on the blackboard, understanding concepts and socialising with his fellow classmates. He started bunking classes and clearly said, "I don't want to go to the school".

We looked into the matter and found out Kushal had poor vision and suffered from learning disabilities,especially dyslexia. At home, instead of playing with toys, he was more interested in breaking toys, understanding how they worked and putting them back together. As a well-rounded solution we designed a home-school experience to teach him practical,everyday skills and hired trained tutors who taught him through demonstration of concepts.

From the difficulties we faced while trying to get Kushal an education that would suit his capacity and needs, we understood that there was a lack of essential policies for children with special needs. We formed a trust through which we founded a special school for speech and hearing-impaired children. As this was the only school in the region, children used to travel long distances to attend the school. So as a solution, we started a hostel for such students. Over the years we also started a regular zilla parishad recognised school in addition to the special school.

As Kushal became an adult, we worked on his social skills by giving him tasks such as hand-delivering a letter to a family acquaintance, such as the Dean of a college/a Collector/a Pharmaceutical Company Director/etc. He was required to use his formal communication skills when he would talk to them. Once he was back home he would use his informal communication skills to tell us about his experience while having to narrate the correct order of events. We also sent him independently to carry out procedures like getting his own license.

As Kushal approached an ideal age of marriage, we asked around in our doctor community to find a suitable girl for him. My pediatrician friend suggested another doctor couple's daughter, Janhavi, who is also an adopted child. After initial discussions, they both agreed and got married. The initial 3 months of the marriage were very stressful for Janhavi as she got to know more about Kushal and his dependency on his parents. She became unhappy in the marriage as she was unable to understand the situation. She left for her parents' house and decided to stay there for 6 months. In this time period Kushal used to travel to meet Janhavi and stayed in touch telephonically. Eventually, us parents decided to have a meeting to clarify all of Janhavi and her family's doubts about Kushal and worries about her future security. We suggested that Janhavi could start her career as a teacher in the school started by our family.

Janhavi moved back into our house and in the next 3 months she was happily pregnant with our grandchild. Janhavi successfully completed the D.Ed, B.Ed and M.Ed degrees and is currently the Principal of both our schools. Kushal on the other hand, is the sole proprietor of an agro-based industry established on the family owned land of around 25 acres. Both of them are extremely successful and content with their healthy 7-year old boy, Milan. We all have come a long way as a family and are extremely content and proud parents and grandparents.

THE BEST IS YET TO COME

Having been together for eight and half years before finally getting married, my husband and I had always spoken about adoption. Two miscarriages later, we realised it was probably time to consider what we had always discussed. That's when we decided to file for adoption and over a year later, we were blessed with a beautiful baby girl more than ten years ago.

Rachel was everything we had prayed for, an ever smiling face and a happy child. We couldn't have asked for more.

Three years later, we were blessed with our baby boy, from the same Adoption Agency as Rachel. That's when the questions started. Rachel was part of the entire process and she looked forward to spending time with Justin at the Adoption Agency. They bonded well and we were really happy considering that we had been afraid about whether or not she would accept him.

The day we brought Justin home, the first question caught me off guard. 'How can you take him away from his mamma?' she asked. 'Wouldn't you cry for me if someone took me away from you?' Her words pierced my heart and I was torn between assuring her that I would cry bitterly if anyone took her away and making her understand that Justin's mamma was crying but wanted us to take care of him. The senior social worker advised us to explain to her that the scar would always be there on his mama's heart but it would heal after sometime, just like a hurt that she got. Rachel soon accepted that Justin was a part of our family and life moved on. Justin and she got along extremely well and have always been there for each other from the beginning.

Two years later, it was time to welcome home Rachel and Justin's cousin, born to their aunt and uncle. The children had been looking forward to an addition to the family and were extremely glad when she was born. However, the baby coming home almost immediately after birth confused Rachel tremendously. She insisted that the baby be sent to the Adoption Agency to stay there for a while since that was how it was meant to be. We laughed it off and explained to her that her cousin was a part of the family and she would be coming home.

This sudden change in the family dynamics and the whole process brought in a lot of unpleasant feelings for Rachel. She loved her cousin dearly but even at that young age, she had understood that there was something different about her and Justin and this little new arrival.

While Rachel was in Upper KG, things started going downhill. She would have bouts of forgetfulness and it took a toll on her academics. There would be days that she would forget her alphabets and numbers. She couldn't focus at all. Her teacher felt that we weren't giving her sufficient time and were not helping her with her studies. Being from the teaching fraternity, my husband and I knew that academics wasn't on our list of priorities at that time. However, her teacher felt that we were making excuses about her being adopted. She even mentioned that she had taught many adopted children during her long career and had never heard excuses like these. It was a difficult time for us, especially for Rachel because she herself didn't know what was happening.

Rachel would cry bitterly at night and she wasn't sure if she wanted to be held by me. Her younger brother, being extremely protective of his sister, was always there to lend a listening ear. One night, she finally broke her silence and asked me if I loved her. I hugged her and assured her that I, daddy and everyone else loved her very much. She then went on to ask about her first mother and why she had left her. Being the adoptive mother who had always decided on being open about the adoption, I was well prepared that this question would be thrown at me sometime, the only difference is that I thought I had time till her teenage years to answer that question. Hearing it when she was merely 6 years old left me numb. It was time to think on my feet and come up with an answer that she would understand without throwing her life out of sync.

In the dark of the night, I explained to her that her mother loved her but she had her reasons for giving her to us. She demanded to know the reasons and she couldn't comprehend why I knew nothing. I tried explaining to her that I had never met her. She then asked if her mama had gone to Jesus. I replied that I thought she was well and when the time was right, maybe we would meet her. She asked me in a rather stern tone for a 6 year old, 'You took me away from someone and you don't know anything about her?' All through the conversation, I had tried to be really strong, but these words shook me to the core and I couldn't help but just hug her and cry softly, not wanting her to see my tears. The last question she asked that night was if we would meet her if she hadn't gone to Jesus. I could only say, 'Yes my love, we will.'

This conversation took place soon after the movie Mowgli had released, a movie we had watched in the theater as a family. My son had been listening in silence to the whole conversation. When he realised that Rachel wasn't ready to accept what I was telling her, he suddenly jumped in with his views. He said, 'Eh Rachel, our mama is like Raksha and we are like Mowgli. We are so lucky.' It amazed me that at three and half he was able to put two and two together and come up with this to comfort his sister.

We've had our ups and downs thereafter too with Rachel not wanting to associate herself with me. I've had my heart broken with words like 'She's not my mother, she's my maternal aunt' and 'You look so funny, you dress so funny'. There was a time that I was on the verge of a breakdown and wanted to just move out of her life. Timely intervention by experienced people in the field helped me understand what Rachel was going through and helped me pull myself together.

Today, Rachel and I share a pretty comfortable relationship with each other and I'd like to believe that the worst is over and the best is yet to come!

I'd also like to add a piece of advice that meeting an adoption therapist over a regular counselor or child psychologist would go a long way in helping an adoptive parent understand their child better.

DIFFERENT PATHWAYS TO LOVE

Our adoption journey started long before the actual adoption of our son. A long time back, my husband's former boss had adopted a child and he had been to the Adoption Agency for either an event or the handing over ceremony. After experiencing the whole atmosphere of the orphanage, he immediately decided to adopt a child in future.

Sometime after the birth of our daughter, I wanted a second child and my husband suggested his wish of adopting the second child. It felt like destiny had worked out the tiny wish I'd made as a medical student. When I was 22, I was interning at a government hospital, my assigned ward was next to a Child Care Agency. It had struck my mind multiple times how it would be great to give a loving home to a child in need.

My husband and I were in agreement and now came the rest of the family. It took a whole year to convince my mother-in-law. She didn't understand the need of having a second child if we couldn't conceive one. She used to say, "Why do you need a second child at all? I am happy with my one granddaughter." The other reason was, she didn't agree morally with the concept of adoption. She looked at it as legitimising other people's 'mistakes'. She thought that us adopting a child would suggest that we accepted that people could be irresponsible, and society is there to take care of the consequences of irresponsible parents. I tried to convince her by understanding her approach. We promised her that we would opt for a known Hindu background baby.

We finally started the documentation after she gave us her consent. Soon enough, the process started and a social worker did 2 home visits. Since we already had a biological daughter, we could legally adopt a male child. Additionally, since I am a doctor, the social worker suggested a baby who was returned by a family because the baby had severe medical problems. She told us that it was unfortunate on the baby's part as he was fully normal otherwise and got the label of "ill baby" because of this one phase of sickness. As we did not have any stringent preferences regarding the baby, we decided to take a look at the baby.

His health condition made him susceptible to infection and thus he was kept with a foster mother. The baby was very dark, with bulging eyes but had a very cute, smiling face. My husband expected the baby to get inspected under our daughter's paediatrician. The visit was planned and the social worker, the baby and my husband went to the clinic. The social worker was carrying two big files of the baby's previous medical records. The paediatrician examined the baby and found that he is lacking in major physical milestones, the baby was 14 months old but couldn't even sit properly. The various medical reports also revealed that the baby had problematic amino acid synthesis in his urine. She made a remark that this may lead to mental retardation in longer course, but a trial may be given for adoption. My husband was in a state of shock as he dropped the baby and social worker back to the foster home.

The social worker was sympathetic towards his mental state and said, "Don't worry, we may suggest you another child". My husband says that the next 8 days were the worst days of his life. He was riddled with the thought that had the baby been his biological child, could he have rejected him? Finally,

I reassured him that we can treat the baby to full recovery so we should adopt the same baby.

It was decided, he was our baby and that we would be taking him home on my mother-in-law's birthday. To solidify her support, I showed the baby's birth details to a trusted astrologer and he gave us a wonderful and hopeful feedback. As his amino acid problem was incidental, my husband asked the institute to give us 3 consecutive urine reports with a gap of 15 days. The first one came on the 2nd October which was normal, the second time, it took time as the foster mother found problems while collecting the sample. The report came on the 15th oct, and the report read everything was normal as well. We were relieved and said that we didn't need the 3rd report and brought our baby home as planned. The whole process happened really quickly for us as he was labelled a 'special-child'.

When we arrived home with our precious baby, the house was full of our relatives and neighbours. Our daughter had been telling everyone that her baby brother was coming home, and our neighbours were really curious as I had not shown any signs of pregnancy. Our son's beautiful dusky skin, his big curious eyes and the most innocent smile won everyone's hearts in a beat.

The next few months were full of his baby antics. He loved raising his eyebrows and did that to everyone who passed by. When he started crawling instead of crawling ahead, he used to crawl in reverse and go around the entire house. He also won over the toughest family member, my mother-in-law so much so, that they had a special connection no one else understood. Everyone in our family had a very positive and loving reaction to his arrival and that helped us smoothen our journey a great deal.

Once he was home, my husband started giving him massages to cure the bowing of his legs, I started giving him ayurvedic medicines for his respiratory improvement. Within 3 months he was walking and almost running on his tiny baby feet. When we took him back to visit the agency, he ran inside the room on his own two feet! All the social workers were stunned and asked us what magic potion we were giving him. The physical growth he started then has only taken an upward curve.

We were advised by the agency to start introducing the concept of adoption when our son turned 6, through simple bed-time stories. We followed the advice by heart and used the same story that was told to us in the pre-adoptive session. He made peace with the fact in whatever manner his tiny mind understood the concept fairly and quickly and never asked any other questions. I understood that he'd completely understood the concept of adoption when we were watching 'The Jungle Book'. As soon as the scene where Bagheera dropped baby Mowgli off with the wolf pack and the wolf mother accepted him as he was, I found him looking at me and we shared a meaningful smile.

When he started school, he was in the same school as my daughter. The school counsellors identified that he has learning disabilities. He was diagnosed to have prominent ADHD. A behavioural child psychologist suggested that we repeat his academic year as early as possible, so he won't feel any humiliation about repeating years. As a precaution we changed his school and admitted him in senior KG again in a different school. His motor skills also needed training, so I used to sit with him and practise his writing with chalk and slate. When he was in the 4th standard, his teacher suggested enrolling him in an activity like taekwondo to dissipate his hyper activity. Gradually after starting his taekwondo classes, he started focusing more and was able to sit in one place for a longer time. His confusion between 'b' and 'd' went away and so did his problems with spellings like 'able' which used to be 'abel'. But even today, he functions better in small groups, or one-one teachings where the teacher can give him enough attention and encourage him to give the answers. He still needs positive reinforcement to keep working ahead and a constant reminder of his priorities.

As he became a teenager he became vocal about his adoption. When he turned 15, he started mentioning that he is adopted to all his friends by himself. He even invited his friends to attend a few events like birthday celebrations, Diwali in our adoption agency. Once, I was trying to find the vaccination records of both the kids and he asked about a big file that I took out. I told him honestly that it was his pre-adoption medical file. He just shrugged and said very casually, "Okay, I'll look into it if I feel like it". He is 18 now and has had no follow up questions about his biological parents. He chooses to live in the present and holds no curiosity towards his past. He accepted us as his family in a heartbeat and sees nothing beyond this concept. Just the way we have forgotten about the adoption, so has he. We have left the fact of his adoption so far in the past that even writing about it felt a little odd.

We were told that after a while the baby starts to look like the family and really, after a few years people started saying that he looks just like his grandmother. A few months back, he shaved for the first time and it was so shocking to see how much he looked like my husband's younger version.

Recently turned 18, our son is doing very well in his life. His happy-go-lucky attitude has made him a favourite amongst friends from different social circles and of both the genders, his taekwondo teachers and even with his cousins. He's the trusted guy that mothers feel okay to send their daughters with - "Oh, he is there, no problem then, you can go." I am lucky that he still remains a mama's boy; anyone can be upset with him, but he can see his Aai... mother... isn't allowed to stay mad at him for long. Now the biggest mission in his life is to take the whole family to Ladakh as soon as he gets his long awaited driving license.

I feel like my motherhood has achieved a good balance after raising a son and a daughter. Both required different techniques and had different challenges. All I wanted were 2 compassionate, humble, well-behaved, polite children and I got them. He has brought tremendous happiness in our family with his mischievous smile and constant jokes. His positive energy keeps the whole family's mood light-hearted and active. We feel very proud to call them our kids and even prouder when we get recognised as their parents.

MY SECRET CHILD

When my first marriage failed and I returned to my parental home, I was in a state of depression. It did not seem possible that I would be accepted by any other marriage partner. My self-esteem was very low because of the rejection I had faced. However, I was doing very well. At a conference in Mumbai, I met an older man belonging to another culture. He was kind and mature and we became good friends. I was surprised and joyful when he proposed to me.

We had to make a lot of adjustments to understand each other's ways, especially with food, as I was a vegetarian and he was not. But we worked it out and enjoyed a happy relationship from which we hoped to become parents. Unfortunately that did not happen, which was one of the reasons I was rejected by my first spouse. Still, I had hoped and prayed I would move forward from my medical issues. I feared my husband would also reject me for my inability to conceive. Instead he was very caring and sensitive to my feelings.

Adoption was not our first choice at all. Neither his family nor mine would ever accept a child born to unknown parentage or who was not genetically connected to us. It was enough that they had accepted our marriage, we could not think of broaching the adoption option to them. We longed for a child to complete our lives and were in despair.

We travelled out to bigger cities in our quest to find a baby in our rather secretive circumstances. We were told that Nursing

Home adoptions were illegal. We were also bewildered by the large number of rules, regulations, documentation and exposure of our personal lives which would be required in an adoption process. Could we hope to ensure secrecy in our family? To our family we would have to pretend that we had a biological child. Anyway, we enlisted our names with an adoption agency as this was our only way forward.

For nine months I went around with a prosthetic on my stomach to make me look pregnant. We moved out of our town in the last two months of this false pregnancy. We had completed all of the adoption process with the adoption agency. They said the child would have to go through the legal period of waiting, and then come to us as pre-adoptive foster parents. Only after that our adoption case could be filed and heard.

As luck would have it a premature baby girl had been admitted to the agency. We happily accepted her though she had big medical challenges. She had to be repeatedly hospitalised and her life hung in the balance. I spent days and nights with her lying next to me receiving intravenous fluids in her tiny arms. Taking care of her in the hospital was like building an umbilical cord... it really connected her to me in a very deep and intangible way. The day she was discharged and all the legal process was completed I really felt I had given birth to her. I joyfully threw away the prosthetic that I had tied around my waist in a simulated pregnancy. My child did not grow inside that prosthetic but above it --in my heart.

That was twenty-three years ago.

Both our families welcomed her with extreme happiness when she entered my parents home in my arms. They showered her with gifts and blessings. She showered them in return with her hugs and laughter, always a happy little girl.

She grew into a very attractive young woman and after getting good academic grades she chose her own artistic career path. She brought us happiness and good luck too.

As my husband and I both looked very different from each other, people did not really question the difference in her looks. She was so well integrated into the extended family.

I did not feel guilty about the pretence that she was not our biological child because I never felt that I did not conceive her. She was so intimately connected with me. And everyone was happy. We had told the adoption agency that it was going to be a secret adoption for our family and we promised to comply with all regulations relating to follow-up of her progress. We regularly sent the reports and arranged for the social worker's visits. They understood our situation and cooperated. They also were happy to see how well this weak baby was now doing in our love and care.

The years have gone by too fast. The nest is empty again, as she is pursuing her career path in the metropolis. But we have been truly blessed to have known the tremendous joy of parenthood through this unusual route. At the same time it is good to see how much more open our society has become towards adoption. I still ask myself how it is possible to tell your own beloved child that she was not born to you but to another woman who could not take care of her.

I live with only one fear and one prayer...that my daughter should never unearth this secret.

THE CIRCLE OF ADOPTION

We, Sachin and Anjali, parents of Purvaja, are pleased and honoured to have received this opportunity to share our wonderful journey of parenthood. We got married in 1997. The first few years of marriage flew by as we settled into our respective professions. Soon, like every couple, we were eager to start a family but after a year or two, we realized that we would need medical advice. After consulting various specialists, we went through a series of investigative procedures and treatments, finally landing at the doorstep of an IVF specialist. We were advised IVF and as we prepared for our first cycle, we mutually decided that as a couple, we must be sure about every decision during the process. We decided that we would not go through more than 3 IVF cycles. If they were to fail, then we would opt for adoption. The decision to adopt, therefore, did not come out of any desperation or trauma – as is the case observed with most couples facing infertility issues.

Since there was no hesitation there weren't any unrealistic expectations. All that we wished was to adopt a healthy girl child. We were also encouraged by our cousin and his wife, who had also decided on adopting a son a few years back. Soon we registered for adoption, and after the registration procedure, we settled down for the waiting period. Shortly after, we received a call from the adoption agency, and we travelled to Pune to visit the center. We were assigned a social worker who counselled us about the entire process of adoption and we were introduced to the most beautiful, adorable 4-month old Purvaja. After the first meeting, we travelled back home and made all the necessary preparations to bring our baby home. Within two weeks, Purvaja was home.

The process of bonding and attachment was completely natural, easy, and required absolutely no effort by the family members. Purvaja was a bright and active baby and soon charmed into the hearts of her grandparents, uncles, aunts, cousins, and our entire extended families and neighbourhood. During early childhood, Purvaja occasionally suffered from minor ailments. Though initially frail and pale, she soon gained weight. Her early development, physical and mental, was age-appropriate.

She started preschool at the age of two and a half years and she easily adjusted to the new surroundings. Most adoptive parents worry about when and how to introduce the concept of adoption to their child. Some feel that it should never be revealed while some believe that it would be better accepted when the child grows older. We disagreed with both these views and believed that the concept should not be "introduced" or "revealed" to the child. Instead, the child should grow up with the idea. We first told Purvaja her story when she was around 3 years old. She was quite fascinated, and it soon became her favourite bedtime story. As she grew out of the age for bedtime stories, the magic of the story faded.

Soon, school, and extra-curricular activities took up most of her time and very naturally, the aura around the word "adoption" dimmed, and it became a non-issue. Now Purvaja is 12 years old, on the threshold of adolescence. She has been learning Kathak and Classical singing for the last 6 years and will now go to grade 7. Initially, she did not seem to have any curiosity about her story. But for the last two years, she has started asking questions about it.

Her most frequently asked questions are:
- *Did I come out of someone else's tummy?*
- *Who is my first mother?*
- *Where was I born?*
- *Was I found on the road? – Or in a dustbin?*
- *God does not drop kids there*
- *How did I get to the orphanage?*
- *Did the police take me to the orphanage?*

When parents are faced with such questions, the first instinct is to deny/avoid the questions or spin a yarn which is far from reality. Occasionally they shut the child up. But these tactics cause more harm and sometimes, permanent damage. We as parents have decided that every question that Purvaja asks must be answered with complete honesty and must be conveyed in a manner appropriate for her age, understanding, and awareness. So, most of her questions are answered honestly, while a few are deliberately left unanswered if either of us instinctively feels that she is not ready for the answers. But even that is conveyed with an explanation, such as "I don't think you'll understand it right now, but I promise to tell you when you are a little older".

We can certainly claim beyond any doubt, that the last 12 years as parents have been extremely fulfilling and enriching for both of us. Purvaja continues to thrive, but underneath the bubbly, happy surface, we do sense that she has many insecurities and doubts. She now doesn't like to speak about adoption, she has never revealed the fact even to her closest friends and has stopped asking questions. She also has confessed, in a rare unguarded moment, that she feels ashamed that she is an adopted child. We have also observed that, apart from her dad and both the grandfathers, she is not comfortable with any male around her. This disturbed us initially, but we have chosen not to react or reassure her too vehemently. As parents, we understand that in this age of hers, these things are bound to create confusion in her mind, and she requires time to come to terms with the realities. The fact will never change that she is an adopted child, and we are adoptive parents – we have to live with this fact.

The desire to know our roots is one of the most primitive urges of mankind, and no adopted child is an exception to this. Instead of avoiding/restricting this urge of the child, we believe that parenthood should promote a bond so strong between the child and parents, that over a time, the child should feel the roots within the adoptive family. We would like to emphasize here that this bond is probably stronger than the "flesh and blood" bond. It is a popular belief that "we adopt the child" – however, time proves that "the child adopts us as parents!".

PARENTS FOR EVERY CHILD

We had been married for quite a long time and the much longed for pregnancy did not happen. The elders in our family encouraged us to think about adopting a child as we all felt there is no happiness without the presence of a child. We decided to adopt a child, a child of our own, on whom we could imprint our culture, values and who can turn out to the best possible personality in the world.

On the recommendation of family and friends, we found our way to a reputed childcare center in our city. They offered adoption services for children who had lost their birth families due to unfortunate circumstances. On our visit to the institution, we were explained the legal process of adoption. This was more than 25 years ago when there were no 'waiting lists' for parents who were seeking to adopt a child, especially a girl child.

We visited the institution where they provided us with brief information regarding the adoption procedure and requirements. My family was impressed. They provided all the required help and support to complete the adoption and make the journey smooth. During our first visit to identify our child, the institution introduced us to a tiny baby girl who immediately attracted our attention, with her contagious sweet smile. Right then and there we finalised our decision to welcome this little girl as our daughter and we abandoned our plans for further search. We had found the child of our dreams!

A week later, on an auspicious muhurta (timing), we entered the threshold of our house with our daughter, with a big welcome from our extended family and friends. The child was smiling and expressing her happiness with cheerful gestures. Everyone greeted the child and showered her with their blessings. Our house was filled with joy. A beautiful name was chosen and finalised by everyone in our family. The naming ceremony ended on a joyful note.

Since receiving her from the institution, we were surprised that she never cried. This got us worried. We decided to make her cry, for example, by making her wait for her feed so that she could express her need. We had to be sure that everything was normal. One of our relatives, being a doctor, advised us to take her to a known pediatrician to understand if there are any health problems. Going through the x-ray the doctor confirmed that the child is suffering from Tuberculosis. This was a shock. He strongly recommended that we should return the baby back to the institution. We decided to take a second opinion and took her to our family Ayurvedic Physician. After examining her thoroughly and going through the x-ray reports, he laughingly confirmed that the child has got a lot of cough and nothing else. After his treatment the X-ray test was normal and we never went to any pediatrician thereafter. Our daughter was growing normally requiring less medical attention. We got her admitted to a playgroup, where she attracted the attention of all her teachers and classmates for her active participation in various activities in the class. She joined dance class, karate and also learnt swimming, drawing and music. She had multiple talents and she used to enjoy all her extracurricular activities. She used to be the star of the playground when she went down in the evening. Overall, she was a happy and cheerful child.

Her mother started introducing her to the idea of her adoption through stories at the age of 2 years. When she turned 5 years old we explained to her that she is god's gift to us. We told her that you are "swayambhu" which means a being who is self-manifested from unknown and divine origins. She seemed to have accepted it. However, she was certainly a bit confused, upset and worried. Nevertheless, she never asked any questions related to the topic but kept everything in her mind.

We shifted her to a renowned school in 5th standard. This was a rather difficult and challenging time in her life. Unfortunately, she was treated badly by some students and teachers due to the fact that she was adopted. They constantly taunted her. Sometimes it was so bad that our daughter refused to go to school. She somehow completed that year.

The next year, we changed her school with her consent, hoping she would have a better experience. Though the admissions were closed my daughter got admitted on merit by impressing the school authorities so much with her previous certificates, medals and most importantly, her positive attitude. They selected her on their sports quota. She won many medals and certificates in different games and competitions. She also took part in various school activities and school programs. The sailing was smooth till the 9th grade.

In her 10h standard school management noted her absenteeism in the class. She would go to school by the school bus but not attend the class. She disconnected herself from everyone in the school. She suddenly stopped interacting with her classmates and her teachers. She also lost her focus on sports performance as well as her studies.

In this period of time we also observed that some cash was disappearing from the house. We kept her informed about these episodes, as it was obvious that she was involved. She used to get terribly upset and annoyed. She started shouting and smashing glass articles. She also made a few statements like, "You are making such allegations, as I am your adopted daughter". This was the first time she said something like this. It continued for some time. We observed that all these problems started when a few of her schoolmates had again started teasing her about her being adopted. They used to tell her that you don't have real parents like us and raised queries about her bloodline. A few among the mischievous students troubled her by tearing her books, putting garbage in her locker and many more such evil actions. The hell she was going through was beyond description.

Now it was time for her to start college education. She decided to stay in our vacant flat in the city. In the meantime, we started homeopathic and psychiatrist treatments. She willingly responded to the treatment. In her new place she was nicely managing her routine. We observed a lot of improvements in her behavior. This change might have been because of her new friends circle that she had formed. All boys and girls were coming from different, decent families who behaved well with her and always extended their helping hand. In the later part of her final year of college she met with an accident and broke the bone in her leg in two pieces. This happened in the morning. She got herself admitted in a well-known orthopedic hospital on her own without anybody's knowledge and help. The doctor informed us on the phone about the accident and requested us to rush, as she needed immediate operation to be performed. We rushed to the hospital to find my daughter laughing and entertaining the staff with her jokes and stories. She came out of the accident in the shortest time possible. In this condition she appeared for her final exam and got through with 1st class. She did not accept any concessions offered by the college.

After college, she got good opportunities during her internship. She was now out of all her problems and leading an independent life. She travelled to Singapore with a travel agency for the first time. Later on she visited different countries such as Australia, Dubai all on her own.

One day she gave us a big surprise. She told us that she had applied for a course conducted in the best countries in Europe just for fun and was selected out of 50 students in India. The school admits only one student from every country for the course for the class of 25 students. We were thrilled. The course was for 2 years including internships.

The school staff was extremely happy with her performance. She passed the university degree and was selected for a work placement in the United States of America. In this period she was trained for the post of manager and received rotational training in different states in America. With the expiring of her Visa and strong desire to meet us she returned back home. We witnessed her convocation in Europe where her teachers and Principal met us and spoke about her good performance and activities spontaneously.

One of the teachers made mention that they have included her performance as a model case in their next year's curriculum presentation. We also visited her workplace in Europe and met her colleagues and her boss who were impressed by my daughter's work performance during her internship. We just cannot express our feelings in words about how happy and proud we are as her parents today.

Currently our daughter is working on completing her further studies up to PHD overseas and settling there. She wants to take both of us with her. After her independent dreams are fulfilled she desires to get married with a suitable match.

In conclusion, I think adoption is the best thing we can do for children who are not ours biologically. All you need is love, patience and the ability to accept them for the unique individual that they are. Our route to becoming parents through adoption was tremendously enjoyable; perhaps more enjoyable than the biological one.

Thank-you god for all the blessings.

GENES

My husband and I love children. Due to some health problems, I was unable to continue my pregnancy and we both decided to go for adoption. We will fix that, we both felt.

We decided that we would only bring a baby girl child home as I have three sisters and only relate to girls. I approached an organisation and collected all the information and procedures required for adoption. We completed all the documentation and were informed that we can see the child. In the 80's there was a huge choice to select a child. However, we had decided that the first baby who would look at us and smile, that would be our daughter.

As we did not have our own child, we had no right to select or to reject any gift that god would send us. Also, we felt that a child is not a product of a saree center where we go and select a dazzling garment.

In accordance to our strong principles we decided upon the first baby girl who smiled at us. She was looking at both of us with a special look in her eyes that seemed to recognise that we were her parents. She was indeed very sweet and charming and our decision was final.

We took her home and my in-laws were very happy and accepted her. My neighbours and relatives were also very happy and supported and welcomed our decision. With god's blessings my child was very healthy and I never faced any health issues. We took all the care required for her food and wellbeing. As it turned out she was a healthy child.

When she was 2-3 years old, I started telling her stories and through those stories I indirectly started telling her about adoption. My younger sister also adopted a baby girl when my daughter was 9-10 years old. In my society there were 3-4 children who came through adoption. So, it was very easy for us to explain to her about adoption although she never asked questions. There were no issues relating to her academic life and she was very clever and participated in all activities.

We had told her about adoption but she might have forgotten about it. Once someone from her friends circle told her about her adoption and then her behaviour changed a lot in her teenage years. Then we took the help of a counselor but my daughter never shared anything with her.

Many years later my daughter opened up about the incident that had hurt her deeply and after that sharing gradually things became normal between us. During the times of her trials, we always remained patient and affectionate. During this time, despite her problems she was never distracted from her academic pursuits and remained and performed very well in her student years.

In her adolescent years, we did face some issues with the opposite sex and that was definitely a tough time. At that time, my mother in law also was not well and hospitalised so we were not able to give our daughter the time she required. However, with help of a counsellor and medication we overcame the issue successfully.

From the beginning I have observed that she was very

aggressive and had a short temper.

When she was 4 years old, seeing traffic parked on the wrong side of the road, "When I will become a policeman, I will crush all these vehicles". Interestingly she always wanted to join the police but we never allowed it. Eventually she studied cybercrime investigation and works in the police department, fulfilling her childhood goal.

She is an extremely bright child who never lets anything distract her from her career goals. She did BCA and then MCA. Simultaneously, she did her graduation in Japanese language and got a scholarship to visit Japan. Currently, she is working in information and cyber security and has done various global certifications. We often wonder, where did she get this strong rooted connection with the police?

PRASAD... OUR GIFT FROM GOD

It was an auspicious day during Diwali when we brought our nearly 9-year old Prasad home. My younger sister, my aunt, my sister-in-law and our neighbours were all present to receive him. After a traditional welcome and blessings, he was welcomed inside the house to become a member of our family. Prasad watched with a wondrous look on his face.

Prasad lost his parents at a very young age and was brought up by his uncle and aunt. They had advertised in a newspaper stating that "A brahmin child available for adoption" and given their contact details. They were unaware that this method was illegal. Fortunately, the vigilant social worker saw this ad and contacted the family to advise them of the lawful process. Thus, Prasad found his new parents through the formal adoption process.

Now our entire focus was on our next goal. We wanted to take him out of his present school and get him admitted to a different school which had a primary and secondary section. I went to meet the Principal of the primary section and explain our problem to her. We could say this was a coincidence. It was like a higher power had planned all this! Some time back the Principal of the secondary section of the school had come to our shop. He had come to know that we outsourced the stitching of our bags and enquired if we could outsource the work to his students. We gave the job to his students. On this background, the Principal of the primary section said: "I will give admission to your son in our school. Be assured". In this way, Prasad got admission in the primary section of the school. She also added that she would speak to the Principal of the secondary school and that I should continue collecting and submitting the documents required for completing the adoption process. She did not stop here, on the school's behalf, she personally applied to the government officers for a name change on records to his present name - Prasad. We were rushing around to complete all the government and legal processes.

Diwali holidays were over and now we took on the role of parents. Now we cast ourselves in the mould of parenthood. Between the two of us, based on our workload we agreed on who would drop Prasad to school and pick him up. Sometimes Prasad chose who would drop him and bring him home and we went along with that. So, in a way at times the system was planned and at other times it just fell into place. One-day when I went to pick him up from school, this boy was sitting on the bench barefoot.

"Did you go to school today without your chappals?"
"No, my chappals tore."
"Both your chappals tore?"
"No one of them tore so I threw away the other."
"Come, show me where you threw them."
I was watching his expressions and I felt that something was not right. The chappals were lying under his class window behind the building's compound. I went and picked them, and he looked bewildered.
"My child, the chappals did not tear but they were torn, isn't it? Tell me how they were torn."
"I was bored so I tore them up." Saying so, he showed me how he did it.
I said "Fine, wear them as they are now. When we reach

home, we will show them to your mother, and we will do as she says".
On hearing this he was very frightened. "No, no, don't tell her I will wear them as they are".

At that time, we noted the change in his mindset. I set his mind to rest and assured him that his mother would not scold him or punish him. The adverse behaviour of the woman in his orphanage as well as his paternal aunt who had looked after him before he came to us, had a very deep-rooted impact on him. For many days he wouldn't allow his mother to touch him. As a result, I used to bathe him. In the evening, all three of us went to a shop and bought him new chappals. That other pair of torn chappals, however, remained home.

He was growing up and our business was also flourishing. His relationship with us was strengthening. An unwritten rule was that the answers to all his questions would be prompt, sensitive and satisfactory.

How does one get parents? Is it true that it's destined? It was a balancing act to explain it all to Prasad in a way that he would understand. But we succeeded. Prasad used the same words at a parent-child gathering arranged by the Agency. He used the most important sentence we had used to speak to him in the gathering very firmly. "My destiny gave me my Aai and Baba on that Diwali. I was very happy. I burst many crackers, hung a Diwali Lantern and ate a lot of special sweet and savoury Diwali treats".

I would definitely like to share one thing that we noted about Prasad. At a first glance, he looked a lot like his mother and as he spent more time with us, his likes and dislikes with regard to food were a lot like his mother. His rebellious and rather mischievous nature was like mine. What is yours comes to you? Prasad's biological mother died when he was born. God made her a medium for bringing Prasad into this world. We were deeply moved after listening to this. For a moment one can only imagine what the family, his birth family must have been feeling. Whether to celebrate the newborn or mourn the death of his mother who had left a family behind suddenly. All this happened while the mother's eyes were closed forever. No words. One breath stopped and the other took his first breath.

A human being who has nobody has God to take care of him. These words personify Prasad. His grandmother looked after him well. For the first few days, he was in a village.

His grandmother fed him Kheer. At first, his grandmother made kheer for him on the sly as the grandmother and Prasad lived in his paternal uncle and aunt's home. They were not greatly welcomed there. So, grandmother gave him treats without the knowledge of the uncle and aunty. The uncle worked on a high post in a private company and his wife put on airs because of that.

Prasad was 7/8, years old and treated like their servant. He had to get the flour from the flour mill, buy vegetables, draw water etc. He was given capital punishment for making mistakes. (That was the reason why for many days he would not allow his mother to touch him.) On our first visit, we took some sweets and wafers for him. He savoured them. To date, he likes the kheer his grandmother made him and the sweets we took him on our first visit. They were the taste of love and nurturing.

Sometimes he lived in an orphanage or at times at home.

Such was the way he was brought up. And we found it difficult to raise him considering this upbringing (the chappals story would perhaps give you an idea).

One day a friend of ours brought him home and asked my wife if she had given him permission to go to a certain town. She denied this and asked him why he was asking. The friend narrated that he had stopped Prasad and asked him where he was going. Prasad told him the name of the town and told him he was going on his bike. The friend had found money in Prasad's pockets. He told the friend it was his mother's. The friend had then decided to bring him back home. My wife was shocked after listening to all this. Prasad had pilfered money from the cupboard saying it was his mother's. Then everything was explained to him quietly and what the consequences would have been. He was really frightened to hear it. He had not even imagined that these things could happen.

He had a lot of anger in him. One day things did not go according to his wishes. He shouted loudly, gnashing his teeth, "Go tell the whole world I am not your son, proclaim publicly. Take me back to the Adoption Agency, call the aunty (social worker at the Adoption Agency) give me back to her". We quietened him down saying "Yes, yes, that's the first thing we will do in the morning". At such times we have to manage the situation in the best way possible.

This boy though had an aptitude for business. During Diwali one year he had borrowed Rs. 100/- as a loan from his mother to sell some edible items from a particular shop. We had forgotten all about it. After a week he returned the Rs. 100/- he had borrowed from his mother. He had sold the edible items by going door to door. We just asked him how he had managed so much stuff. He said it's easy. We asked him how he did it. We were surprised by his answer. So, let's hear it from Prasad himself.

"Suppose I ring the bell, and someone opens the door. Then you introduce yourself in short and tell the reason for your visit. If a man opens the door you show him certain things like Amba Barfi, Jackfruit 'gare', kokum sharbat (that both would enjoy). If it is the woman at the door you offer her pickle, kumbaya, dried mango etc. Once they wish to buy some wares you start displaying other items you have."

Separating goods to sell according to the gender of the person really shows the sharpness of his brain. From the profit he made by the sale in Diwali, he bought me cloth material for a shirt and a purse for his mother. The next year he hammered in some nails on a wooden rod and hung lanterns on them. This time some of our relatives tried to tap his trade secrets, so we had no choice but to interfere. "Prasad we should never reveal to the customer from where we are getting our ware. Just show a sample and ask how many pieces they want and accordingly deliver it to their home." The person who was talking became quiet and without saying a word bought what he wanted and patted him on the back praising him.

In the 10th standard, Prasad's close friend told me that Prasad did not attend the class. He told us that revision classes were going to start the next day. I said, "How can that be? Every day in the morning he leaves saying he has a special class."

When Prasad came home in the afternoon we talked to him gradually. At last, he confessed that he had been bunking classes. We said, "From tomorrow we are going to drop you to the class. Won't you be happy when others comment 'At your age your parents are coming to drop you?'". He cried a lot and promised he would not bunk again and kept his word. As a result, he had a good score in the 10th exam.

At home, our screen-printing business was doing well. As his marks were good we got him admitted for a printing technology diploma. In his last year, he drew supplementary drawings for 8 to 10 students (later we found out that he had earned some money from it). A teacher at the Institute had failed Prasad in the oral exams in the subject he taught on purpose. Both of us were very angry about it but by that time it was too late. The students for whom he had made the drawing had passed their exams and got their Diploma. This hurt him a lot. Finally, we met this teacher. He told us all that had transpired and asked that Prasad should enrol in his class by paying his fees of 1500/-. He agreed to have Prasad appear again in October. The only thing he said was, "Study hard". He recovered what he had lost through the fees and detained Prasad for 6 months. Then in October he sat for the repeat exam, got good marks, and got his Diploma.

Soon after his exams, he appeared for a campus interview for a good company. The senior officers from that company liked his answers. After asking him questions related to his education they asked him if he smoked and he replied, "Yes, sometimes when I feel a strong impulse but not regularly". The officers said, "Mr Prasad you were honest about it. The others come for an interview and their mouths smell of smoke, yet they lie about smoking."
Prasad replied, "Sir how will telling lies help? I felt at peace telling you the truth. Besides at my age, there's nothing wrong in smoking, only it should not cross limits."
"Suppose there is some problem with production while you are working here what will you do"?

"Sir I will first check and try to solve the problem myself by using the knowledge I have and what I have been taught. If I still cannot solve it I will take the help of my colleague who is an experienced worker. If the problem still remains then and only then I will come to you for help. "

"Suppose you join work, what will you do?"

"During the first few days I will observe the nature of work. I will study units from the manufacturing unit up to the marketing unit. Only then I will be able to say something". Later on, when he actually started working the workers warmed towards him and the production increased by 2.5-fold. This is where he went wrong. The Union Chief developed animosity towards him, and Prasad left the job overnight.

I remember an old incident which later turned into his hobby. Today he is still continuing with his hobby. Kiran Purandare' s fascination for Nature is well known. 'Nisarga Wedh' is the name of his Institute. We were taking on some work for them at our printing press (Prasad's mother had a prosperous screen-printing business). At that time Prasad's name was listed as a participant for a trip to the Bharatpur Birds Sanctuary. Till the last moment, Prasad was insisting that his mother should go in his place. The trip contributed a lot towards his interest in Nature. He joined ' Nisarga Wedh ' Wildlife ' and he became a strong support for these organizations. His interest in bird watching increased and he became a favourite guide for the children.

His striving, bold, courageous nature helped him go ahead but sometimes it landed him into trouble. One day he said, "I am going to a famous dam to watch birds" and drove off on his scooter. After one and a half hours there was a call in a frightened voice, "Please come here immediately. There has been an accident".

We took all the money we had at home with us and as parents we were responsible, and it was our duty so both of us started on a motorcycle. Everything was uncertain. The news was not very clear. In the end, we came across Prasad sitting with his head between his knees. On seeing us he started crying. He had just a slight scratch on his elbow. He had rammed his bike into a worker. The worker had been admitted to a nearby hospital. The Doctor whose hospital it was turned out to be a close friend of a doctor friend of ours. He informed us that it was a very serious accident and there was serious damage to the spinal cord. It would be a very expensive operation and the worker may not survive it. So, give him Rs. ten thousand and send him to his town immediately. Your son has a temporary license, and this is a police case. I have somehow managed to hold them from taking any action. Pay my fees later on but send the Worker to his town. I handed over the money to the man accompanying the worker. After two hours I paid the Doctor his fees and we were on our way back home. Prasad drove his scooter.

After leaving his first company he joined a computer company. Now and then he used to declare that he will live separately. Then after a while, he would come back to live with us. This went on for some time. Later on, however, he stayed separately for three consecutive years. There was no communication between us. It looks bad but it was a fact. This was at a time when Prasad's business was not doing well, and we had troubles in the family. Before this separation, my father had passed away. It seemed like a final separation.

Prasad then met a girl whom he wished to marry. It was a love marriage of their choice. However, the girl had one condition, that they should live together with his parents as a joint family. She expressed this wish because he had told her the whole truth about his past and adoption. She felt strongly that he could not exclude the parents who had given him so much love and care.

My father always said, "Our grandson lives in Gokul" and we started living together again. We got him married in a splendid manner. Now we have a lovely grandson and granddaughter. Our daughter-in-law is a physiotherapist and a lecturer in a renowned college. Prasad organizes exhibitions. He is also a District Sales Promotion Officer and besides salary, he earns a commission on Sales, plus, he has the Dealership of another company. At present everything is great. Both our son and daughter-in-law respect us and take good care of us.

With all its challenges, our adoption has been a very fulfilling experience. Prasad is truly our gift from God.

THE SEED

A seed germinates in watered soil...How can this seed germinate in dry, rocky land? One needs to take care of a seed that is sown to help it grow into a sturdy plant....

These are the opening lines of a song from a Marathi film based on the life of an orphaned boy. If a seed is nurtured in the right way, in fertile soil, in the sunshine of love and care, it will grow into a beautiful plant. Similarly, a baby when loved and cared for, will grow up to be a fine person.

Our journey began rather unexpectedly but with a lot of love many years ago. I will never forget the day they (two of them) became our beloved children who brightened up our lives. I remember what they wore and what they looked like when they first came home.

Actually, the first one arrived as a foster child who was supposed to leave India in a couple of months. However, there were some obstructions and so the baby stayed on with us, as our very own child. That was God's plan. Uma became our precious bundle of joy. My husband too fell in love with her right from the beginning and she was the apple of his eyes. She still is.

When Uma was around two and a half years old our second one, Gabdulya, joined our family. When he came to us it was little Uma who accompanied me. Right from the beginning my husband used to be very busy and came home quite late at night. So, I became their loving parent and hands-on caregiver.

I realised it was important for my children to be aware that they had come to our family in unusual circumstances. In order to gradually make them aware of those circumstances, I started telling them stories of Lord Krishna, how he was born to Vasudev and Devaki but grew up in the home of Nanda and Yashoda with all the Gopals of Gokul.

In order to help the children understand the reality of their life story, I started taking them to the child care home from where we had adopted them. Gabdulya was three years old when I began to share the knowledge with Uma and him that they had lived at the children's home when they were very little just like other babies were living there when we visited. Then, with my husband's consent, I brought home babies for foster care. When we brought the new baby home I took both of them along with me. I explained that they had lost their parents. Though they were quite young, both participated in taking care of the new baby. We fostered quite a few babies.

The children were now a little older and they bonded well with each other. In fact, they could not live without one another. On two or three occasions all four of us passed by their birthplaces. We shared with them the important information that this was the place where they were born.

I was under a false impression that by now they had a fairly good idea that they were like Lord Krishna. We were their parents now and we loved and cared for them. They were ours forever. Then one fine day disaster struck. Their whole world turned topsy turvy. We were left suffering the after effects of a personal Tsunami. My daughter was 9 years old and my son was 7. The children found documents related to their adoption. Though we had shared adoption with them in so many emotional ways, the legal reality came as a shock to them.

My daughter's grades (she used to be first or second in class) dropped dramatically. She had a sudden urge to see her birth parents. So, I explained to her that we would do our best to find them when she turned 18 as that would be in accordance with the law. For the whole year, she seemed not quite herself. However, things began to be normal after a year or two. But I believe, though she behaved normally, and her grades improved again, she must have been undergoing an emotional turmoil. This manifested later on when she was studying for her professional exams.

One day my son, who was till that time a happy, cheerful child, suddenly came to me sobbing hard. He said," In any case, I would have had to live on the streets, so I am going now". He picked up his bundle of clothes and opened the door and just walked out. I did not realize he was serious until he almost reached the end of the street. I was in shock. I ran after him and caught hold of him just before he reached the end of the street. I convinced him that he would never have to live on the streets and that we all cared for him and loved him a lot. We were a family. Tai, his elder sister, was our dearest daughter and he was our most cherished and much-loved son. Somehow I convinced him to come home with me. I remember the tee-shirt and shorts he wore that day. From that day onwards he became reserved. Hardly smiled. His laughter disappeared. Gradually his nature and behaviour changed.

EDUCATION

Gabdulya's grades dropped very low and he just managed to pass every year. There were other behaviour problems as well. He played truant. I also consulted a clinical psychologist for a while. Here I must confess that at that time I did not wish to consult the Social Worker in the Institution. I wrongly thought they would blame us, his parents, and hold us responsible. It took many years to realise that some of the children do behave this way. This is not because the parents are at fault but because they are not sure about who they are or why their birth parents left them... a sense of rejection which haunts them.

My son's problems continued till nearly the end of his 10th standard. When the school threatened to retract his form for the 10th Board examination I had to plead with the teacher. My husband and I sat him down and gave him a clear picture of what would happen if he just managed to pass the 10th by scraping through. He would then be left with doing only menial jobs and have to fend for himself as he would not get any admission to a good college. We could not look after him for his entire lifetime. The choice lay in his hands.

Of course, being an intelligent boy, he passed the 10th Board examination with a first-class. Later on, in college, we did not have to ask him to study. He always cleared all his college years with distinction. He chose the line he wanted (though I believed he would do well in another stream of education). I was a bit worried about his choice at that time, but I kept quiet and we allowed him to choose.

Finally, he passed his very difficult professional exam with flying colours. He worked in an International Company for a couple of years. Then he left it and joined another reputed company as a partner. My daughter wished to be a doctor right from the time she was a child. She held her Grandfather in high esteem and wanted to follow in his footsteps and take up medicine. She also wished and did go to a foreign country for Martial Arts. However, she had to change her line on her return and and had to give up her dream of becoming a doctor. She chose another career and got through the entrance exams. During this time, she, unfortunately, became close friends with a group of girls who were not very serious about their studies and their goals. No amount of efforts to convince her that she should give up these friends had any effect on her. She would not listen to any advice. It was quite a few years before she got through the professional exam.

I think this was also the time that she kept her thoughts and brooding to herself. She never shared those thoughts with me from whomshe had not hidden anything. There was a barrier. Anyhow, slowly, and surely these friends disappeared from her life. Free from their influence, she was once more my very own precious daughter.

Here I must mention that all the while when their world turned topsy turvy and all hell broke loose for all of us, I was not aware why both the children had a hard time at the same time in life. It was much later that my daughter shared with me the fact that both of them had come across the details about themselves and it had hit them hard that they were not our biological children. So, though I thought that I had shared the facts with them indirectly, for them it had not sunk in till that time. Or as in my Gabdulya's case, he is still in denial and does not think or talk or share his feelings with any of us.

Both my children are gems, and I don't say this because they are my children. Their actions in these hard times show me that they are wonderful people. They have a loving caring, sensitive nature.

MARRIAGE

At the time when we were looking for a suitable bridegroom for my daughter, the attitude of the boys was negative when they were informed about her adoption. But again, God had His own plans for her. A boy whose family we knew well, had known my daughter since the time she was in college. He asked her for her hand, and she gave him her consent after a few months. Today she is happily married. She is the exact opposite of my son. She is a cheerful lady always bubbling with laughter. Hard-working, intelligent and makes friends very easily.

My son was quite young when he came across a girl who was non-Maharashtrian. We were worried as he was very young, had not even finished his graduation and had no financial standing. As he passed his professional exam there was no way we could say No to his choice. Perhaps it was my perception that she was not a very kind person. That was the only reason we were against his marriage to her. Today though, she is a much better-adjusted person and cares for us. So, all's well that ends well. My son has settled down in life and is happily married. He is blessed with a son and as a father, he pours all his love into the care he gives his son. Yet deep down he is still searching why 'he' should be an 'adopted' child.

Along this special journey today I feel that we should give moral support to our children at every stage in their lives. Show them that you love, trust and care for them. We allowed both our children to make their own decisions and stood by them even if their decisions were sometimes wrong. Freedom to choose is very important for a child to develop and gives her/his confidence. As parents, I think we did our best to give our children a happy life. Giving quality time to your children is an essential requirement of parenthood.

Nowadays adoptive parents have a lot of information about the children they adopt. That is a good development as parents can better understand and fulfill the needs of their child by adoption.

Today I am happy that more and more children have parents all over the world and hope that one day no child will be without loving parents. That is my dream.

TWO PATHS TO PARENTHOOD

Embarking on the adoption process is exciting, scary, intense and emotional. My husband and I decided to adopt a girl child soon after our marriage in 2003.

We applied for the same in a reputed Adoption Agency in 2004, and although while applying, adoption seemed like a seemingly simple procedure to us, we were fraught with endless paperwork, a home study report that evaluates the conduciveness of your home environment and a serpentine queue. The staff at the Adoption Agency were absolutely fantastic, very professional and took us through our journey with extreme ease and care. Kudos to them!

We thought we would have to wait for a year or so for our bundle of joy to arrive and can never forget that morning of May 2005 when our social worker called to say they had found a match in a neighbouring district for us in 7 months. Our happiness and excitement knew no bounds.

My husband and I were very clear from the very beginning that we will not choose from three different babies, as was the norm then. "We weren't going shopping for a daughter" is what we always said and felt and informed the Agency about the same. Our daughter is destined to find her way home, we strongly believed.

Can never forget the day we held Aleena for the first time. A beautiful little 4.5 month old in a lovely floral yellow frock.

When my husband went to take her, she grabbed his finger in a tight grip. That was a moment I can't describe in words. There were tears flowing down our cheeks. A Divine Signal. Our daughter had arrived.

But we were in for a rude shock when the next day during the mandatory ENT check-ups she was declared 100 % deaf in her right ear. The Adoption Agency then told us that since we had asked for a healthy baby we can't take her as now she would come in a different category of children.

We were not willing to give up. We wanted Aleena no matter what!! We were determined that even if she had a problem, she is ours to love and we will take her home. We were told she would need an expensive surgery when she would be 5 years and we were ready for that too. We put up the fight with the Agency for a week and repeated the ENT test with a different doctor. This time she was declared 60% deaf. There!!! We knew what it was. The child had a cold, and that's why her ears were blocked. Our prayers were answered, and The Adoption Agency finally relented, and we brought our angel home.

Her homecoming was like there was a wedding in the house. I got her nursery ready within 2 days, with flowers and all her necessities, bought baby clothes, toys and all other essentials, family and friends all there to welcome her, congratulatory messages flowing in. We were all set for this new, exciting journey in our life.

And what a journey it has been. Aleena is a 14 year old teen now and we are supremely proud of her. She is a school topper, a guitarist, a singer, a horse rider with finesse, a footballer. She plays inter-school football matches and is very popular with family and friends. These children of God are very resilient and if given the right environment with the right people, they can absolutely soar.

When she was 2.5 years old, my husband and I decided that it would be wonderful if Aleena had a sibling. So then when Aleena was 3.5 years old I gave birth to Aliya, my second daughter. Our small family was complete.

There are two fundamental questions at the heart of adoption – can you love somebody else's child, and can they love you? With hindsight, I know both are possible.

I felt I didn't just have to learn how to become a mother, I also had to earn the right to be one – a common feeling among adoptive parents. But you have been better prepared than most to become parents, having been through a rigorous assessment process in which you have had to confront your motives for wanting a family, and assess how good you'll be at it. As for the thorny issue of whether you're the "real" mum or dad – you have fed, washed and clothed your child, dried their tears, read to them and loved them. You can't get more real than that.

Be prepared for awkward questions from strangers, insensitive acquaintances, and inquisitive children. It is helpful to remind yourself that your child's personal history is their story to tell, not yours.

We tried telling Aleena about her adoption, but our situation was a tad different with having one adopted daughter and one biological. We were equal parents to both and didn't want this truth to topple our apple cart. I was afraid.

We knew there isn't anything like the right time to tell your child about adoption. We wanted to make it as simple and positive as we could when we did. Aleena was already 11 years and we hadn't yet told her or her sibling Aliya. I just didn't feel it was the right time and my fear kept delaying us telling her the Truth.

When she was about 12 years old while playing Truth and Dare with her friends, in a Truth situation, her friend told her about her adoption. She came home but didn't say anything to any of us for the longest time.

We noticed her getting very sensitive and we thought it was all a part of growing up. Till one night she came charging into our bedroom after a typical sibling fight and yelled "I know I am adopted and was waiting for you to tell me!" I sprang out of bed and hugged her and in the midst of all the tears and hugs, we told her about her adoption in the most gentle way we could.

She understood and handled it all very maturely. We left the onus on her to tell her sister and cousins whenever she was comfortable. We would not be the ones to tell them, we said. After about a month or so she told Aliya about it and her younger sibling just turned around and said, "So what didi? We all love you. You are my sister and that's never going to change. It makes no difference that I grew in Mama's tummy and you in her heart." Knowing about her adoption hasn't changed anything for Aleena. She hardly had any questions. For her we are her parents and that's the only Truth for her.

So, although I didn't tell her the Truth in her earlier years by God's Grace it all panned out well for us.

We can't believe just how lucky we have been. She is the perfect child for us. I am a PAP – Proud Adoptive Parent.

Loving an adopted child is the same as loving a biological child. That is what my own experience has taught me.

ADOPTION, A DIVINE GIFT

We got married a little later than most people in our society. I was 35 and my wife was 30. Both of us agreed that we should adopt as soon as possible. Both our families supported our decision. Our family Doctor asked us to meet Dr Y and accordingly, on his advice, we went to the Agency.

As Teaching was my profession I was naturally drawn towards children and was always in contact with them. I was also associated with some social organisations. As such, I had a soft corner for 'adopted children'. I did not have any misunderstanding or resentful attitude towards adoption. Both of our families were religious and traditional but we did not follow strict conventions, were not prudish or puritanical. Our family followed a pilgrim tradition, singing devotional songs to the Gods. My wife's family were connected to another famous Temple. However, what was special was that the traditions in our families did not come in our way of adoption!

One of my colleagues at the school where I was teaching had just adopted a baby. Her whole family was happy. Her adoption helped us to take our final decision. She guided us on each step of the adoption process. Her support was the reason we did not feel any pressure during the process of adoption. The police verification in the process got delayed so we went to the police station in person and spoke to the young police officer. He gathered some information about us and said he would come for a home visit. The next day the police officer visited our home, he didn't come inside, just peeped inside and left. We went to the police chowki to bring the verification certificate and asked him why he had not come inside and asked us any questions. He smiled and replied, "When I entered through the door I saw the big idols of 'Panduranga and Mauli' and did not feel it necessary to ask any more questions". In that way, our Gurus and Gods supported our decision to adopt.

We came across positive responses like these very often. We visited our Agency once or twice and they came to see us for a home visit. They told us that it will be sometime before our baby comes home. We had opted for 'open choice for gender'. We were okay with either gender. In fact, if our child had been biological we would have had no choice. We were fully prepared to welcome 'our baby'.

However, we got the opportunity to join a pilgrimage to Kailash-Mansarovar which had been our dream so we could pay our homage to Lord Shiva. Just then, after 9 months of waiting our Agency called to say that they had a prospective baby for us. We had to make a big choice between pilgrimage and parenting. We opted for the latter.

We went to see the baby. They showed us the baby and placed the baby in our hands and the baby who was solemn up till then, smiled sweetly and turned towards me and fell asleep quietly. Our Social Worker who was standing nearby said, "you did not choose the baby, the baby has chosen you". Our home was instantly filled with joy.

We were the first to experience this process of adoption. Later one of my friends, who was also a teacher like me, and some of our relatives, also adopted children. I came to know of their experiences too. But what surprised me, and I admired, was the work Dr Y, our Social Worker and the attendants who took care of the babies, were doing.

They closely observe the prospective adoptive couples, their natures, how they live and their social awareness. They had some information about most of the babies who were admitted to the Agency and they observed each baby and this helped them to decide which baby would suit which couple and which baby should be shown to which couple. Their experience never went wrong, and the baby right from its resemblance to a parent up to their bonding with one another would be so strong that parents forgot their child had been adopted. In truth, this is the true outcome of the understanding and insight of sensitive and well-trained social workers.

Ours was the same. Vasant has blended well with us. He is 13 years old today. We have shared the fact of his adoption with him. We shared it with him gradually step by step. Parents should not reveal the fact of adoption with their child in one sitting. Vasant has accepted his adoption truth very easily. The social workers at the Agency arranged workshops for adoptive parents from time to time. In these workshops, cum counselling sessions discussions were conducted on various issues related to adoption and that is why today one sees the impact of these meetings. How a parent/parents share the fact of adoption with the child differs from family to family as well as the child's nature. The same method does not apply to everyone.

Before Vasant became a part of our family, we had received guidance about touch therapy in a workshop. If a baby is not your biological child, your comforting, loving touch creates a bond between you when you bathe him, massage him. My wife and I have both given an oil massage and bath to baby Vasant. Today Vasant and I share a very strong bond. The roots of the strong bond lie in that touch.

Other couples whom we know, who adopted just before we did or just after we did are in contact with us even today. We were able to form a supportive fraternity. Our Vasant and their adopted children also formed friendship bonds. We share our experiences, problems with one another and discuss them so that if any problem arises, we can solve it. We had a life-shaking experience when Vasant was a toddler. The school van drove right over him. Being a small child, he was safe between the wheels and came out without a scratch. At that moment, he was reborn.

In the last 12-13 years our many experiences in society, with very few exceptions, were very positive and pleasant. At times we have been amazed at the reactions of people who were known to be puritanical and traditional. I will narrate one such experience.

In our home, we practice traditional worship of our deities at Narsobachi Wadi. My father's greatest wish was that at least one family ceremony should be carried out at Narsobachi Wadi. Unfortunately, he passed away before my marriage. We decided to perform Vasant's thread ceremony at Narsobachi Wadi in a very simple manner with just our closest friends and relatives. There were about 30 to 40 of them. The atmosphere at the Wadi was very traditional and orthodox. But we had decided that we would mention to the most respected, senior and highly learned Guruji, the fact that Vasant was our adopted son. We were a little worried about his reaction.

However, with a gentle smile on his face, he said, "A biological son acquires both the virtues and the vices of both the parents genetically. But an adopted child only picks up the virtues of the parents as there is no genetic connection! Genetically a child will be a singer if the parent is a singer and so on. However, in the case of a child who is adopted it all depends on your nurturing and your values guiding him in the right direction." What a great message that was!

I have noticed many times that our nurturing has an impact, consciously or unconsciously, on Vasant. I am interested in history and I have researched on 'Vande Mataram'. I have even written books on it which have been published. With this purpose, I have given audio-visual lectures on 'Vande Mataram', National Flag and National Anthem. Taking notice of this, Vasant has started appreciating historical stories. Not just that, at the age of 8 years when he was in the third standard he gave a speech using a PowerPoint presentation on our National Flag in front of his classmates! Later on, he made a similar presentation before PVG and a Rotary Club! The interest that was created in the subject encouraged him to learn about it and present this confidently before people.
Both of us are not interested in sports or exercises but Vasant loves being on the playgrounds. From the age of 4, he is training in athletics. He has participated in an International marathon under the age of 10 and stood 9th in the running race. We have left the decision of whether he should participate in competitive sports to Vasant and his trainer. We do not insist. He can choose what he wants. There is no pressure from us.

Traditionally our family has been studying and teaching bhajans (devotional songs). My Uncle went to America 40 years ago and had taught bhajans. In our city, International music students had received guidance from him. These bhajans sung in our home have influenced Vasant and he plays the cymbal whenever we sing bhajans. He has an inborn gift of rhythm. It's not easy to play the cymbal. We did not pressurize him to sit for the bhajans but he had imbibed our tradition on his own initiative.

Vasant likes drama. He loves to act and he has participated in elocution competitions in school and won many prizes in it. His speech is sometimes not very clear, but he learnt Sanskrit Sheela's and recited them clearly in the memorizing and recitation competition in school and got the first prize. He has an inclination towards Art subjects, and he does well in school studies. We have never burdened him with our expectations so his independent personality has blossomed. The feeling of being adopted has not proved to be a hindrance for him. In these progressive times, adoption is not something out of the ordinary, but it gives us the same joy as a biological birth would have given. In adoption, the mother does not undergo the pains of labour but the joys and even the pains of parenting! The baby comes through our hearts and accepts us as his/her parents....that is a unique and wondrous experience. Perhaps this was Lord Shiva's gift to us!

HANDLE WITH CARE

Thirteen years of marriage had not resulted in any child for us. We had undergone all possible treatments but without success. With each month, the time for us to become parents was passing by. We were anxious and depressed.

One of my friends had a similar problem. One day she invited us to her home. It was the day she was bringing her adopted girl home. We went to her home and were moved by the magical atmosphere prevalent there. Although we had not been blessed with a child of our own we felt that God had reserved this experience for us to enjoy.

We were certain that all doors had not been shut. Our decision to adopt was finalised. Our Doctor endorsed our desire to adopt. He said it was a good decision and he would help us with whatever we needed. When one undertakes any good work, many people come forward to help.

While we were gathering information about where to go we came to know of the adoption agency. We had many apprehensions. We had already undergone a lot of trauma so we were worried about what sort of people we would meet at the agency, what sort of questions would they ask us. And then one day we finally steeled ourselves and went to the Agency. There we met Social Worker Mrs X and our worries disappeared.

We already knew Mrs. X, but we did not know that we would

meet her here. Previously we had a whole lot of questions and everything appeared very difficult but the moment we took our decision our world turned 360 degrees, and everything appeared to be easy.

We completed all the procedures and gathered the various documents that had to be attached to our application for adoption. This is absolutely a necessary part of the procedure of adoption from the point of view of security of the children. Along with the legal process, we had started informing our family, relatives, friends, neighbours about our decision to adopt. They all joined us in our happiness. We wondered that if only our decision to adopt filled us with such joy then what would be our state when our baby is actually with us?

I started imagining what my daughter would look like. When we had filled the form, we had requested for a fair, smiling, and playful baby girl. We were told by Mrs X that the Social Workers have such a good sense that they would only suggest a baby that would match us. We had been told we would perhaps have to wait for 7/8 months before we would have our daughter. But we were lucky. We got a call from the Agency almost immediately.

We rushed to see our baby. The attendant had dressed her up like a little fairy. She was three and a half months old then. The attendant placed the baby in my lap. 'She came, she saw, and she conquered!'

I was completely lost to the world around me. I was certain that a strong bond was formed between us that day. The other formalities were completed quickly. Mrs X, other social workers and the attendants helped us a lot and very soon our baby daughter was home.

We had informed our neighbours and friends about her arrival. They had decorated the whole building with lights and decorated the house with flowers. The whole house was full of people and they kept coming to meet her till late at night. Everybody wanted to pick her up, caress her cheeks, give her gifts and she allowed them to do it all. She was happy, we were happy and the whole world seemed full of happiness because of her arrival.

Every day our baby was growing, and her father was always in a flurry to capture her antics, her babble, baby talk, her first steps in his camera. Time flew and before we knew it she was growing from one stage to another, with her determination, her studies, and her minor and major illnesses.

Our Social worker had advised us to start sharing the fact of adoption at the earliest. Our niece helped us with this delicate and difficult task. It was successful since they were both very attached to each other. We had heard that sometimes when children find out they are adopted they have strong reactions. That made us afraid. Our daughter being an introvert did not react strongly. She asked me a few questions about her past. But since rules dictate that all such information be kept confidential I could not give her any answers. Every adopted child will have some doubts but if we give them answers without being fearful they quieten down. Then I told her all about how she was welcomed home with a lot of pomp, how her father had recorded everything she did, all the initial stories and gradually her mind was put to rest. She has adjusted so well in our home that everybody has forgotten about her adoption. She is the favourite of all because of her quiet and cheerful nature.

When she went to the 9th standard she started finding

Science and Maths difficult. We understood her issue and stood behind her and thought that she should appear for her 10th standard exams through the National Institute of Open Schooling (NIOS). NIOS allows a student to appear for subjects of his/her choice. In the 10th std,she studied at home and did well in her exams. She got admission for arts in a well-known College. She has nearly completed her junior college. She behaves like other children of her age. As she is an adolescent we have adopted a 'handle with care' behaviour with regard to her. The two of us are constantly together. All my merits and demerits are reflected in her. Her eating habits though have been picked up from her father. All children are the same.

Everybody faces problems of some sort in life. Excess use of T. V., I pad, smartphone and similar things has made it challenging/strenuous for parents to bring up their children. We too faced these obstacles to an extent in our lives but all three of us worked as a team and overcame them and we have come this far. I am certain that by God's grace everything will be fine in future too.

After reading this article one will assume that the 17 to 18 years must have been a breeze, but that was not the case. We had to face many problems on our journey before we reached the present time. She was excessively stubborn, found school and studies boring, was lazy, did not help with chores at home and many more things led to arguments. It was a balancing act to get her out of these undesirable habits without getting angry or quarrelling. Her excessive use of smartphone distressed us greatly and as a result, her father suffers from skin problems and I have diabetes. We attribute our ailments to stress.

Bringing up children these days has become complicated. Being the only child makes them prone to mental problems. We were considerate in understanding our daughter's problems as at the time of her adoption she was three and a half months old while her father was 37 years old and I was 35 years old. This was a slightly bigger age gap compared to other parents. Due to this age difference, we were able to have more patience and had better control over our reactions. We could help her solve her problems. We spent many days and nights in finding solutions for her problematic behaviour. The atmosphere of the whole house was shaken, words became arrows that wounded, pillows were soaked with tears, we faced the mornings with swollen eyes. Many such incidents occurred. The home atmosphere is constantly in turmoil. But we go on living, providing each other with strong support.

There shouldn't be any discrimination based on 'adopted' or 'biological'. Every child's disposition is different. They should be allowed to grow freely. We should continue being there for them whenever they fall short of anything. From time to time our Social Workers help us gladly and there is no embarrassment in asking for their help.

If I was able to clear the doubts in the mind of even one parent by expressing my thoughts then I will feel compensated. Challenges are a part of parenting through which both parents and child grow up. It is a roller coaster ride without a dull moment!

WAITING FOR THE GOOD NEWS

We had been married for eight years and all our friends and relatives pestered us with questions like : are you expecting a baby ? when are you giving us the 'good news' ? 'when can we expect the 'pedhas ' (sweets which are distributed at the birth of a child).?' It was very pressurising and difficult for us to deal with.

We had undergone a whole series of medical tests and treatments, some of which were expensive and beyond our means to diagnose why we had not conceived a child and explore available treatment. At that time medical science had not developed new techniques for reproduction. Even if they had, our condition was not conducive since both the fallopian tubes in the case of my wife were blocked and we were given only 50% chance of conception even after treatment.

Around that time a couple known to us had adopted a boy. We had accompanied them to bring him home so we became familiar, to a certain extent, with the idea and process of adoption. For the first time, I thought to myself about adopting a child.

Our relatives went to the extent of suggesting that I should marry again. I was in total disagreement as it was not my wife's fault that she could not bear a child. Her body was Nature's creation, so why should she be punished for it? I spoke to my wife about adoption. At first she was hesitant but she gave her consent. After that I wrote to my parents and my brother, gave them information and asked for their permission. We also asked my wife's relatives. In my family only my father welcomed our decision with happiness and praised us. All the rest vehemently opposed our decision to adopt. Her relatives did not have any objection to our decision.

By then we had made our firm resolution. The only question which remained was whether we should adopt a girl or a boy? We gave it a thought. We saw that people were choosing to adopt a boy when taking into consideration the need for support in their old age. On the other hand what we considered was that even if a boy grows up in an orphanage and has to leave it after he turns 18, he will not have significant problems looking after himself. But what about a girl who is not adopted? What would be her future? How will she stay safe and secure? Many such questions came to our mind. Obviously we could not take on the responsibility of all girls but we could be good parents to at least one. With this one thought we decided to adopt a girl. We completed the process of adoption and in the true sense became parents to a three month old baby daughter.

All our friends admired us and the baby. Days passed in appreciation of our daughter. Sometimes she fell ill and suffered from a minor cold, cough, fever. Experienced parents told us that all small children suffer from such small illnesses and we felt reassured. We fed her meals on time. We greatly experienced and enjoyed her antics. In my home town all with the exception of my father, were against our adoption. So for two or three years we avoided visiting there. However, with time they slowly started accepting her and we saw a change in their mind set. We were happy and satisfied that our daughter now enjoyed the love of her grandparents.

People who knew about our adoption never brought up the topic when we were around.

We celebrated our daughter's first birthday as best as we could within our means. Even if our financial capability was not good we took care of all of our daughter's needs.. We were delighted that all our friends were fond of our daughter. Once my daughter was suffering from high fever. Since it appeared to be really high we took her to a well-known Paediatrician in town but by the time we reached his clinic he had already left. The compounder told us that the Doctor would come back only at 4.00p.m. We were distraught. I was under a lot of stress so I threatened the Compounder that if anything happened to my daughter I would throw him down from the third floor. The Compounder probably knew about children's illnesses because he wiped our daughter with a wet towel and surprisingly her fever came down and she started to play. The doctor upon his return told me that I should not get frightened if our child gets a fever. He told us that for a child under five years of age with fever one must wipe her with a wet towel and put cold compress on her forehead. We came back home with a lesson learnt. My wife's days passed on happily in giving a massage to our daughter, giving her a bath and feeding her dal rice, giving her milk.

My daughter was now about three and half years old. Her mother took her to the nursery, waited there for a while and brought her back home. Gradually my daughter adjusted to the nursery. We were delighted listening to the sweet sound of her silver anklets. We were happy to hear her lisping. With her lisping she had made us her parents, winning our hearts completely. This was the ultimate moment for us and we had forgotten she was 'adopted'.
Nearly seven years passed by happily taking care of our

daughter. I decided to leave my job and start a business of my own. We moved to a different and new city. A new city but close to one we stayed before. I started my business there. We admitted our daughter in the first standard of Zilla Parishad (ZP) school (school run by the local administration). Self-defense classes for Judo and karate were being held on the school grounds. I admitted her in these classes with the permission of the coach with the aim that she would be able to defend herself in the future. My heart swelled with pride and I had tears of joy when she won a gold medal in karate competition in the second standard. She never looked back after that. Along with her education she became a Black Belt (First Dan) in Karate and went to Nepal for an international competition. Along with that she completed her professional course [D. Pharm]. Our financial condition was bad at this time but a benefactor helped us. He was like an angel. I have no words to express my gratitude to him. I salute him.

These years passed by quickly and we lost track of how fast she grew up. In our eyes though she was always a little girl. She was never demanding or obstinate. God should bless all parents with such children.

Over the years we didn't realize how things changed, our roles reversed, and instead of us taking care of her she started taking care of us. We were proud of this change in her. Our daughter grew up slowly, she had almost completed her education now we were thinking of her marriage. But... To get our daughter married meant we had to disclose her adoption to the bridegroom's family as she had to share her future with this family. Just as it was necessary to tell the bridegroom's family, so was it necessary to tell our daughter about her adoption. She had never heard about her adoption from me. Her mother had given her some idea indirectly.

Actually we should have told her together as her parents but I could not gather the courage for it. We did not want to hurt her with this information. I then took the help of the Director of the Adoption Agency. They called us and gave her some ideas in general about the children in the children's home and adoption. They told us to go home and gave us guidance on how to explain adoption to our daughter.

Even then for a week I could not bring myself to share this fact with my daughter. Finally with a heavy heart and with a big lump in my throat I did share her adoption story with her. With tears flowing she hugged us both and told us that you are my mummy and papa, I don't care about anything else. My birth parents may be rich or millionaires but I will never leave you and go anywhere. I will not get married and leave you. In fact, I will look after you as a son. And then she hugged us both and cried.

We explained to her that it is the duty and responsibility of every girl's parents to get her married and settled in life. Soon we started getting marriage proposals for her. But as soon as the prospective groom and family were informed about her adoption they would start making excuses like 'we will let you know', or, 'my father is against it', 'uncle says no' or 'mother has refused'. Such rejections came from well-educated families. These responses and reactions do not suit families who claim to be descendants of reformers like Mahatma Phule or Savitribai Phule. They have no right to claim such heritage and should not do so.

Any way we started looking for grooms from inter-religious inter-caste communities. In the process a boy from a cultured family asked for her hand and we got them married. The boy is good and the parents-in-law are also good. Once again the benefactor, our angel stood behind us and supported us. We will be forever indebted and grateful to him. God bless him with a long and healthy life.

Today when the world is in turmoil with the COVID-19 pandemic, our daughter calls us every day and asks us how we are doing. When she calls us with such deep concern for us we feel that our life is truly blessed and meaningful.

Our daughter has given us a beautiful and smart grandson. When he lisps and calls us Aaji, Baba we feel very happy and satisfied. If we had not taken this decision at the right time who would have called us Mummy, Papa, Aaji, Baba?

There is just one thing I would like to say based on my experience and that is do not regret that you cannot bear a child and do not feel guilty about it. Consider this to be God's wish and adopt a child. Believe that this is God's Grace and His blessing for you to go into parenthood by a different path. This child is as much your own as any biological child, for you to love and take care of. You will find Heavenly happiness in this. The right values and upbringing can make a girl or boy an ideal child. Without any doubts in your mind, don't bother about society, learn to swim against the tide and abundant happiness will be yours!

TOMMY'S TREE

I have recently celebrated an important landmark— my Eightieth birthday. Perhaps I have been blessed with such a long life because my warm hearted wife and I lived close to nature surrounded by forests and hills in a beautiful landscape. Yet these forests were also home to restless rebels like the Naxalites. As a journalist and a professor whose field was national service development, I interacted with their children as well as many other angry and restless youth, ruffians and goons. It was my task to reach out to them, alter their misguided perceptions and bring them on a harmonious path through counselling and support which they so greatly lacked. I had nearly 150 students a year under the National Service Plan, for nearly 20 years.

The students realised that I, Sir, was always supportive, fair and just. I gained their trust and brought them on a positive track with positive social values, steering them away from drugs, alcohol, violence etc. In all my efforts I was supported by my wife who was also dedicated to the cause of upliftment of troubled youth.

So engrossed were we in our mission and interaction with such a wide range of people that we somehow filled the gap of our involuntary childlessness. Our sorrow became secondary to the involvement with our work. However, as our youth began slipping away, friends urged us to think about adoption. It was a thought but we did not make any effort towards this.

An eye surgery took me to a big city for treatment. It was through this medical institute that we were directed to visit a children's institution nearby. As a journalist and a professor it was very interesting to understand the circumstances of children in institutional care. But as a prospective adoptive parent I had some reservations. We were not young, did we have the energy and the capacity to parent a little kid with a traumatic history?

Anyway we went through the required process. We learnt about a 4 year old boy with a very unusual life story at this institute. Gopal was born to a young mother who was the secret partner of a well-respected medical professional. She worked as his secretary and from their affair the little boy was born. He funded her luxurious needs and when he refused to indulge her she threatened to inform his wife about their relationship and their child. She wanted him to leave his wife and when he did not agree she went and told the wife that her husband and she had a son. It was a very painful and complicated triangle of which the little boy was the victim.

Gopal lived with his mother and knew little about his shadowy father. His mother took him to all kinds of places of luxurious dining when she went out at night. The father said this was not good for the little boy and the best option for all concerned would be to relinquish his custody so that an adoptive family could be found with whom he could have a stable life.

The relinquishment was very traumatic for Gopal. His mother was sad but tough. His father was practical. It was traumatic for the institution to handle the ocean of grief this little boy suffered due to the unstable life of his parents. He was a stranger in an institution. He could not settle down to group care and wept for his beloved mother. The institute placed him in foster family care and there he began to settle down, go to school and take part in family activities. He was a very intelligent kid who even told the agency doctor how an injection should be given. He was well versed in the medical profession.

We felt a connection to Gopal the very first time we set eyes on him. Once the adoption was finalised we began our preparation to take him back with us. When we were about to sit in the rickshaw to go to the station, the Rickshaw driver started the engine. Gopal screamed in fear and distress, shouting, "Please don't leave me!" We were shaken by the depth of his anxiety.

His outburst was the fear of abandonment which he had repressed till now. He was sweating heavily and his new mother, my wife, held him close to her heart and comforted him. Even today we have not forgotten the sadness in his eyes. In the night during our journey he kept waking up and groping for a touch of his mother.

Our long journey by train to our home was over. We took a rickshaw from the station. The Rickshaw stopped and the curious children in our neighbourhood surrounded us. We introduced Gopal to them and told them that he would now live with us forever. The circle surrounding us was that of the middle class and poor children but they had rich minds. The parents too were warm hearted. These children looked after Gopal like an elder brother. Even now Gopal and these adults (who were young then) are his friends. Gopal played, laughed and was obstinate like any other child. But his mind seemed uneasy.

One evening Gopal was playing with a train and a toy joker was beating a drum. Girl friends were present with their dolls. Just then a guest asked him a lot of inquisitive questions: What was his real name? What was his hometown? What was his father's name? And such probing questions. It was unexpected. Gopal was very upset and could not control his anger. He threw the train down forcefully and broke it. He also banged the joker on the ground. He felt humiliated and provoked and ran out of the house. We watched calmly. Two of Gopal's friends ran, one before him and one behind him. I too, followed them at some distance. After some distance had been covered he slowed down a little as it was getting dark and the boys lifted him in their arms and brought him back. When Gopal was home he lifted the broken joker in his hands and caressed him many times. After a little while he hugged his mother.

Barring some such exceptional undesirable incidents, time passed by happily. His friends took good care of him. He too was completely engrossed in their company. One day Gopal asked his mother if she ate non-vegetarian food. Both of us were vegetarian. Gopal said that the next door neighbours were cooking mutton and he loved mutton. His mother asked him if he would eat mutton. He said yes, he used to enjoy it with his birth mother. From that day Gopal and his father too ate mutton. His father stopped eating it only when Gopal grew up.

A Government Blind School was near our home. We were always invited to the programs of this Blind School. The blind, disabled, orphans of this school got to know Gopal. Some of them became his friends. This Blind school opened his eyes to another dimension of life. It made him mentally strong and he was able to bear sorrow, disdain and derision after getting to know their world of darkness. Every year on his birthday we invited these students from the blind school to a party celebration. We served them with a feast and Gopal and his friends served them according to their capability.

Through my profession I also travelled a lot to interesting projects and places, sometimes to give a lecture or as a chief guest. I made it a point to take Gopal with me. In this way he developed a lot of exposure to real life and was shaped by these experiences and influences.

Ever since Gopal became our son we found that he was attracted to churches. I took him to church every Sunday. Gradually our visits to the church stopped. We had decided to admit him to a church school. The well-educated Principal of this school was my student but Gopal did not take to her and he was drawn to a Principal of another well known school. Here he got fully engaged with his studies. He was a very bright and outstanding student, well ahead of his class and the only one fluent in English! We tried as far as possible to be very considerate to his feelings and sensitivities, even though it meant a great deal of adjustment on our part.

It was the month of May in Vidarbha, a year after we had brought him home. Gopal had fought with his mother in a pillow fight which became quite violent as he had become hysterical, punching the pillow to release some great emotion. After the release he experienced, he dropped off to sleep. Just then in the afternoon, his biological father called us. He informed us that Gopal's mother had passed away. The circumstances were tragic.

When Gopal awoke we gave him the sad news. Gopal demanded we should call his father. At that time mobiles did not exist so we called his father on the landline. Gopal asked him what had happened. At his father's reply he banged the phone down. He was very distressed. After some time he went and hugged his mother. Later on an unusual thing happened. Gopal took the photo of a woman in an advertisement to be his mother. When we contacted the big company in Mumbai and requested for a photo of that woman, the company complied and sent Gopal a big photo of that model who perhaps resembled his attractive mother. For many days he looked for his mother in that photo. In this way the emotional upheavals went on in his life.

At the same time we continued our efforts to nurture and heal him. We were very honest with him and discussed everything openly. Due to this he developed great trust in us. We made special efforts to promote Gopal's love for reading. When he grew up he became interested in a library. He started reading various newspapers in Marathi, Hindi and English language. Later on he started discussing the news or articles, even those that his father had written. In one such discussion on the Mahabharata, he blamed Kunti for leaving Karna to die when she could have given him in adoption to another family. Anything could have happened to Karna in the rapidly flowing river Ganga, he said with great feeling.

I had been invited to give a lecture in a university back in the city where we had adopted Gopal. My wife expressed her wish that I should take Gopal with me to meet his father. Without informing him, I had met his father before and we had shared experiences and talked about his health, medicine, his likes and dislikes and many things concerning him. I had also acquired a photograph of Gopal's mother from his father. Every year the photo is brought out on the occasion of Akshay Trutiya to offer prayers for his mother.

We stopped to see Gopal's father. Gopal refused to go out with his father, but on our return when we were about to leave, he hugged his father and cried. He expresses his hurt that his "father too left him". On his own he never talks to his father but we have still not stopped trying as it is important for his healing.

Gopal had many school friends. He was very popular. I was presented with a Tibetan puppy by a Tibetan man. Gopal was fond of this puppy who was named Tommy. For the three or four years of his emotional turmoil, Tommy's company helped him to deal with his problems. When Tommy died Gopal and his friends buried him and planted a laburnum (Amaltash) tree over his grave, as we had also planted one as a memorial to his mother. Today this tree of golden yellow flowers is called Tommy'sTree.. In this way we supported Gopal's emotional journey.

For the first two years our Social Worker was carefully watching Gopal and us. She visited our home twice. We invited her for our adoption enlightening workshop as the chief speaker. Many parents desiring to adopt attended this workshop in large numbers. It was published and praised in all the Newspapers of our city. Those parents desiring to adopt felt motivated.

Gopal talks of the influence of the 'cultural camps' on him. Cultural camps gave him confidence and eloquence. Many children due to lack of funds cannot attend these camps, he said. To overcome this deprivation, he approached his parents, us, and that year we organized a free Summer Camp for children who could not pay. Many well known experts, people fully dedicated from various fields like dancing, poetry, story narrating, craft, drawing, yoga, writers, and group singers offered their free services to the camp.

Many people who are holding high posts today say that they are in these posts because of these camps they attended. During last year's puja, we celebrated veneration of parents in the camp. 'Support of parents' was the subject and Gopal spoke openly about his biological mother and his parents, giving several examples. The whole camp was moved. This year for the first time in 30 years we could not hold the camp due to the coronavirus.

Gopal's school years were happy and successful ones. He loved to study and had a special skill of conveying a lot of meaning through a few words. He loved reading. He participated in the competition of 'Kishor' magazine in the 9th standard and won the first prize. He was not arrogant because of his success. He had self-restraint and was curious. He loved to serve others and detested dishonesty and this nature made him a favourite of all the teachers. Gopal's 10th and 12th standard results were excellent and we wanted him to be a Doctor. But he did not want to follow in his birth father's footsteps. He chose IT (Information Technology).

For his I. T. Course he was in a famous university in a different city. In his very first year he met a classmate called Suma. They were both very good in studies. Both lived in a hostel and both proved to be good study partners in their studies. During holidays when Gopal came home Suma accompanied him. From a friend Suma became his fiancé. He talked to his mother about how they would marry later on and how Suma would go against her parent's wish and marry him. He firmly convinced his parents. His mother kept warning him that girls and boys may change sometimes and he should not get carried away. Suma's parents knew us but did not visit us very often. Gopal and Suma both graduated with good marks and both got jobs in different cities in America. They used to spend holidays together and visited different places for three years. They spent an intoxicated life of happiness. When Gopal and Suma left for America, Suma's parents were also there to see her off. But there was no mention of marriage.

Gopal was keen to settle in America. He wanted us to live with him there but we firmly refused and Gopal respected our wishes. Soon we started receiving many marriage proposals for Gopal. But he wanted to marry Suma. When we asked for her hand in marriage for our son, her parents refused. Suma too, did not have the courage to defy her parents. It was a blow to our son. Gopal knew that we stood firmly behind him at such a time. His friends saw him through this difficult time. But Gopal recovered and the Suma chapter was closed forever.

We had been receiving many marriage proposals for Gopal both within and out of our caste. Many of the parents of the prospective brides would visit us but before this we were not sure what to say to them. But now things were clear. Gopal's choice among the many alliances was Supriya. She belonged to our caste and came from a good, well settled family. She was a Science graduate. We informed her father and maternal uncles that our son was adopted. But Supriya's father replied that he was not addicted to alcohol and was a promising boy so they had no objections. The marriage was held with full fanfare. Soon Supriya got a job in the same well known IT Firm as Gopal.

We live with our son. His mother takes care of their five year old son and he is nurtured as well as Gopal was, by his mother. It was that unconditional love and nurturing that went a long way to help our son grow into a strong young man who is able to deal with all challenges of life.

Gopal is proud of both of us. He looks after us with warmth and care. We were at peace all our lives and accepted all the experiences in a calm manner. It is due to our attitude that even when I am 80 years and my wife too is getting on in age, we continue to be in good health.

I recall an incident when I was 75 years old and was awarded a prize for journalism at the state level. To receive this prize I had to go very far on a long and tedious train journey. I had fractured my leg but still had a strong desire to go there. It was a difficult journey but Gopal encouraged me and took me and his mother there, taking good care of us throughout. During the railway journey I had a flashback of a scene from another railway journey we had made together a long time ago with a baby boy in our arms. Today Gopal was making the railway journey with us two 'babies' holding on to his capable and caring arms, like the legend of Shravan Baal who carried his aged parents on a pilgrimage in two baskets when they were old and infirm..

ANIMALS ARE FAITHFUL

Alisha: "He came from your tummy and I did not come from your tummy that's why you scold me"
Me: "Why did I scold you now? Tell me."
Alisha: "Rikshani Uncle has come and I am not ready?"
Me: "Is he ready?"
Alisha: "Yes"
Me: "If you had been ready would I have scolded you?"
Alisha: "Um....no."
Me: "Now do you understand why mummy scolded you?"

In the above incident Alisha is 10 years old, about to go to school. We have adopted her into our family. When she joined our family she was six months old. Her older brother Amish was three and half years old. Amish is our biological son. In our family the two of us, both sets of grandparents, and maternal uncle are all highly educated.

When I was studying in college I had this idea that I would have one biological child and adopt the second. It became a reality as my partner in life wholeheartedly supported my view. We all owe our society some positIve contribution, to pay back our debts as well as to satisfy our self-interest. As we had a boy the other one had to be a girl and adoption helped us fulfill our intention.

We were on the lookout for families who had the same intentions and found out about their experiences. Luckily the Adoption Agency referred us to two such families. The meetings gave a reality orientation and helped strengthen our decision to adopt.

Our only criteria was to adopt a girl between 3 to 6 months of age and whose medical information at the time of birth was available. Our Adoption Agency took care of the remaining procedures and we brought our Alisha home, thirty years ago.

Before we brought her home we took our son, Nilay along to introduce him to the baby and as a way of preparing him to accept her as his sister when she joined our family. The grandparents also visited Alisha. Nilay was very happy to see Alisha. The first time he saw her she was wearing a pink dress so for a long time he would refer to her as 'pink baby'.

In his joy he declared to our neighbours that we are getting a 'chakuli' (baby) home. They thought he was very young and joking. Who can 'get' a baby anywhere?!

In the Institution the baby had a different name. We had decided before when Nilay was born that if it is a boy he would be named Nilay and if a girl was born she would be Alisha! So the name of the baby had already been decided.

My brother and my mother had accompanied us to bring Alisha home. My father came the next day. Many of our friends too visited us out of caring, love and curiosity. The neighbors understood the meaning of 'baby'. Immediately they took her to their homes and in their own way welcomed her... And later on she became their darling.

Both the grandfathers were overjoyed to bring the baby home sharing the news with whomever they met! In the end we had to ask them to stop informing everyone, as it might prove troublesome for her later on. My mother was afraid about what will happen if someone exercises their rights on her later in life. But when we told her that everything is legally done her mind was put to rest. My mother-in-law however was always against our idea of adopting the second child. Even as our daughter grew up well integrated with the family, she did not accept this child of unknown blood and caste. She quite obviously differentiated between our biological son and adopted daughter. Thankfully, no one else did.

For six months Alisha probably found it difficult to adjust to all the changes including her new name. She did not sleep well at night, and was constantly uneasy. As a result her health suffered. She often had diarrhoea, her hands and feet had rashes. For the first two months it seemed as though her growth was stunted. There was no growth in the tiny teeth that had appeared. She was rocking to and fro but not moving forward. After that suddenly there was a growth spurt. It was so fast that at 11 months she was running all by herself!

She would have convulsions when she had fever as a baby. She continued having those till she was five years old. Whenever she ate mithai (sweets) she had diarrhoea. Between the age of three and three and a half she had three big accidents.

Once she fell down from the slide and broke her collarbone; another time she got a deep cut on her left forehead while playing at home, and then later on she again suffered a deep cut on the right forehead while playing outside. Around that time her K. G. Teacher noticed she seemed short sighted. Her eyes were checked and it was found that she had a distance vision problem and had a high number. She was hyper active both at home and in school. She had almost completed her Mini Kg but the school informed us that she could not recognize alphabets. We should try teaching her at home and they would re examine her and if she passed she could go to the next class. We taught her at home and she started recognizing them well and she was admitted to the next standard.

We noticed once she wore spectacles her problems of learning alphabets, accidents and her instability disappeared. These problems were probably related to short sightedness. She has a very high number and wears contact lenses now.

In those days, the schools would generally give admission to the younger sibling as a practice. This was not the case in Nilay's school. But once the school knew that Alisha was adopted she was given admission immediately.

Alisha was 4 or 4&1/2 years old when she saw her school friend's pregnant mother. When she came back from school she wanted to know if she too had come from my tummy. I shared with her the information by telling her she had not come from my tummy but from some other mother's tummy. This answer satisfied her for the time being but somewhere in her mind she had made a note of it. Later on when she was 15/16 years old she started bombarding us with enigmatic questions. The example mentioned earlier was one such example.

She saw an adopted daughter of our friend having a convulsion. On our way home she asked me if all adopted children have convulsions? She was sounding us out, (evaluating our reactions?) Around the time she was in 9th or 10th standard she had understood completely what adoption meant. She, however, seemed to have accepted the fact of her adoption. In fact she went as far as bragging about her being adopted. Or it may have been a defense mechanism to hide her nervousness. She teased Nilay that you were born to Mummy and Daddy but I am special as I am the chosen one! In a family function she made a cousin cry by saying I have two mothers but you have only one!

From time to time she went through some medical problems. Many times while playing roughly she broke her bones, and for some time she had to be on medicines for depression. She has to take thyroid medication for the last 4/5 years. There was no obvious trigger for her depression. However the psychiatrist explained that there are certain key points in an adopted person's life when old traumas may resurface. At these times growing adoptees are prone to depression... adolescence, childbirth and menopause being a few of those points.

From her childhood she suffered from an inferiority complex as she had a darker complexion than our family members. She had also asked if her mother had rejected her because she was dark and I used to tell her that her mother had some problem and could not care for her. She was helpless and so she had to give you up to the institution. She did not reject you. I wanted to make her feel that she was not rejected.

Around that time she had asked me if we could meet her 'first mother' and I told her that once she was 18 years old and was wise she could talk about it to the Adoption Agency. Then she asked me if I would accompany her and I said 'yes', but after that she never brought up the topic again.

To convey the fact of adoption to a child is a long drawn process and one can't say how much time it will take. It depends on person to person. It depends on how well the child has accepted and adjusted to the fact that these are my parents and this is my family.

Alisha has a good I. Q. It is above average but she was not interested too much in studies. She believed that school was only a place where she could meet her friends! Later on she acquired a degree but she was not engrossed or interested in the stream she had graduated in. She chose a different line altogether which really she had interest in the care of dogs. We let her join a course so that she could turn this into a profession. During her training she met a young man in whom she was interested. They became quite close, but his parents came to our house and expressed their disapproval of this match. It could have been because she was adopted. Another relationship also fell through because the boy was pursuing her knowing that her father is well placed in his profession. Seeing many young people struggling with broken relationships she decided that marriage is not for her. She is now independent, has got a dog and lives separately. It may be difficult to trust a man. But, as she sees it, you can always trust a dog to be loving and faithful.

FULFILLED

Our only expectations while adopting a child was that the child should match our family. More importantly, our concern was that the child should resemble both of us, the adoptive parents. Further, that the child should be normal. We did not feel the need for any information on the birth mother or background of the child.

We were clear that we wanted only a daughter! Those were times when the birth of a girl was not celebrated, and we thought it would be of value if we opted for a girl child. We wished for a child who was within 6 months of age so that she would be able to adapt with ease into our family.

My mother-in-law was the one first to suggest adoption. She was open-minded, unlike many people of her generation. Our friends who had adopted children and people from other NGOs helped us in the process of adoption and gave us much needed support.

Can there be any process for forming an attachment with a baby? There was only one difference in the process of attachment to our daughter, which was that the child was not born to us. Our daughter was only five months old when she came home. She now had two people to love her and take care of her and we now had her as the baby we had longed for. So, we bonded from day one. The love flowed between us.

Our neighbours had all readily accepted her. My sister,

mother, mother-in-law and others accepted her without much objection. Only my older brother-in-law, who has two daughters, remarked that if we adopted a boy, his daughters would have had a brother of their own to tie a rakhi.

Being adoptive parents, we never really thought about her birth parents. We just accepted her as our baby who came from a different route into our lives. Where she came from was not of any relevance to us. She was our daughter.

The parenting journey poses some challenges for all parents. There were a few minor incidents as we raised her. Sometimes we solved those issues on our own and sometimes our very concerned family friend helped solve them. Now there are no more issues between us.

Although we were aware that children could face and display many behavioural issues in their teens, we were fortunate that our daughter was reasonably balanced and calm. She never indulged in habits which we did not approve of. She never stole, was never violent and did not have any addictions. We don't think she suffered from buried emotions like feelings of rejection or loss. She did not brood over her past, to the best of our knowledge, and accepted her life as it was.

The big issue we faced was that she did not study. She enjoyed playing with her friends all the time. She would say she was getting bored at home. When I would tell her that the friends you play with are not going to be around during your exams to help you, she would think that I was comparing her with other children. This would distress her, but in truth, we were not comparing her to the other girls, we just wanted her to do well for her own sake.

However, in school, she was considered to be a slow learner and was taught in a separate batch. This made both her and I feel bad. It affected her self-esteem. But in order to get out of that situation, she needed to study. In spite of explaining this to her, she was not able to understand and accept that she needed to put much more effort into her studies. She did not understand what was meant by comparison. We never told her that a certain child has got so many marks so you should also get such marks.

Her drawing was very good but despite that, it was very difficult to prepare her for the drawing exams. After school, she concentrated on her studies and worked hard in college. Finally, she got a degree in Fine Arts. She worked very hard; she did a course in Graphic Designing. She completed her MA in Indology. She worked for three years at a firm.

At present, she is freelancing. This is not a satisfactory career journey, but she is proficient in her job and does good quality work. While she was working, one of her projects got the first prize! Because of that award, she got the opportunity to participate in the Arts Festival at Cannes in France every year. Another of her projects won the second prize. We were so happy to see her talents unfolding and receiving recognition. Art is not an easy or lucrative career. In spite of her efforts and her talents, she is still not financially independent and that is a little worrying for us as her parents.

Overall, our parenting journey through the path of adoption has been satisfactory. We faced challenges similar to those faced by any other 'normal' parents, those who gave birth to their children. In our unique path to parenthood, we developed a deeper understanding of love and life. We feel fulfilled as parents and as a family, our life together has been happy!

BROKEN TRUST

My husband and I were both professionals. We lived in a metropolitan city and had demanding careers.

Our respective careers took us into parallel worlds.

When we met at home after long days in the office we were often quite fatigued. We did not really think about having children due to our career demands. However the extended family urged us not to wait too long and to start thinking about parenting. A biological child did not happen perhaps because of our stresses.

We were into middle age when we took the tentative decision to adopt a child, preferably not an infant.

Our search led us to an institution for children. A little girl about three years old, had been found at the railway station. Her parents could not be traced through all the efforts made by authorities. We heard her traumatic background story and expected to meet a pathetic looking child. Instead we were introduced to a rosy cheeked, smiling little girl. In no time she became our girl.

She came home to us and life suddenly became very different in our previously empty and childless home. I had to cut down on my career and focus on our newly arrived daughter. She was rather easy and adjusted to us very smoothly. Surprisingly she even seemed to develop trust in us, which we had heard could be a long process for children retrieved from trauma. Our daughter had a special bond with my husband, her new father. Perhaps she also retained a good memory of her birth father, though she never recollected her past.

There was quite a big age gap between my husband and me. Along with that gap our careers also took us on separate paths in which we met diverse people. In time I came to realise that my husband was seeing another woman professional with whom he shared a lot in common. This was painful knowledge for me but I went along with it as I did not want to upset our home life. My daughter was growing up well and nearly approaching the teens, an age at which an unsettled family would have hurt her a lot. Rather sadly I told myself that my very handsome husband would of course be happy with this beautiful woman. In comparison I was quite ordinary. I was not depressed but sad.

One day in the course of their common work, my husband and this woman had gone on a long car drive. I got a phone call in the afternoon that the car had met with an accident. I went to the hospital but it was too late to see him. He had passed away. The woman had escaped with some injuries, but she was also in shock.

My daughter came home from school to the horrifying news of her father's death. She was completely devastated.

I had to work very hard after that, seeing to his work which was in a mess. There were big loans and hardly any money in his account. Perhaps he had given away most of his savings to the woman. It was my task to clean up both his business affairs and his personal affairs. I had to stand on my feet and prepare to support our 12 year old daughter who had been brought up so far with all that money could buy.

My mother moved in and I spent long hours in his office. To compensate for my absence I bought material gifts for my daughter hoping it would fill the gap this tragedy had created in her life. She cried heartbreakingly for the father she had tragically lost.

In school too, she could not focus and spent much of her time crying. One fateful day, trying to console her, a close friend asked her, "Why are you crying so much? He was not your real father anyway"

I was in my office when my little teen came home from school early, phoned me and demanded, "Come home. I want to see an album of my baby photos!"

I understood what had happened. Someone had told her that she was adopted. We had not yet shared this fact with her. Somehow we thought she was aware of it as she had come to us as a three year old, not a baby. We postponed discussion about adoption till a future date. But life does not wait.

When I came home I finally had to share her adoption story with her. She cried. I cried. We both were in grief..deep grief. The losses were too many.

She lost not only a series of her family members - both birth family and adoptive family - but she lost something very valuable. She lost her trust in us, in her life. If her parents could not have been truthful then who in this world could she trust?

After that day our relationship went into a terrible storm.

Some days she was soft and sweet but other days she was rude and aggressive. Daily her demand for material gratification increased. I had to work harder and harder to fulfill her growing needs.

As she grew up further, it got worse. She became out of control and violent. The violence became so severe I used to lock myself up in one room to keep safe from her abuse. I sought help but she would either put up a very sweet and docile front to people or lock herself in her room refusing to meet them.

She developed relationships with rather weak boys whom she could control. She also seemed to support and nurture them or manipulate them with material gifts which they could not afford. Her only relationship was with these friends who were not of our social level.

I continued to spend on her to meet her extravagant demands, just to buy myself peace, but it did not end there. Peace never followed. She was interested in the contents of my Will and I even thought of dis-inheriting her. But of course I did not. Instead I have poured in all my earnings to give her higher education of the best quality. I still hope and pray that she will come out of this chronic state of anger and depression and build a new life for herself.

She is a young adult now. With all the difficulties I have faced she still remains my daughter.

HEAVENLY BLESSING

OUR DECISION TO ADOPT

My wife and I were inspired to adopt after the birth of our biological son, Soham. My wife's cousin had initially adopted so we were familiar with the concept. Being from a Koregaon in Satara district we wanted to gauge the reaction of the people around us. We started asking around in our family and friend circle and we got a strong, positive reaction. We felt relaxed but no-one in our vicinity had done something like this. As the word spread, the way it usually does in small towns, we got a surprisingly encouraging response. Everyone looked at us as if we were doing a great deed by providing a home for an orphaned child. We simply replied by saying that we need the baby in our lives more than the baby needs us.

We were very specific in our preference for a girl child. As we had a biological son, Soham, we wanted the perfect balance to create our family of 4. We wanted to make sure that Soham wouldn't feel neglected with the upcoming arrival of the baby, so we made some preparatory arrangements. We invited our in-laws to help us out and it was a good decision as grandparents have a lion's share in raising both our kids. After all the procedures, our baby Radha finally came home.

EARLY STAGES AND EDUCATION

I worked as a professor in a senior college hence, my routine really suited the kids' needs. My wife has completed her B.Ed. and used to take tuition classes from around 8am-11am. She used to make everyone's food before her classes and then

I used to help get the kids ready. I used to give them their baths, comb and braid Radha's hair, fill their lunch boxes etc. For the longest time my daughter thought I cooked the meals as well and she used to rave about it to her teachers. In the evenings, my wife had her evening lectures so when I came back from the college, I used to join the kids for their after-school activities. It may come off as rather unconventional for the father to do such things, but I am very happy that I got the opportunity to do it all.

Soham was initially enrolled in a convent school. It was a really rigid and disciplinarian school. We enrolled Radha in a Marathi medium school and later felt that both our kids should receive equal education. We moved Soham to Radha's school and he was much relaxed in the new environment and blossomed there. Radha had to take a lot more efforts than Soham in her studies. The hard work took a little longer, but she is diligent. She has that strong will that makes her take the necessary effort. She used to have a tough time in memorising concepts, but the correct nutritious diet helped her overcome it to some extent. Radha has always been much more athletic than academic. She excelled in whatever sport she took up and even represented her school at district-level competitions.

After school, she finished her undergraduate degree in Koregaon itself and started her PG Diploma in the nearest big city. She used to travel everyday by the state transport, she was so determined about the diploma that she didn't see the travel as a challenge. Due to her interest in sports, she wanted to move to Patiala to pursue her passion further. We weren't fond of the idea of her moving so far away from us. Incidentally, she found out a residential course about Yoga-therapy in the same city as the PG Diploma and we encouraged that whole heartedly. During the course, she had to re-sit an exam and she was very upset about it. We convinced her that it is Yoga-therapy, and it has medical purposes, thus she has to be perfect in it, thus, it is infact a good opportunity that she has to give the exam again. Being a level-headed person, she immediately got the point and was excited about the course again.

TELLING RADHA ABOUT HER ADOPTION

When Radha started 6th grade, she became quite mature and understanding. We got home a puppy for the kids, but she was never too fond of it like everyone else. We started explaining the concept of adoption through the puppy's story. We told her to look at how the puppy was away from its mother and now our family was responsible for raising and taking care of it. The puppy was living happily with us and we were very happy to have it in our home. This way we conveyed it to her that the birth-giver is important, but the caretaker is much more important. Once she understood the concept of adoption, she wanted to know if the people in our family were aware about it. She was told that everyone was aware, and we pointed out how it is not an issue for anyone. Everything depends on our perspective and we loved kids and simply wanted a sister for our son. Nothing else matters to us or our family, they love her just as much as her brother. There was only one hiccup where she used to feel bad about her height. Everyone in our family is quite tall and she's 5'1. She used to feel a little left out, but I pointed out many people around us and the extended family who are short as well and it stopped being an issue in her mind. Since then, everything has been on the positive end of things.

HEALTH

In terms of her health, she has had a healthy growth and

was very athletic so she made sure she stayed fit and in good health. She would need her mother every time she needed to get a vaccination as she was quite afraid of them. Radha's already made her mother promise that when she gets pregnant, her mother has to stay with her the entire 9 months of the pregnancy. She used to get a lot of abdominal cramps during her menstruation and we used to get worried. During her PG Diploma, when she used to travel to the big city, we were very extremely worried for her wellbeing, but her determination helped her through the travels. She learnt a lot about the world through those travels and meeting people from all walks of life truly enriched her personality.

MARRIAGE AND FUTURE

Both our kids got married through an online matrimony service. Radha is a very charming girl and wins over everyone around her. She is still connected to friends from her nursery school. We had around 1000 people in her wedding because she holds everyone close to her heart and could not bear to leave anyone out. We advised her to prioritise her in-laws after her marriage and not her social circles, but she has won them over as well and is loved by everyone wherever she goes. Soham is happy as well but we haven't been able to judge our daughter-in-law's personality. It still appears as a big mystery and now she's trying to create some issues between the siblings related to the adoption. Our whole family has put the adoption so far in the past that we don't understand how it matters in the present day. Soham promises he has everything under control.

Apart from that, we are very happy about our decision and thanks to Radha we could complete our little heaven and give it a meaningful balance. We would recommend the process to everyone out there looking to complete their heaven.

THE MOST NATURAL BOND

We brought home my brother Aditya when he was one and a half years old and I was six and a half. Apparently, I was so excited to get a baby brother that I had run around our entire neighbourhood spreading the news. As a result, not only my relatives but all my neighbours flocked to our house when baby Aditya came home. Overnight I was a 'tai', an elder sister, which was quite exciting for me. However, that was not the only change in my life.

Baby Aditya's arrival meant that all of a sudden my house, my toys, my parents, my grandparents, the love and affection I got, were not entirely mine. They were his too. I didn't see my mother's stomach grow for nine months as a natural preparation for the arrival of a baby. Instead it involved directly welcoming a baby who was already a one and a half-year-old, not an infant. Thankfully, my parents did not deem me too young and involved me as much as they could in the process of adoption.

I remember when I saw Aditya for the first time in his foster home. He came out in the arms of his foster mother with a mop of curly hair and wearing a frilly pink frock. The first thing I said about him was, "But I asked for a brother, not a sister!". The girlie frock was misleading!

The fact that I got to pick if I wanted a brother or a sister was the most exciting part of the process for me. Knowing that I had such a unique choice that no-one I ever knew had, made me feel so extraordinary and valued that I was elated by it. That made the whole process fun for me. If the choice actually existed, I don't know, but the feeling put a different spin on the situation for me.

As young siblings, it was all fun and games between the two of us, but outside of that, I've fought numerous arguments for Aditya, with our family and friends equally. With friends, it used to be some silly teasing or usual kids' stuff, but I used to get so worked up, I used to yell at them and walk off haughtily in the middle of our games. My friends were always puzzled about my reaction, but I never bothered to explain myself.

The tricky bit was at home, with our Aaji, my grandmother. She was a very loving grandmother and spoilt us with so many gifts but if she was angry it was hard to judge which nerve she'll hit. With Aditya, it was the usual scenario where she undiplomatically declared that all the good habits are nurtured (upbringing by the family) and the bad habits are nature (inherited from birth parents). I tried explaining to her that his behaviour of shouting, being mischievous are standard young boy habits but she remained unconvinced. I used to plead, shout, cry to make her stop calling him things like "ungrateful" or "showing his true roots" and such. These fights used to usually happen when my mother was in her evening clinic and it was just us kids and Aaji. I used to run myself ragged fighting for him and within ten minutes he and Aaji would be chatting amicably and watching tv again. I used to get caught in these bipolar reactions and become the only one getting very rattled and deeply upset by the fights.

My mother eventually asked me to stop getting involved and made me see that Aditya is one tough-skinned boy. Whatever impressions he had upon him as a baby, he is a fighter. He's not as sensitive and even as a nine to ten-year-old, he knew when to take things to his heart and when to blow it off. He was the perfect match against our Aaji as he gave equally unexpected reactions to her unexpected scolding. Although I have to add that this friction reflected only 10% of our Aaji. She loved Aditya quite a lot and no matter what she said at home, to the outside world she was as protective as one can be.

As I entered my teens, I became a bit of a recluse. I would stay in my room and hear our parents and Aditya laughing over something and having a happy time in general. My mind would start thinking – They are much happier without me, they don't even care that I am not in the room, they don't even miss me, they don't want me, I should stay away and let them be happy, they're a better family without me. Comparisons began in my head relating to him being the Special One who was the one they had chosen to adopt, while I was the biological one who just happened to be born.

I would spiral to this weird place where I used to think, I bet they're glad they brought him home because I'm such a grinch. I started feeling like a misfit in my family. Funnily enough, I never blamed him for anything. I always thought it to be my fault. Fortunately, as my teenage angst settled and I became a calm girl again, things went back to normal. Simple pranks didn't turn into emotional meltdowns and I was having fun again. I started purposely sticking around instead of running to my room and my parents made sure to involve me in the conversation. It happens even today that I'll hear Aditya and my mother laugh over something but now I'm glad he's the reason the atmosphere is light and humorous in the otherwise quiet family.

Growing up, in the early years, people used to be surprised when I would say Aditya is my brother. I got used to it and would immediately explain that he is adopted. It is said that over time adopted children start looking like their families. It happens because of something called 'Attunement' which explains how children learn facial expressions from their families and how they look the same because they react the same. As Aditya stepped into his teens and his facial features started changing, people said he looked a lot like our Aaji. This used to make him smile and somewhere give a feeling of truly fitting in. Additionally, he has always been insecure about his dark skin tone but our Aaji has imbibed in us that dark-skinned people look smarter and it has had a lasting effect on him.

Now he is an eighteen-year-old college-going, motorcycle -riding boy whose Instagram means the world to him. I keep teasing him about his involvement and how he goes to great lengths to keep his social media friendships. Whenever he comes to me for advice or to share something upsetting that has happened, I tell him to be honest about his feelings and not mix up being a people's person with being a people pleaser. All he says is, "How can I be rude to them? I'm never rude to anyone!". Hearing that I start teasing him about how he cannot do it to outsiders but is so comfortable with snapping at his own family. To that, he said something which left me astounded. He said, "You guys will never leave me, I know that, but they can. So that's why I'm so polite with them and try to get along with everyone". I was so surprised because in whatever articles/stories I had come across regarding adopted children, they said the opposite. I rationalised it by thinking that maybe he has successfully accepted us as his family on a deeper subconscious level and I should leave it at that.

Our relationship has taken many turns and it has really become positive in the last three years. I had gone far away for my post graduation, and being apart actually helped our relationship. I've become his secret keeper and the first person he dials for anything. He matured a lot without the presence of his elder sibling to cover for him.

Adoption has been a personal journey for the majority but when we started getting invited for pre-adoption events to share our journey, it started feeling like a fabulous story. When I used to be asked to speak as the biological child, sitting on that stage I used to feel like a mini-celebrity with everyone giving importance to me. So did Aditya and at one point it started feeling very unusual and important. That is when our mother started politely refusing to attend the events. She encouraged the institution administration to give a chance to the newer families. She very wisely took this step to keep us away from the publicity with a view to keeping us grounded.

This really helped us siblings look at our story as a 'normal' family again. Over time, it helped me refuse to look at adoption as any act of 'social service', or 'what a brave step'. Taking that appreciation away made it feel normal again and now it also feels awkward when someone appreciates the fact that our family has an adopted child. Why am I getting appreciated for loving my brother? I asked myself that question.

When I was filling in complex application forms to enter university, my father urged me to mention my adopted sibling in my Statement of Purpose for a university. It just didn't sit right with me. Adoption was an unusual route for a family with one biological child, but I did not feel comfortable mentioning it as something special anymore. I have a sibling and that is that for me. Thankfully, the people around me have a very calm attitude as well and do not fixate on adoption as something out of the ordinary.

Some may think, is this what it is? Does the adoption factor never really leave us? I think, even though it feels like it never vanishes, it only grows in positivity. Somewhere along the line of casually mentioning adoption like it is not a big deal made it easier for Aditya to own his narrative. Looking back, I don't know if all my protectiveness comes from a special place of shielding him from the possible social judgement or if it is something usual. To me, it is the most natural sibling bond ever.

There is nothing to question about the reality or the strength of this relationship.

BEYOND FANTASY - OUR ADOPTION JOURNEY

"Adoption begins with loss. There is grief and this child had to lose something before he came to us. There is no white-washing this fact." This is the first notion I share with an aspiring adoptive family. We have all moved beyond fantasy to the reality of adoption.

I usually ask my son his permission before I put anything out on our lives now. After all, he is a teen. Before I go on, a few caveats for the readers: When I say 'I', it is not only me I refer to. We are a couple and my husband is pretty phenomenal. Without his complete support and the way he stands behind me, informing himself through workshops and seminars and trusting me to summarise for him, I would be a shell of who I am. My 'I' here is mostly a 'we'. I certainly did not do this on my own.

The anonymous sharing of our story is not just about our child but about our parenting, in order to inform those who might walk parts of the same path. Anonymity has enabled us to be completely honest and protect the privacy of my son in a society which attaches stigma to some of the challenges we encountered.

Our son joined us, 16 years ago, less than a year old, a smiling, puffy cheeked baby. The first time we saw him, my husband held out his arms and the little cherub jumped into his arms with a huge grin. We went in prepared to say yes and we did. As a couple with a biological daughter, then herself under 2 years of age, we could adopt the opposite sex under HAMA. These were days before the JJ Act was enacted and we were very sure that we wanted the child to have every right he would as our legal child, just as our biological child would. Parenting a boy would be fun too, we truly had no preferences except that we would like a child who was younger than our daughter. So 'under one and a half years' was ideal in our minds.

Living where we do, we had the advantage of a couple of colleagues who were adoptive parents. They inducted us into a parent support organization that had us attend sessions by experts, experienced parents and adoptees. We thought we were prepared and I have to say, we were in a way, we knew whom to go to if we needed to. It would turn out to be 'when', not 'if'.

As a baby, he was really easy. He slept the night, falling asleep at the times the institution's shift ended, waking up really early in the mornings. He was sitting when placed, soon he started pulling himself up. The puffiness from the water retention dropped off to show us a dimpled face with the cutest smile. I have to mention here that the reason our wait was short was because several families had 'rejected' him because he was dark in complexion. Some families were themselves of the same complexion!

The kids grew up well together – two kids under 3 with diapers and toilet training and school admissions, life was hectic in the nicest way possible. Our support systems were friends, my parents and the many kids who lived around. Our son, Prateik, said large words precociously, was active, ate well, slept exceedingly well and was the baby everyone liked to notice.

When it came to school, he followed his sister into her Montessori school without much of a fuss. While she needed me to go and sit near her classroom for a few days, he walked in, holding the teacher's hand without even a backward glance. He bounced out, full of talk, every day. The first parent teacher meeting got us thinking – he had issues following rules, would get upset really quick and in general, needed more than the other kids in terms of the teachers' attention.

At home, the terrible twos had started before time and he was a dynamo. He had two settings – awake and out and nothing in-between. He was like water when you tried to pick him up, running where walking would be useful, flowing in and out of our hands without any quiet times. When the school gently pointed out what he was doing, we went to see a psychiatrist. The doctor wrote down 'borderline hyperactivity' and suggested that we talk to the Spastics Society. Not for us the hardcore stuff, we decided (a decision I stand by to date) and decided to give him activities that would help. Drums for the fingers that never stopped drumming on surfaces, swimming for the super active body and life went on like this, with ups and downs in school the whole time.

I read books, relearned what parenting we had done already, worked on my own approach based on my childhood and the unconscious parenting presets that had given me, engaged him, tired him out, sat with him, read to him and was involved without trying to helicopter to the level possible.

When Prateik entered Grade 1, suddenly there were temper tantrums, there were defiant outbursts, there were parent teacher meetings every week. We began taking him to a counselor who was an adoptive parent too. As someone working in an area completely unrelated to education or child development, I trusted her to figure it out for us. Twice a week, I would pick both kids up from school and directly get ourselves to the counseling sessions. We were interviewed together as a couple as well as individually. We had no idea what was happening inside and when I asked, I was told that it was a combination of methods. Daughter would do her homework outside the counselor's office, we would read, talk, spend time and have a good time. After all, she was a kid too, needing my attention and we made it a point every day, husband and I, to spend time with each kid separately and jointly. Looking back, I wonder how we did that but that is a habit that stood us in good stead. Now both kids think we are partial to the other, so we did do something right!

The counseling sessions carried on, with no change in school. We continued on for just under one year. In the middle of that, I was told that I was the one who needed counseling, the child was fine. I have nothing against counseling but didn't appreciate someone railroading me into it. If I had a penny for the number of times I have been told by professionals that I was the issue, I would be rich. My being the issue would have been the easier option, removing myself from the situation would have seen a change then, right? We would have at least identified the problem and be closer to a solution!

In any case, this trust was misplaced and the sessions were cut off over the phone, without even a final session. Son wasn't bothered and we were back to square one. The issues had escalated at school, all behaviour related. I would get him onto the school bus and sit on tenterhooks for that day's report. We tried many things – I read parenting books, adoptive parenting books, special education resources, asked for patterns, suggested solutions. The school was on board initially but soon, it clearly was a child they did not want to handle. There were kids with higher needs around but for some reason, this kid had the ability to push their buttons with precision. It isn't an exaggeration to say that I was close to a breakdown by this time, the benefit was that there was weight loss! We have to scrounge for the silver lining always, huh?

In the meantime, life went on with music classes and dance classes and lots of fun activities as a family. We brought home a puppy and she ended up being the best person in our family, with everyone unanimously agreeing on this! Of all that went right in our adoption journey, our pup was a big one. To be fair, I brought her home for me. I had the kids and waited until they were older, did everything to make ourselves stable so that we could have the pleasure of a dog in our lives again. This is something I recommend unhesitatingly to a family: please bring a dog home. The pup teaches like we parents never can, brings in empathy and the experience of unconditional love in a practical, everyday way that all the words, lectures and classes fail to.

By the end of Grade 2, we pulled him out of school to figure him out. The levels of anger we saw were scary. At 7 years old, we, as adults, were a bit scared of what he could and would do. In all this, mind you, not once has he been physically aggressive with his sister, through everything. He has said very scary things, stuff that it was hard to see in a child his age without wondering what his future would be.

Through all this, the one thing we did right with no second guessing and self doubt was how adoption had been disclosed to the kids. My daughter Sunaina was under 2 years of age when Prateik came home. The weekend in between our referral getting approved and bringing him home was all about getting her adjusted. She was used to seeing me pick up other children but her father picking up a child was cause for a bout of 'what the heck' crying. We went shopping on that Saturday to get the baby coming in some clothes and toys of his own, in addition to what he would share with her. The whole time, we had her carry around a doll, named it with Prateik's nickname and kept reinforcing it as our baby.

Sunaina, being who she is, this worked. It might have not for a more demanding, less adjusted and attached baby! From when they can remember, adoption was a word in their vocabulary. The first time I told the story to Prateik, he was a baby and had no idea what was being said. With all the preparation, all the reading and listening, it was an emotional thing for me and I am glad I said it to him at a time when he had no idea what was being said. I liken starting early with this versus later in a child's life to catching a stationary train to boarding a moving one. Early on, I got the chance to get many kinks out of my system and their questions came at a pace that I was confident of answering.

We told them that he was born in another aunty's stomach and came home to be our child. We tried several books but the one that felt most comfortable for us was a photo album that started from when we got married and went on to past his adoption to a few vacations we took. The day our daughter was born was there and the day he came home was there too, with the one baby picture of his we have from his first month.

Over the years, he has processed his adoption in several ways. He has asked at 4.5 years if 'she was bad', referring to his first mother. There were times when we would be just out of sight and he would have stopped to put on his shoes and he would cry, saying "I thought you left me!" He said stuff we wouldn't expect a child to say. It has been a lesson to me in how children internalize stuff. If we were not open, maybe we wouldn't have heard these thoughts. I am happy we were open though since his processing of the events in his life are critical to his well being and I would much rather start earlier than later. We speak openly of adoption in our home and despite all this, he sometimes starts off with "no offence to you or anything…". Kids worry about hurting their parents and to me, this means I need to communicate my security and comfort with him asking anything about anything, really. That's parenting, isn't it? Being secure enough to answer all questions?

As time processed, he would both feel proud AND use adoption against us. There were times when he has said that he was so upset with himself for having chosen us. It was usually when we had said a firm "NO" to something he wanted to do. We laugh it off and now he knows that it isn't a 'card' to use. Adoption just is and with its complexity and life long impact, it isn't going to win him any extra sympathy points.

Coming back to Grade 2 and pulling him out of school to figure out what the issue was, we found out that his fine motor skills were below developmental level. Through his school years, I read books on discipline and adoption, collaborative problem solving and learned that there are specific reasons behind behaviour. If someone is really resisting something, it is likely to be because it was too difficult for them. I planned a cutting activity with him and with a single tear running down his cheek, this usually angry kid revealed an important part of himself to say, "even a nursery kid can cut better than me!" We bought all kinds of scissors to provide his fingers support and learned to go to experts to help us peel back some layers on this. Occupational therapy was the answer, sensory processing difficulties being the issue.

Some 60 sessions over 3 months later, he could write and do several fine motor activities with dexterity. A child who taught himself to cycle on his own at 4 without training wheels wouldn't be the most ideal candidate to suspect motor issues. All it took was for the assessment to put him a foot off the group and the issues began to show.

This is one thing I would love for parents to know – sensory integration is how we do everything we need to in everyday life, from standing, picking something up, playing a sport and everything academic. When children face traumatic separation, nutritional deficits and other difficulties early in life, we don't know which parts of which skills are likely to be issues going forward. Checking for sensory issues early on is a great way to go – fixing anything we find is easier the younger they are, are mostly fun play activities done with a bit of conscious observation and save the child a ton of pain when they step out of the home.

This story talks a lot about Prateik's difficulties and this is a conscious choice. There is a lot out there about how fantastic the journeys are for many families. Mine too was awesome and knowing all that I do now, I would not do it differently even for a second. I would want to know more and be better prepared from the beginning though and that is the reason I have opened up about very private and personal difficulties. While adoption is wonderful, I will not gloss over the difficulties that most adoptive families deal with. When enough people don't talk, even in adoptive circles, parents feel like it is their fault, it is something they are doing that is wrong. I don't know why denial is so deeply ingrained in us on these differences. When a child has gone through tough stuff early in life, is it so hard to understand that there will be some issues to handle going forward? Does that make the child any different or any less ours and lovable?

So my son is humourous and wonderful, thinks laterally in ways that tell all of us trying to 'think out of the box' that he hasn't even seen a box, is a natural sportsman, is kind and sensitive, loves and feels deeply and is super intelligent. Right along with his difficulties that hinder his everyday relationships and make it hard for him to follow the rules, deal with authority and trust easily. If we were to unpackage ourselves, this may be our profiles too, based on our childhood history and adult experiences. We all like to think we are 'okay' despite childhoods being whacked, punished and humiliated in schools and homes. A cursory glance at the levels of anger and reaction in our streets routinely discredits this 'okay'. Many adults don't know whether they are hurt or angry and yet we expect so much more from kids.

Working on sensory skills helped him gain confidence, showed in his writing skills and helped him on several levels in school. However, he couldn't outrun his reputation, however much he tried (remembering that he is a tiny kid still and learning a few skills didn't get rid of all the other issues in one fell swoop), behaviour issues were a staple complaint. Some parts were definitely unlearned skills on his part, the rest was equally definitely a school system that wasn't going to work with him. We have come to a level where systems will work with kids who have academic issues but behaviour related difficulties are still looked on with judgement versus observation.

As things got worse and worse, we took him to a specialist in another city. We had resisted medication with all we had until now but had no real answer to her asking us why this child wasn't being given all the help he could get. He got a formal ADHD diagnosis along with medication. This was our last resort and looking back, a selfish way of being. We resisted medication from our perspective. The meds helped him and might have been even better for him, if we had taken the advice earlier on. If he needed glasses, we wouldn't have thought twice. Yes, this is medication, yes, there are likely some minimal side effects, yes, it needs thought and planning but on the other side is his well being outside, his self esteem and less hindered life in school. If I were to go back to change something, we would have started medication sooner.

The other piece of advice we received and took to heart was that he needed a different school, one where he wouldn't be marked for life from his previous behaviour. In the meantime, I went back to school myself and got certified to be a special educator. By now, it was evident that depending on others to help my child wasn't a great long term strategy. As someone unhappy in my current profession, I had no qualms trying something new and ended up loving it. That silver lining – this is a massive silver cloud for me, working through all this helped me find my calling so much later in life.

A new school closer home, professional sports and my working in the same school were our next few years. Try as we might, we couldn't stay under the radar. The behaviour difficulties continued. What also happened is that anyone could trigger him off while themselves staying under the radar. So it became fun for kids to get him angry and he would get caught every single time. He would take something to try and help someone and get reported to the teacher.

Teachers who understood and were secure themselves could work with him. With them, there were no issues, there were even amazing efforts and performances in academics and projects. He would do extra research to get a smile and nod from them. Others who wrote him off were in turn written off by him. It works for adults when they write off a kid. It doesn't work for a kid when he writes off an adult and therefore doesn't believe that they are an authority figure. Add to this underdeveloped skills in regulating emotions, a skewed sense of fair and it is a perfect storm, set up to mess with a set of parents' peace of mind!

This went on until we decided to pull him out of school. He was now 11 years old and getting hardened to being the bad kid. We wanted him to stop surviving (he was barely surviving in any case) and wanted him to thrive. His strengths were rarely the discussion, they were the small part that followed a 'but.....' with a detailed listing of his unlearned skills. What's worse, we parents were supposed to handle situations that happened in school as well. Whatever we did and practiced at home, school situations need to be handled by school authorities and hopefully those who were interested in resolving solutions, not branding kids as problems. I was sure that I couldn't handle it if he fell to pieces later on, that I would be able to pick up and piece them back, if we continued on like we had thus far.

The effect all this had on me is still evident, some 5 years after the fact. To date, when I see certain names calling me, my hands automatically shake. Once, at a dentist, the school was calling me in my professional capacity, my son wasn't even in school and my heart races, my hands shook too much to be functional and I had to calm myself down, reminding myself that he is here with me and couldn't be the reason for the call.

Any teachers and school authorities reading this, please do text before calling and give parents a chance to be prepared for the conversation. Anxious parents aren't going to be of use in any case, if you want problems to be solved. I would also suggest not calling on a Friday to set up a meeting on Monday. That weekend in between is hell.

The stress levels at home came down tremendously with homeschooling. Learning became the focus. It isn't like we didn't have issues, we did but there was flexibility and solutions for as well. My husband's words were our maxim: I don't want his schooling to interfere with his education. The past few years have been largely skills building. Sure, we have had issues with self-regulation and anger. With the lack of pressure from the schooling, he has been able to work on these skills and make strides. The plan was always to get him back to school for Grade 11 and 12.

Seeing how well things were going, I made a mistake. There was (still is) an alternative school run by a special educator. They asked for fresh reports, we gave them those. He attended school for a week before both parties agreed to attending school. This ended up being a huge mistake. The school was unprofessional in the extreme from the beginning and it isn't like my child behaved his best. However, this time around, every little thing was picked apart and it wasn't only my child who was the devil. There were complaints from teachers about him even on days when he was absent. This time though, we knew better than to suffer it for long – 6 months, including holidays before we decided enough was enough. This school has a fantastic public image and a founder who will aggressively jump at your throat at the slightest sign of an issue.

What I learned after this time was not to believe appearances or paper qualifications. Anyone who will take to publicly making the child's name known to other parents can't be a respected educator in my book. We have done everything – medication, counseling, all kinds of parenting practices, techniques like journaling, mindfulness…you name it and we have done it.

What worked best for us was sports, hanging on and telling him the truth as it is about the world, his strengths and his issues. He wants to make sport his career and we support that completely. Homeschooling helped him do that during the day and get further in his goals. We have seen and walked through clinical depression and medical issues that seem to be genetic. At certain times, it feels like we just recover a bit from a body blow and there's another waiting around the corner.

If I have to distill a few practices, maxims and my truths, they are:

Support yourselves as a couple and stand firm behind each other.
- Trauma is a real thing and shows up every day in adoptive families, whether or not we recognize it.
- Every child goes through it to some extent, different shapes and forms and while it can't be obliterated, it can be mitigated to a great extent through loving and kind parenting. The good news is that even epigenetic changes can be reversed with positive experiences in huge volumes.
- Read up about core issues from adoption to understand why taking a 'no' is hard and why trust is an issue.
- Detach a bit in order to parent better: everything isn't our fault and it isn't possible to be the parent we need to be if

we make it about ourselves.

- Alternative schooling that will give a child the time and space to catch up on skills is more important than marks based academics.
- Any and all difficulties kids have can be worked with and every child who is worked with progresses.
- Observing the difficulty in order to work with it is critical.
- A child having to deal with the impact of early childhood losses isn't an 'adoption' problem, adoption is very much still a solution.
- Adoption isn't charity, it is parenting. If charity is the motive, donating money or things is the better way to go.
- Minimizing others when they talk of difficulties doesn't make anything go away. All it does is stop people from talking. Every time I have shared, there have been a few who nodded along. Until we speak to each other and share, it feels like we are alone or the only ones with those issues.
- Adoptive parenting is different: deal with it.
- Different isn't bad, it just is. We are all different and that's the best part.
- Behaviour issues are signals that the child is finding something difficult.
- Looking at behaviour as a signal tells us that the child isn't there yet, that they will when taught.
- We need mental health specialists who see adoption as a facet to our issues. Denialism and parent blaming from professionals is a signal to us that this isn't the right person. While every issue isn't related to adoption, several are related to early childhood deficiencies and events and they need to be addressed accordingly.
- All children need to be given consistent boundaries lovingly, our children through adoption need this to experience safety.
- Placement of a child in a household is just the start of

adoption, which is a life-long journey.

- When children can, they will. When they don't, we teach.
- Thinking of the worst-case scenario and extrapolating it to the future is useless, I found out after lots of falling down, others might want to be smarter.
- Get a dog or volunteer with animals/causes that the child feels strongly about: a sense of belonging and contributing is hugely helpful.
- Sports, sports, sports or music, dance, theatre – finding the child's passion is a great way to give him/her a safe space, maybe even a potential career.
- It is important to deal with our adult issues enough to parent the child we have, not the one we wish we had.
- As a doctor recently told me: if we see anything as an elephant, it is an elephant. If we see it as an ant, it is an ant.

I write in hope that others do better than I did and I wish you all tons of fun in the journey. We are doing well now with a 16 year old dealing with uncertainty and exams in Covid times and I didn't think that was possible several times, sometimes several times in one day! He wants to go back to school next year and we work towards that, hoping that this time will be the lucky charm.

DNA

My ten year old daughter and I were sitting in bed under a warm blanket on a cold December night. We were watching a popular crime serial on TV. A baby girl was lost and later found by the police. A woman who claimed to be her mother was traced. The police said they would be conducting a DNA test to establish their connection.

My daughter asked me what DNA testing implied. I explained to her how it revealed blood ties. The next morning my daughter woke up and stated, "If I got lost the police would not be able to trace you by a DNA test."

She was my daughter by adoption. My blood did not flow in her veins. But my love did. If only there was a way to gauge the power and strength of this connection. Instead adoption is always being scrutinised to establish its reality...

'But who are your Real parents?' is a question young peers ask my daughter time and again. She came to us as an infant and transformed our lives as only infants can do. We kept in touch with the child care center from where she was adopted. I explained adoption through bedtime stories of our universally loved infant, Sri Krishna. He had two mothers. Devaki had given birth to him and Yashoda had brought him up. She put two and two together with her intelligent little brain.

"So you are my Yashoda Mother," she stated. Questions

followed. "What if my Devaki Mother turned up one day and knocked on our door? What would you do? Would you throw her out? Or would you return me to her?" She was completely tense as she awaited my reply. Neither option was acceptable to her.

"I would be happy to meet her because she is your birth mother. I would tell her she is also a part of our family circle. I would thank her for giving birth to My daughter! Sometimes two mothers are needed to fulfill the needs of one child". "So you will not send me away ever?", she asked. "Never!", was my firm reply, " We will always be together!"

Life took a tragic turn two years later when this mother and twelve year old daughter were separated by the sudden passing of the devoted mother. Her grandmother and father took over where her mother had left off. There was no DNA tie. But the ties of love are enduring…

DISMANTLING WALLS
TO LET IN DIVINE LIGHT

I am a pandit at a temple dedicated to Mother goddess. The divine Mother is known for her abundant blessings to devotees to fulfill their desires for worldly happiness. My wife and I had been married for many years without the blessing of a child. We performed all possible rituals and prayers. We fasted. Everyday of the week we invoked the planets to release us from our karmas,and fulfill our great desire and need for a child. But no child was conceived. It was a great irony that the boons Divine Mother gave to others were denied to us who served her religiously.

At the same time my wife underwent medical treatment which was very painful and even life threatening for her. She developed an emotional disorder and went into depression, manifested in total withdrawal and indifference to the family and life around her. We were not young as we had spent many years in the hope of having a child.

One day we saw a short film on television relating to adoption. We knew the producer of the programme and he referred us to an adoption agency known to him. Previous enquiries at adoption homes had been rejected because they felt we were too old to adopt a baby. This agency told us they would enlist our request for a child if we were willing to accept a child between 4 to 6 years old. We were aware that adopting an older child could be challenging as older children retained memories and already had developed in a certain way, but we had no option and had to accept this condition.

Quite suddenly we were told about a lost and found child who had been left in a timber market place. This boy was about 4 to 5 years old. All efforts to trace his family had failed. The little boy himself gave the story that his Uncle had brought him on his motorbike, asked him to get off and wait near a shop till he returned. He drove away and never returned. The shopkeepers saw him crying and took care of him. They called the police who then brought him for shelter to this institution.

He did not share his name or any other details as he was in a state of trauma and shock. After a while he did explain how his Uncle had left him. An extensive search by the police, through TV, radio and newspapers, led nowhere. He was apparently nobody's child...

He settled down in the institution and started going to school. Everyone observed that the boy was very well mannered, disciplined and sweet natured.

This was the child who was referred to us for adoption. When we went to see him he came straight into the arms of my wife. Seeing them bonding immediately I too did not waste time with too many questions and doubts. Shortly afterwards he came home to us in foster care prior to confirming the adoption.

His behaviour was very gentle, loving and cultured. We had not expected this from a child found on the street. He seemed to have been brought up in love and had positive family concepts. He settled down easily in the family and my wife and he continued to share a special bond.

Gradually, as he gained confidence he started opening up

a bit about himself. He told his mother that he loved gulab jamuns.His mother started making them regularly. They were not the best but they were made with love. One day our son gently told his mother not to take so much trouble to make this sweet. He shared that his birth mother used to make them for him as she was an expert, and both of them used to enjoy sharing the gulab jamuns. He was careful not to hurt his adopted mother's feelings.

He used to speak to us in Hindi, not in the local Marathi language. He was exceptionally well behaved. We wondered about the parents he had lost. By storytelling and paintings we got some clues about his past. My wife asked him to draw a house. He drew two houses, one small house and one big house. The big house did not have a door. There was no access. Only the small house had a door. He told his mother, 'You should also know how people live in small houses.'

At dinner time one evening he cried a lot. He said he was remembering his birth parents. "My mother used to cook very tasty food. We had a hotel where people would come to eat. But one evening when we were eating my parents had a very big fight with each other. My mother took a piece of glass and cut her wrist. My grandfather, Ajoba, came and took me away to stay with him. When we went back after a few days my house had vanished. So my Mama took me to his house. One day he took me on his scooter and left me somewhere. I lost him. I lost my house and I lost all my family. I cried loudly. The police came and took me to a shelter for care."

That was his story as he recalled it.

One day he asked his mother, "What is this bindi you put on your forehead? My mother never put on a bindi. She used to wear simple black clothes only."

He asked this new mother to remove the bindi, which was a huge challenge for my wife to comply with as a married woman could not be seen without a bindi on her forehead, according to our Hindu tradition.

Between the mother and son they came to an understanding that she would remove the bindi when they were alone at home, but outside or in the presence of others, she would put it. So half the day she removed the bindi. But if the doorbell rang, our son would run to his mother and put the bindi on her forehead before the door was opened! He was very sensitive to her needs and also remained sensitive to the mother he had lost. He revealed that violence had taken place in his home and his mother had suffered a lot. He rarely mentioned his father.

Our family used to go to the temple once a day in the early morning to offer prayers. Our son asked, 'Why do you pray only once a day, you should pray five times a day.' Then he started demonstrating how the prayers should be performed. Gradually it dawned on our family that our son was probably a Muslim, born to Muslim parents. This was a shock to us all as we were devout Hindus from a family of priests. We respect other faiths but in no way could we integrate another stream of faith into our family. Prejudices began to develop. Even my wife began to feel prejudiced against our son. The family said, we are priests of such a famous temple and now like a cruel joke we have landed up with a Muslim child! What irony! Not one of us even had knowledge of other faiths and certainly we were not open to any acceptance of such a deviation from our caste and bloodline. It was a huge crisis. This led to a lot of soul searching and many questions about Life, God, Faith, Blood, Genetics, Paap (sin), Punya (good deeds) and Karma. Suddenly I, who was an expert on religious philosophy, had no answers.

We did not know how to proceed. But we continued to look after him, though a gap had developed in our relationships. It was rather sad to see my wife's withdrawal. I did not feel the same.In spite of my deep prejudices and strong beliefs I had a love for this unusual child who had come into our lives. The question remained if he was my son or an alien who had come to mock my time tested traditional values and faith.

One day we had to make an unscheduled visit to Pune to meet a relative in a suburb. As we were walking through the narrow lanes trying to find our way in an unfamiliar area, our 'son' suddenly began to lead the way with confidence. After some further distance he began to run as though he knew the way. He was excited and very sure of where he was going. My wife and I looked at each other quite bewildered. Then we got into a panic and started sweating. How was our boy so familiar with this area?

Our panic increased. What if any of his birth family links were located somewhere in this area? Should we follow his lead back to his roots and let him go?

Was this the opportunity we needed to resolve our dilemma? Time stood still. It was a moment in Destiny. The very thought that He would abandon us was terrifying...not only for me but for my wife too. It was in that moment that we both realised that he really was Our son.

We ran to our son and told him where we had to go.
We diverted his attention and told him we needed his help to

find this relative who was sick. He turned his attention back to us and together we found our destination. We also found each other and the bond we shared.

We had been introduced to adoption on a TV show called 'Bin Bhintin Cha Ghar', meaning a Home Without Walls, without barriers of prejudice.

That was the lesson Divine Mother was teaching us through this child who did not come from his mother's womb but through her heart....teaching this life lesson to the priest who served her everyday.

We have to dismantle the walls of our false and narrow beliefs to let love—and God— enter our lives.

At last we became parents..REAL parents.

PART 4

MESSAGES FROM THE HEART

MESSAGES FROM THE HEART:
LIFE LESSONS LEARNT

The experience of parenting through adoption shared in the preceding pages has revealed some interesting patterns, reinforced some beliefs and provided us knowledge about significant issues and challenges in domestic adoption. One of the greatest challenges comes from the area of social prejudice which is encountered by each one involved in the adoption circle..the birth giving mother, the parent who could not conceive a biological child, and the very innocent child who carries the burden of prejudice in a traditional society.

Perhaps the greatest lesson learnt is the need for adoption conversations. This requires very good communication skills as well as the need to be equipped with vocabulary with which adoption related ideas can be shared.

Communication relating to adoption is not a one-time event but an on- going process of sharing information in an effective manner. Communication about the facts of adoption is not a theoretical exercise but an extremely delicate and sensitive process as per developmental stage of a child. New questions emerge as the child assimilates the complex issues of adoption with increasing maturity and understanding.

Diverse ways of communicating are needed and parents have to be resourceful and creative in their response to the child's need to understand the circumstances in which he or she came to be adopted. Parents have used fairy tales and fables to introduce adoption, particularly the stories of divine children. When it comes to the need for more factual information some parents visit the child care center from where their child was adopted. Seeing children in the institution, their own child could experience that world and receive explanations about the realities of loss of birth families and the journey to adoption.

We also see that parents who have open communication with the child impart a sense of confidence into their child as compared to those who would rather close the topic of adoption. Parental awkwardness/ secrecy in addressing the child's concerns signals anxiety.

As some parents have observed, there are no perfect answers that any adoptive parent can give relating to the child's questions or traumatic past, but at least discussions can bring concerns into the open, rather than festering inside the child.

Children who suddenly turned violent were generally those who learnt about their adoption from outside sources, very often in a twisted and unpleasant manner. Many Parents believed that they finished their job of sharing the fact of adoption once and for all and they closed the door on continuing the conversation as their children went through different stages of development. This left their growing children confused and bewildered and they did not know where to turn when their families refused to acknowledge their vital need for information and explanations about how and why they lost their birth families. Children who are not given proper explanations imagine horrific things about the reasons for their loss of blood ties. Reality is indeed very hard to accept but fantasy can be even worse as children imagine their parents must have been criminals or immoral beings. This is hardly ever the case. Single motherhood, socio-economic concerns, ill health, domestic violence and above all lack of opportunities for education and a supportive environment are the widespread underlying causes of disruption of birth ties.

The first challenging question children have asked their adoptive parents was: 'Did I come from your stomach?' The first truthful answer is 'No'. It is most challenging for parents to answer the questions which follow this reply, because it is at this point that children are introduced to Another Mother's stomach, an unknown mother.

This discussion needs to continue through many stages of growth particularly the teens. Parents are relieved when their children do not ask adoption related questions, in the false belief that they are 'not interested'. But the truth is that almost every child wants to know their own story. It is one of the responsibilities of parenting by adoption to share this story with sensitivity and empathy.

Those who participated in adoption preparation workshops or sought pre and post adoption counselling, found themselves better equipped to deal with adoption related issues as they gained so much from the experience of other parents and experts. They developed a support network for different stages of their parenting journey.

It is so inspiring to hear how parents have responded with such acceptance, devotion and effort to fulfill special needs faced by their children, relating to emotional, physical or educational challenges, by training themselves to acquire new skills to meet their needs. Some parents have even taken training in remedial learning to fulfill the needs of their child, which has involved taking time off from their chosen careers or completely changing their tracks to respond to their commitment to their child. Parents feel that greater understanding and support from society is very much needed, but lacking. Also parents who have to deal with challenging circumstances need to keep time for self-care if they are to continue on the path of reconstructing relationships, which is involved in adoption.

We have also seen that authoritative parenting has not been the way to deal with behaviours which really have emotional roots. In the end parents have had to go beyond discipline to recognise where their child's behaviour is coming from... not bad genetics but a traumatic and unaddressed early life experience. Parents who were in denial of their child's past trauma have often had to open up to it and give space to their child to grieve. Being a good listener is very much a part of adoption conversations as children need freedom to express their feelings, share their perspective and be heard with respect even if parents do not agree with them.

Although adoption does entail acceptance of differences we can understand that a family in domestic adoption feels much more comfortable in society if the child's looks somehow 'matches' the family. This helps assimilation into the larger family network and also the child does not have to answer awkward questions from peers about the marked difference in looks and is accepted literally at Face Value. This can be a special concern when a family has a biological child and opt to have another child by adoption. Even though both children are loved by the parents, the extended family and society are constantly making comparisons which can be hurtful to either siblings and very damaging to family harmony. Grandparents are known to experience loss of continuity of their bloodline...generativity. Yet we find that after early difficulties of acceptance of adoption, they have become close to the same grandchildren in later years.

Along the way prudent parents recognised and accepted that their children had very different talents and abilities from the family by adoption. They encouraged their children to follow their own path rather than forcing them to fit into the family mould. This was very supportive to their children and went a long way to help the children to build their identity and self-esteem, which is one of the most vital areas of concern in raising children. As children reach adulthood parents look forward to their children settling down. But when it comes to finding a marriage partner by the traditional route of an arranged marriage, many prejudices surface from the potential partner's family. It is a common experience that potential partners back off when they hear about the adoption factor. Yet it is very interesting to note that in the end a partner of much better character and values does surface and most marriages thus arranged have been rather successful. Many adopted young people have also found caring partners of their choice who do not harbour prejudices about adoption.

Most parents have taken the adoption route when they were confronted with involuntary childlessness. They also had to confront their loss for the dream of a biological conception and continuation of the family bloodline. For some, marriage did not happen but they still wanted to parent a child. For all parents, couples or single, adoption opened up a new vista in their lives, another path to family building. Most parents have attributed the adoption to a divine source...a unique relationship which has manifested from another realm and can only be attributed to the mysteries of the Universe. The challenges have been tough but their own human growth has evolved from the despair, the conflicts, the confrontation, the provocations, the paradoxes and above all, the joys of this quite amazing relationship which has taught us that the 'stomach' and the 'heart' are both routes to parenthood, and, in the words of a parent, ' Love is eternal'...

A mother was taken aback when her young daughter came home from school and asked her, 'So you are my step mother?' This is how her friend perceived her relationship with her mother by adoption. Her mother then had to do a lot of explaining about their relationship. Unfortunately adoption requires a lifetime of explanation.

Once the legal bond of the parent-child relationship is secured it is really unnecessary for the adoption prefix to remain. In fact adoption is not a label but it refers to the circumstances due to which a child is transplanted into a family by a legal process.

The Voices from the Heart that we have heard through these pages have clearly demonstrated that parenthood is not a qualification of the body but a quality of the mind and the heart. This book is our tribute to those parents and children, grandparents and families who have opened their hearts to a relationship which surpasses all limitations, expectations and boundaries to embrace another dimension of life and love....

~ Dipika Maharaj Singh
Founder Director, SPARCC

ABOUT THE AUTHOR

Dipika Maharaj Singh has dedicated her life to the service of vulnerable children residing in institutions. In 1969, she started out as volunteer at a century old orphanage where she experienced the loneliness and despair of family-deprived children living in bleak conditions. This motivated her to set up a child care programme to provide qualitative care to crisis affected children, and to develop rehabilitation services through foster care and adoption. In 1973, she helped to establish Shreevatsa, a child care center, under the flagship of Sofosh, Sassoon Hospitals, Pune. She served as managing committee member and Vice Chairperson of Sofosh until 2015. She has been advisor to numerous child care programmes and centres, including BSSK, Pune.

Dipika has played a pioneering role in child development and adoption and has been actively participating in the movement to promote adoption in India as co-founder of the Pune Consortium of Adoption and the VCA , which became a national model recommended by the Supreme Court of India to promote adoption. She has developed ethical practices and contributed to evolving policy on adoption. With special concern for the plight of mentally and physically disabled abandoned children, she fulfilled her vision to set up care homes to serve their special needs.

Dipika has been speaker in innumerable national and global forums and seminars and written papers and articles for journals in India and abroad.

Dipika is Founder and Managing Trustee of LKJha Foundation, providing educational and social support services for disadvantaged families. She is Founder Director of SPARCC, a project of the Samarpan Foundation , which offers a wide range of adoption support services including publications.

In over fifty years of honorary work, Dipika has left her silent presence and footprints in child care centres, child development programmes and, most relevantly, in the hearts of countless children who began their lives in institutions.

SAMARPAN FOUNDATION : SPARCC

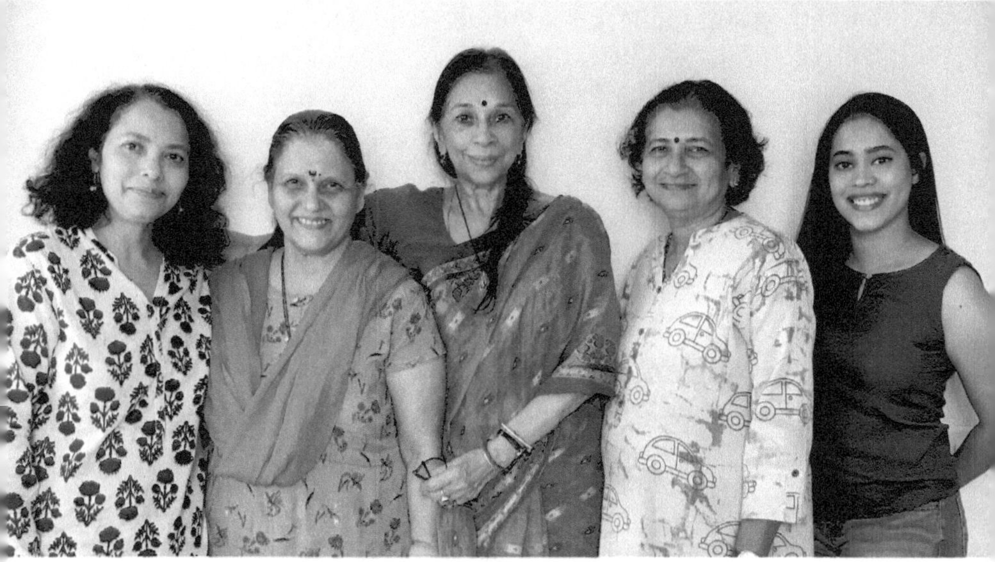

The Samarpan Foundation is a not-for-profit humanitarian organisation with global services to support social initiatives relating to health, education, environment, women, children, animal welfare, etc.

In October 2015 a new project, SPARCC: the Samarpan Programme for Adoption Research Counseling Consultancy and Care, was initiated to support the security and well-being of family-deprived and disadvantaged children in our society. Based in Pune, Maharashtra, SPARCC offers specialised services to children and families created through adoption, as well as consultancy to organisations working to rehabilitate children through adoption. SPARCC conducts workshops for aspiring parents, offers pre adoption and post adoption counselling services and gives hands on assistance to adoption applicants to understand and complete online procedures. SPARCC has a fraternity of adopted young people called Bright Sparks who provide peer counselling. It also publishes adoption - related publications, assists organisations in the preparation of Home Study Reports and Post Placement reports. SPARCC also supports education and nutrition to children from disadvantaged families. All the activities of SPARCC are conducted by its well qualified, reputed and highly experienced team of social service providers.

For more information, please contact SPARCC at:
Email - sparccindia@gmail.com
Website - www.samarpanfoundation.org